BOUND AND DETERMINED

WOMEN IN CULTURE AND SOCIETY

A series edited by Catharine R. Stimpson

CHRISTOPHER CASTIGLIA

Bound and Determined

Captivity,

Culture-Crossing, and

White Womanhood

from Mary Rowlandson

to Patty Hearst

THE UNIVERSITY OF CHICAGO PRESS   Chicago & London

Christopher Castiglia is assistant professor in the Department of English at Bryn Mawr College.

The University of Chicago Press, Chicago 60637
The University of Chicago Press, Ltd., London
© 1996 by The University of Chicago
All rights reserved. Published 1996
Printed in the United States of America
05 04 03 02 01 00 99 98 97 96   1 2 3 4 5
ISBN: 0–226–09652–1 (cloth)
ISBN: 0–226–09654–8 (paper)

Library of Congress Cataloging-in-Publication Data

Castiglia, Christopher.
    Bound and determined: Captivity, culture-crossing, and white womanhood from Mary Rowlandson to Patty Hearst / Christopher Castiglia.
        p.   cm. — (Women in culture and society)
    Includes bibliographical references and index.
    1. American prose literature—Women authors—History and criticism.   2. Literature and anthropology—United States—History,
3. Women and literature—United States—History.   4. Indians of North America in literature.   5. Culture conflict in literature.
6. Race relations in literature.   7. Imprisonment in literature.
8. White women in literature.   9. Abduction in literature.
10. Rowlandson, Mary White, ca. 1635–ca. 1678—Captivity, 1676.
11. Hearst, Patricia, 1954–   . I. Title. II. Series.
PS152.C37   1996
818'.08—dc20   95-20049
                                                                            CIP

A previous version of chapter 6 appeared as "In Praise of Extravagant Women: *Hope Leslie* and the Captivity Romance," *Legacy* 6, no. 2 (Fall 1989): 3–16. © 1989 by the Pennsylvania State University. Reproduced by permission. A previous version of chapter 5 appeared as "Susanna Rowson's *Reuben and Rachel:* Captivity, Colonization, and the Domestication of Columbus" in *Redefining the Political Novel: American Women Writers, 1797–1901*, pp. 23–42. Edited by Sharon M. Harris. © 1995 by the University of Tennessee Press.

♾ The paper used in this publication meets the minimum requirements of the American National Standard for Information Sciences—Permanence of Paper for Printed Library Materials, ANSI Z39.48–1984.

FOR CHRIS

CONTENTS

In the opening passages of the book of Genesis, Eve speaks but twice. First she tells the serpent what God's commandments to Adam and Eve in the Garden of Eden have been. Next, after she and Adam have disobeyed these orders, she blames the serpent for treacherously leading her astray. God then metes out his dreadful punishments for their transgressions and expels his creations from the Garden forever.

A powerful myth asserts that America is the new Garden of Eden, with the American man a new Adam, the American woman a new Eve. What, Christopher Castiglia asks in *Bound and Determined*, his fascinating and provocative first book, was this new Eve supposed to say? Because the old Eve spoke so destructively, the new Eve was to say very little—if anything at all. Silence and passivity best became her. But what, Castiglia goes on to inquire, happened when the new Eve actually spoke? Fortunately, she not only spoke but wrote. In doing so, she evoked vital and shattering realities.

Building on feminist criticism, Castiglia first explores the dramatic genre and the development of the women's captivity narrative. Its founding author was Mary White Rowlandson, the daughter of a wealthy landowner and the wife of a minister in colonial Massachusetts. Captured by Indians in 1676, she published the story of her ordeal and survival in 1682. After tracing the evolution of the captivity narrative as white men and women moved westward across the continent, Castiglia offers an astonishing reading of the stories by and about Patricia Hearst, the granddaughter of a very rich newspaper publisher, who was kidnapped by a biracial group of revolutionaries in Berkeley, California, in 1974.

The laws of the genre of the captivity narrative are clear. So, for Castiglia, is one of its primary functions: to maintain the established interlocking hierarchies of race and gender in the New World. He points out that the captivity narrative flourishes during periods of gender and racial tension in the United States that challenge these hierarchies—for example, during the colonial confrontation with Native Americans and during the Civil War. The captivity narrative is to tell of a brutal, murderous band of savages who seize a frail, vulnerable white woman. Traditionally, the barbarians are Indian; for Hearst, they were black. These savages threaten to rape and enslave the white woman. White men must kill them in order to rescue the woman and restore her to civilized society. Once back, she gratefully submits to patriarchal protection and control. Castiglia persuasively shows how white male authority figures—be they ministers, editors, publishers, lawyers, or film directors—enforce generic laws and frame individual women's stories.

The captives, however, subvert and disrupt these laws as they tell their stories. They write beyond and across the rules. Paradoxically, the experience of imprisonment away from home has taught many of the captives about imprisonment at home. Being bound has made them determined to act differently. To be sure, the white women who have been made captives respond to their situation in various ways. Some wait for men to rescue them. Others fight against capture and, if captured, try to escape. Still others become acculturated to the new, once alien society and refuse to leave. According to one account, of 723 female captives, 60 stayed with the Indians and 150 converted to Roman Catholicism, some becoming nuns. Still other captives declined to side entirely with either Indian or white culture, but used their "position between societies to criticize both" (see p. 25). As time passes, the captivity narrative also becomes increasingly secular and decreasingly an example of God's works and will. No matter what the captive's specific response, no matter how much religion did or did not buttress her, her story undercuts gender and racial stereotypes. Her courage, strength, and endurance during her captivity mock the official rhetoric of feminine frailty; her frequent misery after her return mocks the official rhetoric of masculine excellence. Although white women never lost the privileges of being white and of writing in English, their descriptions of their relationships with Indians—very often with Indian women—contest vicious and self-serving representations of the "racial Other." In brief, the captive learns how malleable, how *constructable,* racial and gender identities are.

After reinterpreting the women's captivity narrative, Castiglia moves to a subgenre that mingles history and fiction: the captivity romance. Its origins, he suggests, are in the late eighteenth century, when it became clear that the American Revolution would not extend liberties to white women and people of color. Contained and restrained, these white women became writers who imagined a freer, happier place both in communities of women and in the wilderness, which they refused to abandon to men and masculine fantasies. Like the captivity narratives written during westward expansion, the captivity romance was skeptical—in both bold and subtle ways—of grandiose myths of a frontier waiting for the white man's rifle, Bible, deed, and plow. Having influenced subsequent nineteenth-century interweavings of the captivity narrative with sentimental and domestic fiction, the captivity romance survives today in perhaps diminished but still popular form in heterosexual plots about white heroines and noble Indian braves.

Castiglia argues that the captivity narratives and romances show women once again concerned with the themes of "containment and community" and with border-crossings, "the shifting boundaries of culture and identity" (p. 193). This argument is important because it contributes to a complex understanding of American literature, culture, and society. Moreover, *Bound and Determined* is appearing at a taut, tense moment in American history as people are struggling over the meanings of American history and society; the location of American borders; the land and environmental regulations; race, ethnicity, and gender. In these struggles, some people are sincere, some manipulative, some cruel. In the woods and over Internet, white militia men with stacks of weapons plot to defend a nutty vision of America by destroying government and creating redemptive enclaves of purity and power. The voices of the captives in *Bound and Determined,* these American Eves, are, despite some warpings of time, haunting, impressive. They also stand as warnings from history about what successor generations should do and not do; what moral orders these generations should and should not obey; which fruits they should cultivate, and which strange fruits they must never cultivate again.

Catharine R. Stimpson

ACKNOWLEDGMENTS

A fellowship from the Newberry Library allowed me to complete research for this book; I am grateful to the members of the Newberry staff, especially John Aubrey, for sharing their expertise with me. My chapter on Catharine Sedgwick benefited from the careful criticism of Joanne Dobson, Judith Fetterley, Carolyn Karcher, and Mary Kelley. Emory Elliott's generous and insightful suggestions led me to revise the entire manuscript in significant ways. I was fortunate to find in Alan Thomas a patient, supportive, and enthusiastic editor. Numerous friends, students, and colleagues have lived this book with me and, mercifully, helped me escape it from time to time; in particular, I want to thank Kathy Ashley, Rayne Carroll, Donna Cassidy, Rich DeProspo, Sharon Haar, Naomi King, Bruce Levy, Scott Mendel, Lisa Nelson, Beth Newman, Lucy Rinehart, Augusta Rohrbach, Barry Sarchett, Steffi Siegmund, Julia Stern, Liza Wieland, Liz Wiesen, and the members of my writing group at Columbia—Claire Fowler, Anne Himelfarb, Sam Huber, Eve Keller, Karen Luten, and Dan Manheim—for talking through various ideas with me. I especially want to thank Leigh Gilmore for sharing with me her extraordinary intelligence, compassion, and sense of humor. Barbara Castiglia, Mary Castiglia, Rob and Nancy Castiglia, and Tim and Suzanne Castiglia, continually offered their inexhaustible and particular good humor, for which I give my love as well as my gratitude. My parents, Joe and Gloria Castiglia, first modeled for me the courage and resilience I admire in these captives; without their unflagging love and spirit, none of this could have been undertaken. I share with the captives the great fortune of having had several skilled guides through the discursive wilderness. Jonathan Arac represents for me the finer side of literary scholarship and of the profession in general; his kindness, encouragement, and intelligence have meant more to me than I can say. Ann Douglas first sold me on the study of American culture. My debt to her for setting a standard of rigorous, honest, and intelligent analysis that I constantly strive to achieve, and especially for teaching me the meaning and value of "faith," is immeasurable. Finally, to Chris Reed, my best friend and the kindest, most honest reader an author could hope for, I dedicate this book.

Captivity Is Consciousness:
Captivity, Culture-Crossing,
and the Revision of Identity

The Eagle of his Nest
No easier divest—
And gain the Sky
Than mayest Thou—

Except Thyself may be
Thine Enemy—
Captivity is Consciousness—
So's Liberty.
                    Emily Dickinson, #384

En unas pocas centurias, the future will belong to the mestiza. Because
the future depends on the breaking down of paradigms, it depends on the
straddling of two or more cultures. By creating a new mythos—that is, a
change in the way we perceive reality, the way we see ourselves, and the
ways we behave—*la mestiza* creates a new consciousness.
                    Gloria Anzaldua
                    Borderlands/La Frontera, p. 80

IN 1676 NARRAGANSETT INDIANS DRAGGED Mary White
Rowlandson, the wife of a Puritan minister, from a burning house in
Lancaster, Massachusetts, and held her captive for eleven weeks.
Published in 1682, her story of an innocent Christian woman held
prisoner by dark-skinned barbarians became the first distinctly
American best-seller. Three hundred years later another white
woman was abducted from her home by a group of "dark" men and
later composed an account of her captivity. The woman was Patricia
Campbell Hearst, and her story too became a national best-seller.[1]

While many critics have assumed that the captivity narrative vanished with the Puritans or passed from Rowlandson to such literary sons as Charles Brockden Brown and James Fenimore Cooper, there extends between Rowlandson and Hearst a long and complex line of white women who wrote captivity narratives in America.[2] In addition, some of early America's best-known women authors, including Susanna Rowson and Catharine Maria Sedgwick, wrote novels based on historical accounts of captivity; in these captivity romances, women participate in creating the cultural mythology of the American wilderness, a literary realm that allows white women to wrestle with their placement in the new nation. Even today, romance novels mass-marketed for women frequently feature captivity plots, while the dynamics of the captivity story, especially its exploration of the relationships between race and gender, confinement and community, inscription and collective action, continue to animate American feminist discourse.

Critics have explained the enduring popularity of the captivity narratives in terms of their appeal to white Anglo-America's expansionist racism, engendered and justified in these tales of savage brutality committed by Native Americans against their benevolent and unsuspecting white neighbors. In this analysis, the captivity narratives remained popular even after Anglo-America had won its wars for possession of the continent and its resources because they offered sensational stories of explicit or implied sex and violence. Often invented by authors eager to corner the market created by sentimental novels, the so-called penny dreadfuls, characterized by Roy Harvey Pearce as "mainly vulgar, fictional, and pathological" (1947, 9), thus represent a pioneering example of the prurient appeal of mass entertainment.[3] These explanations are undoubtedly true on some level. Captivity narratives were indeed circulated to justify imperialistic expansion. Asserting that innately bestial Indians were incapable of cultivating land, let alone cultures, captivity narratives seem to suggest that whites need not feel guilty over the extermination of Indians and the appropriation of their land; in fact, Anglo-America's protective possession of "wild" lands became a duty undertaken on behalf of "civilization."[4] Throughout the eighteenth and nineteenth centuries, furthermore, captivity narratives stood cheek by jowl with the serialized fiction and true crime accounts that filled newspapers and anthologies. Later narratives, such as Patty Hearst's, generated both prurient interest in the sexual exploits of the helpless white girl and hatred and fear of the brutal men of color. Her narrative helped create a social climate necessary to counter the demands of radical feminists and black nationalists, and to justify aggression against Arabs who held America "hostage" during the oil crisis.[5]

While one could reasonably attribute the narratives' popularity to the misogyny and racism that fuel aggressive American nationalism, however, such critical accounts necessarily imagine an audience fascinated by stereotypes of the bestial savage and the raped and tormented white woman. Both portraits deny agency to the figures they construct, in the former case by making the "savage" a creature of nature, ruled by bodily rather than reasoned and strategic impulses, and in the latter by making white women passive items of exchange in battles fought by and for men. Moreover, these accounts assert generic and hence ideological stasis: if captivity narratives are popular because they show brutal savages of nature and their vulnerable victims, then they must never depict Native Americans as the subjects of culture or white women as active agents in their lives during captivity. The narratives have been critically assigned, therefore, a fixed genre and, perhaps more importantly, a fixed audience, composed of neither white women nor Native Americans, who presumably could take only a masochistic pleasure in witnessing a caricature of their lives that denies them the possibility of discursive or social agency. In imagining such an audience, critics continue to deny the possibility of a reading—and, arguably, a national—public comprised of anyone but white males.

The question therefore arises: Why, if these accounts are correct, would white women continue to write captivity stories that, while they assert essential racial differences that strengthen their position in a racial hierarchy, also maintain essential gender differences that weaken women's social positions? In order to answer that question, I wish to offer a different explanation for the popularity of the captivity narratives, and in so doing to argue for making these narratives a central part of current critical investigations into the construction of gender, race, and nation.[6]

First, I want to suggest that the captivity stories may have sustained their interest for white women readers through the connections they offer between the plight of the literal captive and less tangible forms of victimization and restriction experienced by their white, female readers. Captivity thus gives symbolic form to the culturally unnameable: confinement within the home, enforced economic dependence, rape, compulsory heterosexuality, prescribed plots. The novels based on the narratives assert the metaphorical usefulness of captivity for women readers by featuring appreciative female audiences within the texts, thereby suggesting the potential value for women of reading captivity stories as a way not only to express other forms of constraint but also to enter a community of fellow "captives."

Beyond embodying the problems facing white women in America, the captivity narrative also offers a story of female strength, endurance, and even prosperity. The captivity narratives, I will argue in the following chapters, offered American women a female picaresque, an adventure story set, unlike most early American women's literature, outside the home. In the American "wilderness," white women could demonstrate skills and attitudes of which their home cultures thought them incapable. As it evolved from a religious document of the seventeenth to a feminist plot of the twentieth century, the captivity narrative allowed women authors to create a symbolic economy through which to express dissatisfaction with the roles traditionally offered white women in America, and to reimagine those roles and the narratives that normalize them, giving rise ultimately to a new female subject and to the female audience on which she relies.

Above all, I want to suggest that the captivity narratives hold their greatest potential interest for readers excluded from the critical accounts traced above because they refuse to be static texts endorsing essential, unchanging identities and hence fixed social hierarchies of race and gender. Rather, the captivity narratives persistently explore generic and cultural changes, divisions, and differences occasioned by the captives' cultural crossings. To begin with, I will argue in the following chapters that white women have consistently used accounts of captivity to transgress and transform the boundaries of genre in order to accomplish their own ends, even—perhaps especially—when they contradict the desires of their white countrymen. Chapter 4 shows how women writers, in narrating their captivities, have blurred the line between fact and fiction in order to revise gender scripts and increase women's social mobility. A number of women novelists, furthermore, have used the captivity narrative to transform more traditionally "feminine" genres such as the sentimental and the domestic novels and the cultural attitudes they perpetuate. Equally significant for a revision of American literary history are the ways women authors, in writing captivity romances, have used aspects of "women's genres" to revise nationalist frontier mythologies. Writing narratives of collective agency rather than of solitary heroics undertaken precisely to escape social commitments, white women authors criticize and revise rugged individualism (especially constructed in opposition to women, who represent civilization and convention) and a violent, appropriative attitude toward the land (manifested as a xenophobic hatred of Indians and other people of color). In so doing, the authors of captivity romances transform the American Adam into a New World Eve.

Literary genres—and critical accounts of genre—function in several ideological capacities, perhaps chief among them by shaping recognizable social identities.[7] As I have already suggested, accounts of the captivity narratives as unchanging tales of brutality and torture, for instance, cast Native Americans as savage and natural, while representing white women as helpless, sexually vulnerable, and xenophobic. In reading captivity narratives and their critical explications, women and people of color are interpellated within an ideological system that grants agency only to white, male subjects.[8] To insist on a genre's stable borders is also, therefore, as I argue in chapter 1, to assert that subject positions ("identities") are also fixed and nameable. That assertion becomes especially germane regarding the captivity narratives, which were also used to stabilize the borders of cultures and nations by insisting that the narratives document essentially differentiated racial identities: Indians could never be like whites, and vice versa, because of absolute racial differences owing not to culture but to nature. These differences gave rise, then, to imperialistic hierarchies: the "cultural" (white) identity would and should triumph over the "natural" (Indian) one, just as, in the rhetoric of manifest destiny, culture appropriated and "improved" the natural terrain. Ironically, the very

5

philosophy that assured white victory over Indians on the basis of culture's power over nature rested on the assumption that, in determining subjectivity, nature was more powerful than culture.

White women, however, as I argue in greater detail in chapter 2, often had more ambivalent relationships to the rhetoric of westward expansion and, in revising its genres, also rewrote its cultural identities. Captive white women often used the experience of culture-crossing to engage in an early form of what Teresa de Lauretis calls radical feminist epistemology: a rethinking of subjectivity, not in relation to sexual difference alone, but "across language and cultural representations" (1987, 2). Such crossings give rise, de Lauretis argues, to "a subject en-gendered in the experience of race and class, as well as sexual relations; a subject, therefore, not united but rather multiple, and not so much divided as contradicted" (2). Due to their capture, white women found themselves in contexts that necessitated a revision of the discourses of knowledge and identity policed at/as the borders of white society. Crossing cultures forced white women to question the constitutive binaries of civilized and savage, free and captured, Christian and pagan, race and nation, on which their identities were based. Above all, captivity's epistemological "contradiction" challenged Anglo-America's assertion that racial and gendered identities are innate, unified, and unchanging.

The radical epistemology of captive white women begins with their revised relationship to colonialist discourses of race and nation, occasioned by their location at the shaky nexus of white/male domination. To the variable degree that they participated in the composition and dissemination of their stories, captive white women, by generating fear and hatred of the Indians and their allies, helped to further the colonization of the shifting western frontiers. Even the stories white women frequently tell of forming bonds of sympathy and compassion with their captors, particularly with Indian women, inscribe the agenda of integrationist colonization.[9] In these tales of friendship, white women assert their right to assimilate their captors, especially their female captors, into "communities" (often "sisterhoods") that the captors themselves do not define and from which they apparently benefit not at all.

At the same time, captivity caused many white women to investigate and ultimately to challenge the essentializing white dis-

courses of race on which imperialism rested. Captives were frequently adopted into Indian families where they assumed the social
status of dead or captive members of the tribe.[10] Crossing cultures
thus entailed white women's entrance into different sets of languages, rituals, and institutions, marking identities as discursive
practices, not as the products of biology. Captivity momentarily released white women from the ontological determination their home
cultures relied on to naturalize positions of "superiority" and "depravity," of "strength" and "vulnerability." Perhaps more importantly, in comparing Indian cultural practices (particularly those
relating to gender) with those of their natal societies, captive white
women raise the possibility that whites have a cultural identity that
can be named, evaluated, and revised. This awareness, possible only
from the borders between white identity and its constitutive
"other," undermines the invisibility that white identity relies on to
maintain its neutral and normative status.[11] At the same time, captive white women, whose adoption into Indian society was rarely
complete, also deny the binary opposition of white and Indian societies; moving between cultures, at home in neither yet ultimately
constituted from elements of both, the captives articulate "hybrid"
subjectivities that destabilize white culture's fiction of fixed and
pure identity. By contradicting their pure and essential "whiteness"
with different epistemologies, captives present a model of how,
without imagining oneself free of discursive exchange, one can
nevertheless write a new subjectivity, using different grammars of
identification.

7

Of course, since white women profit from imperialist discourses
that privilege whites over people of color, few captives ever entirely
rejected the racial ideologies of their day, and some maintained their
home cultures' essentializing racial stereotypes intact throughout
their captivities. What appears to have allowed many captive white
women to undertake the ontological revisions traced above is less a
cultural altruism than the desire to subvert white discourses of gender, in which white women were far less privileged than their white
brothers. Captives appear to recognize, furthermore, that in the
publishing format and ontological strategies of the captivity narratives, white women and Indians are both appropriated and subordinated to white males. If the captivity narratives were deployed to fix

the meaning of race, for example, those deployments also register the usurpation of white women's narrative authority. Captivity is almost synonymous with the circulation of women between groups of men: the female captive is passed almost invariably from husband or father to Indian braves and back again to ministers and militiamen. The narratives of captives, too, were circulated: as I discuss in chapter 2, almost without exception an interpretive "frame" was provided for the captivity narratives by someone other than the captives themselves. In the seventeenth and eighteenth centuries, those frames were provided by ministers; in the late eighteenth and nineteenth centuries, by editors of anthologies and individual narratives. Even in the twentieth century, as I show in chapter 3, Patty Hearst's "autobiography" was shaped by lawyers during her trial, by a coauthor at the time of its composition, and, following its publication, by Paul Schrader in his film *Patty Hearst*. These editors reinscribe white woman's subjectivity in interpretive frames that may or may not be consistent with the claims of the narratives themselves. Not surprisingly, then, the captivity stories, and

8 particularly the novels, articulate the desire for a different definition of white womanhood in the context of a revision of conventional, appropriative discourses of gender.

Those different gender definitions arise in the captivity narratives through the captives' challenge to racial ontology. Once captives demonstrate that identities are discursive and hence alterable, they increasingly shift their focus of identity, as I will argue in greater detail in chapters 1 and 2, from "race" to "gender" (a shift initiated by the autobiographical narratives, but foregrounded and more explicitly articulated by the captivity romances). That is, the captives move from defining themselves as sharing identity with white men in opposition to all people of color, to defining themselves as primarily "female," therefore sharing identity with other women across racial difference, in opposition to all men. This shift is strategic: while being "white" in the captives' home societies might be more culturally powerful than being "female," the opposite is true among their captors, for whom whites, not women, are the enemies.

Gender identifications inscribed *across* cultures, as I argue in chapter 1, appear to have granted women more mobility, more social prominence, and more economic participation than they had in their home cultures (an aspect of the narratives that made them appealing to women novelists writing at a time when domestic ideologies threatened to render women even more housebound). Ceasing to identify with conventional white womanhood thus allowed women to enjoy what nineteenth-century captive Rachel Plummer called "a more interesting adventure." Those adventures allowed captives to challenge the representation of sexually vulnerable, unalterably xenophobic, and physically helpless women who require the protection and support of white men. In refusing those representations, captives demonstrate that gender, like race, is the product of malleable cultural—and particularly nationalist—investments. Writing against the discursive grain of race and gender in order to experiment with other articulations of identity, captive white women position themselves as subjects speaking to other captives, other women, and hence as agents, not objects, of cultural exchange. In the chapters that follow, I wish to suggest that the captives' experience of captivity and crossing cultures occasioned their revision of identities and of the genres that constitute them, which in turn became a way for white women to survive captivity not only by Indians but by patriarchal prescription at home as well. Those acts of revisionary survival are the principal topic of this book.

9

In challenging the fixity of race and gender, the captives ultimately subvert their intended function as symbols of the stable nation. Captivity narratives were circulated to create what Lauren Berlant has called a national symbolic, rendering the borders of America as the boundaries of the white, female body. To the degree that the captive resists taking on the attributes of her captors, she represents the impermeable, defensible borders of the white, Anglo nation. Readers, who were to attain their identities as "pure" citizens by identifying with the white captive's resistance to Indianization, were thus asked to erase any contradictions between the experiences of captured women and their public, symbolic manifestations in sermons, pamphlets, and newspapers. Yet if, as Berlant contends, national symbols such as the Statue of Liberty often take the form of a woman whose "immobility and silence are fundamental to her activity as a positive site of national power and fantasy" (1991, 27), then captive white women subvert rather than ensure national coherence. The narratives repeatedly draw attention to how and why captive women are framed to produce national power and fantasy, thereby demonstrating the ideological investments in maintaining the white, female body as an object of cultural exchange. Furthermore, the narratives resist that "framing" by showing that bodily boundaries are inscribed, constrained, and transformed by discourses of race and gender that are changing and changeable, not fixed and finite. As the female body becomes renegotiated through the crossing of discursive borders, then, so implicitly does the body of America.

Captives enact other renegotiations of nationhood as well, especially by deconstructing one of Anglo-America's most cherished definitional strategies: the mythic equation of citizenship, subjectivity, and freedom. Capture implies freedom as its constitutive opposite; by calling white women's experience of crossing cultures "captivity," then, one defines return to and life in white, Anglo-America as "freedom." To be free is to be American (a citizen of the "Land of the Free"), and vice versa, while both states require the subject's acquiescence to discourses that normalize the values of white, Anglo-American males. Freedom is a paradoxical state, then, requiring language and hence community to define it, while promising life in a realm divorced from cultural or linguistic determination. Hester Prynne realized the paradox of freedom in *The Scarlet Letter* when she attempts to escape Puritan society in the freedom of the untamed forest, only to discover that she cannot leave behind the scarlet A attached to her bosom. If bodies are interpellated into language and hence cultural value, then all citizens must bear the letter of the law—the letter of identity—on their bodies, as Hester does, and recognize freedom as a tormenting illusion.

Long before Hester Prynne, the white, female captive realized the impossibility of freedom. Rather than calling return to white society "freedom," captives repeatedly expand the parameters of their texts to show their continuing imprisonment, even after their return from captivity, within the subordinating, infantilizing, and immobilizing gender ideologies of white America. Instead of pursuing freedom, captives opt for resolution through revision, using their cultural liminality to create interstitial narratives that recontextualize, denaturalize, and reconstruct the identity-formations of their home cultures. If they can never be free of identity, particularly gender identity, white women, in their passages between captivities, create and circulate a vocabulary that allows them to criticize and revise their constrictions by both whites and Indians.

The gender critique enabled by discursive crossing is perhaps best demonstrated by a recent "captive" who, like Patty Hearst, chose to join her kidnappers and fight the gender assumptions of the culture that produced her. In December 1993, a group called the BLO (Barbie Liberation Organization) switched the voice boxes of three hundred Barbie and G. I. Joe dolls.[12] On Christmas morning, girls across America found Barbies under the tree who mouthed military clichés, while boys unwrapped G. I. Joes who sang out, "Let's go shopping!" In the BLO video claiming responsibility for the act of terrorism, Barbie states that since she could not get an entirely new voice, she decided to switch voices with men. The assertion that no one gets a "new voice" in a world where all articulations are scripted and mass-produced reveals the impossible fiction of freedom, of American "newness." At the same time, however, the BLO offers the revisionary possibility of recontextualizing cultural scripts by denaturalizing their relationship to the bodies that are forced to articulate them. The boys and girls interviewed favored the change, claiming that it made G. I. Joe less violent. Its effect on Barbie went without comment.

The captivity narratives allow Barbie to go on speaking, letting the female body take on different cultural scripts, not only of gender, but of race and nation as well. In so doing, the captives also attempt to make G. I. Joe less violent, undermining the nationalist discourses that justify war by essentializing and hierarchizing racial differences. Captives were most concerned with the impact of crossing cultures, of "switching voices," on constructions of white womanhood. In a culture whose mythology often implies that one must be free in order to speak (American government rests on the impossible guarantee of "freedom of speech"), but where "freedom" is maintained as the prerogative of white males, women would seem to be left captive and hence voiceless. Captive white women have shown, however, that while they are never free, they have nevertheless developed voices with which to denaturalize and

11

revise their home cultures' scripts of identity and to rearticulate American genres, popular rhetoric, and mythology so as to speak the experiences of those marginalized by the dominant national language.

At the risk of continuing a chain of appropriative allegories, I would like to end by suggesting why the captivity stories potentially address cultural experiences not typically accounted for in cultural mythology. As abortion legislation tells women that they have no control over their bodies—no autonomy in a society where they are passed from fathers to husbands, from ministers to legislators—the captivity narratives embody women's loss of control but also provide strategies for enduring and altering their powerlessness. For people of color who daily see themselves represented by the mainstream media as drug-crazed and sex-obsessed, the narratives display and legitimize a resentment of and a resistance to appropriation and stereotypical characterization. While our culture still teaches young white women that their greatest enemies are men of color and that they have nothing in common with women of color, the captivity narratives stress the urgent need for cooperation between culturally separated peoples. The identifications enabled by the captivity story are not with "beings" (I see a person of color or a white woman in that narrative, therefore I see myself); rather, the narratives occasion identification with their analysis of power and its investment in representation, with their critique of patriarchal, colonialist subjectivity and the narratives that engender it, and with their exploration of the empowerment that can come from different narratives, different identifications, and different alliances.

I began by claiming that critical accounts of the captivity narratives reveal the critics' own investments in creating the genres they purport only to name. I am no exception. Women's captivity narratives, I have suggested, evidence an ambivalence about identity: momentarily destabilizing their home cultures' ontological fixity, the captives end by reinscribing gender identity in seemingly more enabling forms. If I have claimed that identity can comprise a captivity all its own, I have also suggested, by naming the reconstitution of identity as a survival strategy, its usefulness as well. Precisely this "double effect" of the narratives is what most appeals to me as a critic who finds that much of his work—including this study—

enacts a critique of "the American character" inscribed and naturalized in our national literatures and literary histories. Yet, as a
gay-identified man, I cannot and do not wish completely to disavow
identity in a society that fiercely polices "compulsory heterosexuality."[13]

My sense of confinement in America is different, almost anti-
thetical to the constraints depicted in canonical American literature, which depicts solitary figures (the "American Adam") fleeing
from the constraints of home, community, and history. Far from
feeling burdened with too much history, I have felt that there is too
little history, or in any case too few versions of history. Far from feeling constricted by socially acceptable ties of family and marriage, I
have been forbidden family and have had my relationships devalued
and criminalized. Above all, far from imagining that "freedom"
exists for me in solitude, I have learned that power comes through
alliances, in numbers. My community is a continuing sign of my restriction, organized as it is under discourses of sexuality that maintain heterosexuality as normative and dominant; in that sense there
can be no true "freedom" either within or without identity. Yet to   **13**
surrender identity-based community is not to surrender "identity";
it is simply to allow oneself to be named more fully within dominant discourse. "Community" has thus taught me to revise—not to
escape—one's name, to perform identity, as the captives do, in order to imagine other relationships of body and discourse, and hence
to render "queer" the language of domination. My interest in the
experiences of captives is understandable in these terms: stifled, isolated, bound and often gagged, the captive white woman paradoxically gains a voice, a mobility, and above all a revised sense of
collective belonging. The captivity narratives therefore express
what is for me a more recognizable story about life in the United
States.

The opening chapters of *Bound and Determined* examine more
than sixty narratives by captive white women in order to explore the
cultural forces at work in their central paradoxes: through their servility, captives gain positions of relative eminence among their captors; attempting a condemnation of people perceived as radically
"other," they end by criticizing the inadequacies of their own cul-

ture; in the experience of captivity, seemingly the most helpless and effacing of conditions, these women gain an agency they would have found nearly impossible to claim in their native culture.[14] Chapter 1 focuses on contemporary critical discussions of a "typical" captivity narrative as an effort to use the parameters of genre to police social conformity. This chapter further explores the variations of textual patterns found in captivity literature in order to suggest what those deviations might tell about social dissent.

Chapters 2 and 3 historicize those textual patterns in three historical moments: the late seventeenth century (focusing on the narrative of Mary Rowlandson), the mid-nineteenth century (focusing on the narratives of Sarah Wakefield and Fanny Kelly), and the late twentieth century (focusing on the narrative of Patty Hearst). Captivity narratives flourish in moments of racial "crisis" in America: the colonial confrontation with Native Americans, the Civil War, the civil rights movement. The same periods also witnessed important changes in the status of women in America, as increased opportunities arose from new tasks presented by life in the colonies, by a public stage attained through the abolition and temperance societies and the increased popularity of women's literature, and by the feminist movement of the late 1960s and early 1970s. Chapters 2 and 3 will examine the frames created for the captivity narratives by ministers, editors, and filmmakers as attempts to limit radical challenges to racial and gender stereotypes by asking readers to view the narratives as documents of racial depravity, needing white male control, and of female helplessness, requiring white male protection. The narratives themselves, these chapters will argue, tell a different story. From Mary Rowlandson to Patty Hearst, captives challenge cultural constructions of race and gender and envision new social arrangements, new definitions of community, and hence new American "selves."

The remaining four chapters examine the influence of captivity narratives on late-eighteenth- and early-nineteenth-century women's fiction, especially Ann Eliza Bleecker's 1793 *The History of Maria Kittle* (chapter 4), Susanna Rowson's 1798 *Reuben and Rachel* (chapter 5), and Catharine Maria Sedgwick's 1827 *Hope Leslie* (chapter 6). These chapters will argue that women authors used the captivity story to invent a literary "wilderness" that promised re-

14

lease from rigid social, and particularly gender, conventions. These chapters also examine the captivity romance as an example of what M. M. Bakhtin calls "heteroglossia," using the captivity story to modify more traditionally "female" genres—the novel of sensibility, domestic fiction—and the assumptions about gender they perpetuate. Using Michel Foucault's theories of "discipline," I explore in these chapters the dialectic of imprisonment and extravagance, restriction and community, central to the captivity romances. In the conclusion, which concerns Barbara Deming's *Prisons That Could Not Hold* (1984) and popular romances based on Indian captivity, I contend that the dynamics of the captivity story remain central to American women's writing into the twentieth century. Tracing the emergence of the images and strategies of contemporary women's writing from the captivity narratives, with their thematization of containment and community and their concern for the interaction of race and gender, *Bound and Determined* therefore provides a basis for a female tradition in American culture.

15

ONE *A More Interesting Adventure: Critics, Captives, and Narrative Dissent*

Such epics follow a well-paved story line which satisfies a host of white male expectations: the white woman is captured by "savages"—and "we all know how they treat their women"; she is forced to live in a state of utter humiliation and abjection, raped, beaten, tortured, finally stripped and murdered. Such little comedies serve to titillate the white male, intimidate "his woman," and slander the persons upon whom the white male has shifted the burden of his own prurient sadism.

Kate Millet
Sexual Politics, p. 286

Carried away unwillingly into the uncharted geography of North America, an author cannot let some definitive version of New England's destiny pull her. Once she senses oscillations of sense close to the face of her hunger, Scripture is a closure. Allegory a grid she can get over.

Susan Howe
The Birth-mark, p. 125

IN HER SHORT STORY "Our Lady of the Massacre" (1986), Angela Carter imagines what an Indian captive's tale might have been had her narration not been supervised by ministerial editors. Carter's protagonist is a young, orphaned girl—her name is "neither here nor there" (1986, 41)—who through poverty becomes a London prostitute. When her greed—and, Carter implies, her disregard for private property caused by men's debasement of her body—

leads her to theft, she is sent to Virginia to work on a plantation. There the overseer tries to rape her, but she cuts off his ears and then flees to the wilderness to avoid being hanged. She survives easily in the wilderness and travels without fear, having "more dread of the *white man,* which I knew, than of the *red man,* who was at that time unknown to me" (45).

One day the girl stumbles upon an Indian woman collecting herbs in the forest. As verbal communication is impossible, the women eye each other suspiciously.

> But I am struck by her looks, she is a handsome woman, not red but wondrous brown, and it came into my mind to open my bodice, show her my breasts, that, though I had the whiter skin, I could give suck as well as she and she reached out and touched my bosom.
>
> She was a woman of about the middle age dressed in nowt but a buckskin skirt and she grunted when she saw my stays— for I still wore my *English apparel,* though it was ragged—and motioned me, as I thought, that whalebone was not the fashion among the Indian nation. So off go my stays and I throw them into a bush and breathes easier for it. (45)

The Indian woman invites the narrator to come to her village, where she adopts the girl as her daughter. The narrator tells her reader that "in this way, no other, was I 'taken' by 'em although the Minister would have it otherwise, that they took me with violence, against my will, haling me by the hair, and if he wishes to believe it, then let 'im" (46). The girl lives happily with her adoptive mother, the midwife to the tribe. She is "cured" of her desire to whore and to thieve, for she now has self-esteem and lives where property is communal, shared even with women. When a brave whom she loves proposes, she accepts, and within a year gives birth to a son. Her life with her new husband is pleasant, for Indian men "are taught to love their wives and let them have their way no matter how many of them they marry" (50).

Then one day the narrator awakens to find the entire village on fire, under attack by the English. In the massacre referred to in the title, the soldiers easily kill the braves they have drugged with rum. They rape and murder the narrator's mother and take the girl back to "civilization." She is sold to a minister and his wife, who ask her to thank the Lord that she has been "rescued from the savage" (55). "Taking my cue from this," she reports, "I fell to my knees, for I see that repentance is the fashion in these parts and the more of it I show, the better it will be for me" (56). The minister spreads the story of a raid on a plantation years earlier, in which Indians killed the overseer and dragged a young girl into the wilderness against her will. In return for her acquiescence in this fiction, the girl is treated like a servant.

> I scrubbed the Minister's floor, cooked the dinner, washed the clothes and for all the Minister swears they've come to build the *City of God* in the *New World,* I was the same skivvy as I'd been in Lancashire and no openings for a whore in the *Community of the Saints,* either, if I could have found in my heart the least desire to take up my old trade again. But that I could not; the Indians had damned me for a *good woman* once and for all. (55–56)

18 The minister's wife—motivated in her matchmaking by a desire to keep the half-breed baby, since she can have no children of her own—suggests that she marry Jabez Mather. But the girl, now rechristened Mary, refuses. In the final line of the story, Mary states: "*she* will never have my little lad for son, nor will I have Jabez Mather for my husband, nor any man living, but sit and weep by the waters of Babylon" (56).

"Our Lady of the Massacre" may seem far-fetched to readers of Mary Rowlandson's captivity account and perverse to those familiar with the critical discourse on the captivity tradition. The following chapters will demonstrate, however, that Carter is one of the most careful readers of captivity narratives. In her revision of the captivity story, Carter identifies and fleshes out from accounts of captivity many clues, previously unrecognized, about how white women perceived their relationship to the Indians, to the "wilderness," and most centrally to their home societies. In their narratives of life among the Indians, white women express a self-esteem—a social and economic self-possession—rarely claimed within their native cultures. Refusing the binary logic of civilized/savage by showing the "conquest" of the Indians to be the result of Anglo chicanery and brutal violence, Carter's heroine, like numerous captive white women, challenges the innate moral superiority of white culture and hence justifies the ambivalence narratives almost invariably express about their authors' return. Captivity narratives frequently complicate the assumption that a return to white society is equivalent to "freedom," the purported "closure" to a captive's text. "Our Lady of the Massacre" ends, like many captivity narratives, by showing life among whites as a captivity requiring women to adopt survival strategies that work against their own interests. A careful reading of the captivity narratives, in which white women represent themselves as having been able to "breathe easier" once freed from the "stays" of their restrictive roles in white society, documents the historical insight of Carter's fiction.

While many captives also represent white women as the prisoners of their white countrymen, they join Carter as well in demonstrating, often unintentionally, how difficult it is to leave the values and assumptions of their home cultures behind. Carter presents life among the Indians as a utopia of communal support and respect, into which her heroine moves without lingering traces of the culture she leaves behind. Because she is devalued within her home culture's hierarchies of class and gender, the white woman, in her adoption into Indian society, apparently brings with her no racial privilege. Indian society thus represents for the white heroine the "freedom" she has been denied at home; among the Indians, Carter's heroine imagines herself freed from the cultural discourses that constitute her as "white" and "woman" in the first place. In assuming a universal and naturalized sympathy between women, however, and by having a white woman initiate and benefit from this "sisterhood," Carter, like novelists discussed in later chapters, romanticizes the happy integration of white women and maternal and eroticized Indians despite this scenario's perpetuation of patriarchal domestic ideology (in which all women are the same) and its inscription of an imperialist allegory of willing Indian integration with whites. When Carter's heroine removes her clothes in order to show what she shares with the Indian woman, she naturalizes that bond through an appeal to the biological while appearing to cast off the trappings of white acculturation, the body itself apparently innocent of cultural meaning.[1] Far from attaining "freedom" from white society

19

among the Indians, however, Carter's narrator, like numerous captive white women before her, expresses her social dissatisfaction through several of the most dominant narratives of Anglo-American culture. Less likely than Carter to romanticize life among the Indians, the authors of captivity narratives frequently chose to represent their lives among both whites and Indians as a captivity, rather than seeing Indian life as a final and absolute resolution to the constraints of white womanhood. And while they often deploy the language of "bonding" or "sisterhood," they are also explicit in using that rhetoric within contexts of coercion, survival, and resistance, hence showing the "biological" to be always already cultural. In so doing, they render inconceivable the "freedom" Carter appears to require for narrative poignancy.

Ironically, while "Our Lady of the Massacre" does not comment on the impossibility of breaking free of the stories that serve the dominant subjects of one's home culture, it does show the ultimate control of those stories over any competing accounts of social experience. By juxtaposing Mary's chronicle of her "captivity" with the version created by the minister, Carter offers a crucial insight into the impossibility of the captive achieving complete agency in her self-representation. In the majority of captivity narratives, editors obscure and revise the captives' stories in order to strengthen flagging religious devotion, to justify westward expansion and the extermination of Indians, and to create the illusion of a stable and paternal nation. In "Our Lady of the Massacre," the minister is motivated in his revisions by his desire to establish a "Community of Saints," a colonialist enterprise requiring a threat against white womanhood to justify a brutal massacre that results in the narrative endorsement of white clerical and military authority. To achieve this end, the minister represents captivity as a story of barbaric savages and helpless white women: the heroes of his narrative are white men, who can eliminate (massacre) the inhuman threat to "their" women and hence maintain their social control. By assuming the right to substitute his narrative for hers, as well as in the contents of his story, the minister asserts his social privilege over "Mary" (and over the Indians, who tell their stories in neither version). Both as narrative and as speech act, then, the minister's account serves to inscribe a social hierarchy based on race and gender. Acquiescence

20

to a white man's story amounts, in "Our Lady of the Massacre," to subjection under white male authority, with "Mary" literally becoming a servant to God, or at least to His human deputy.

Carter thus reveals patriarchal imperialism's investments in the figure of both the captive and her narrative (even as she conceals her own investment in those figures as representatives of white feminism). At the same time, however, the ministerial inscription of white, male authority remains sharply contradicted by the story told by the narrator herself, who shows why she has more to "dread" from the white men than from her Indian "captors." While the minister seeks to fix the captive in a stable narrative position (represented by his assigning her a name drawn from the Christian cult of female sacrifice), the narrator asserts her ability to redefine and hence denaturalize her identity (she asserts that names are neither "here nor there"). In telling a different story structured on different cultural values (communally held property, polygamy, socially assumed racial identity, respect for women) and featuring minoritized cultural agents, the narrator disrupts the appearance of an uncontradicted social story, an illusion apparently necessary for the assignation of subjugating names and for the inscription of social hierarchies. Carter thus foregrounds, first, the rupture evident in many captivity accounts between an editorial frame authored from and authorizing dominant cultural authority and, second, the captives' narrative reconfigurations of alliances and identities in order to attain self-esteem, economic independence, and, above all, options for negotiating their own subject positions. Such ruptures remain the most consistent feature of the captivity narratives, indicating white women's conflicting positions in relation to cultural constructions of race, gender, and nation.

Perhaps the denaturalizing rupture produced by the uneasy collaboration between captive women and male editors explains the persistent desire on the part of critics to assert social order by patrolling the borders of the captivity narrative as a genre. Contemporary criticism continues to assert the "unity" and "conformity" of both captivity narratives and their subjects, shaping a large body of literature into predictable patterns that sustain the colonizing and paternalistic stereotypes endorsed by earlier editors.[2] The critical standardization centers on the "typical" sequence of events in the "classic" narrative. While Phillips Carleton attributes the uniformity of narrative pattern to forces beyond the captive's control, he nevertheless accepts this sequence as evident and unvarying.

> [The captivity narratives] had the primary requisite of form, even though it was a form forced on them: the opening pages usually dealt with the attack itself; after the capture the narrative rose gradually to the crescendo of escape or return. Accidental or not, the form gave coherence to a narrative even in the hands of an unskilled writer. (171)

A more careful reader of the captivity narratives, Roy Harvey Pearce, challenges efforts to "make a single genre out of the sort of popular form which shapes and reshapes itself according to varying immediate cultural 'needs'" (1947, 1). Pearce's division of the captivity tradition into three genres—religious documents, anti-Indian and anti-French propaganda, and sentimental pulp fiction—is helpful in outlining the historical development of the narratives. Yet like other critics, Pearce, while noting diachronic development in the narratives, does not allow for differences between narratives written in the same period. Within the category of religious narratives, for instance, Pearce traces a predictable and artless paradigm.

> The first, and greatest, of the captivity narratives are simple, direct religious documents. They are for the greatest part Puritan; and their writers find in the experience of captivity, "removal," hardships on the march to Canada, adoption or torture or both . . . , and eventual return (this is the classic pattern of the captivity), evidences of God's inscrutable wisdom. (2)

Pearce's terms are repeated by Richard VanDerBeets, who reports that the earliest captivity narratives, "straightforward and generally unadorned religious documents," adopt "a typically symbolic or even typological value":

> The religious expressions deriving from the captivity experience treat the salutary effects of the captivity, especially in the context of redemptive suffering; the captivity as test, trial, or punishment by God; and, finally and most demonstrably, the captivity as evidence of Divine Providence and of God's inscrutable wisdom. (1973, ix)

Almost every description of the "classic" captivity account bears traces of the three assumptions behind Richard Slotkin's summary of the generic narrative, in which

> a single individual, usually a woman, stands passively under the
> strokes of evil, awaiting rescue by the grace of God. . . . In the
> Indian's devilish clutches, the captive had to meet and reject
> the temptation of Indian marriage and/or the Indian's "can-
> nibal" eucharist. To partake of the Indian's love or of his
> equivalent to bread and wine was to debase, to un-English
> the very soul. The captive's ultimate redemption by the grace
> of Christ and the efforts of the Puritan magistrates is likened to
> the regeneration of the soul in conversion. (1973, 94)

First, the captive functions as a "single individual"; her ordeal is divorced from collective discourses of antagonism or identification, of coercion or resistance. Second, critics highlight the passivity of the captive, who is frequently represented bowing down before God's will. In Slotkin's formulation, Christ and the "Puritan magistrates" are unquestionably interchangeable, and the female captive, in losing her will to one, becomes simultaneously subjected to the other. Unlike Carter, Slotkin never entertains the possibility that for the captive this traffic in women within a closed circuit composed of ministers, Christ, and magistrates might form a continuum with and not a closure to her "captivity" among the Indians. Ironically, the "passivity" of the captive white woman apparently renders her as "vulnerable" to the purveyors of white cultural forms as she is to Indians; Carleton describes how "unskilled" captives have the form of their narratives "forced" on them, just as they are forced into captivity by the Indians. The passivity of the captive's body is transferred to her text and vice versa, as Indians and white cultural authorities become interchangeable in their desire to reshape both. Lacking any agency in regard to her survival in the wilderness, her decision to return, or her choice to stay among the Indians, the captive may exert herself only in refusing the Indian way of life. Thus the "climax" of the captivity narrative, as Carleton reports, is "the repulse of the Indians, escape, victory over them" (1943, 172). Slotkin builds his account of American mythology on this assumption, arguing that the captive "had to meet and reject" any symbolic or physical merger with the Indians. The only exchange between captors and captives, Slotkin asserts, occurs in the context of violence.

Based on assumptions that reflect dominant conceptions of race and gender, the conviction that captivity accounts conform to a consistent pattern not surprisingly leads to the assertion that the narratives are expressions of voluntary social conformity. In David Minter's account, for example, the captive becomes "a radically socialized individual, an individual who feels a deep need to conform experience to socially sanctioned patterns and no longer feels any deep resistance to such restriction" (1974, 347). The connection between "socially sanctioned patterns" of human behavior and "typical" patterns of narrative events becomes clear when these social and literary accounts are taken together. Roy Harvey Pearce's argument that the "greatest" captivity narratives are those that conform to religious doctrine and hence to Puritan political and social authority, leads logically to Minter's admiration for "a nearly perfect internalization of a social code" (347). Downplaying deviation or resistance of any sort, overlooking any variations of style, expression, desire, or behavior, critical accounts of captivity contribute to the regulatory circulation of images of white women as helpless, isolated, and xenophobic victims and of Indians as ruthless savages.[3] When narratives consistently represent white men as the sole possessors of divinely sanctioned agency, then "proper" gender, racial, and national orders begin to appear natural and inevitable, the result of unalterable "being" rather than of insistent textual inscription. Social privilege thus depends on narrative control, as editors from the Puritans to the present day appear to have recognized; behaviors, identities, social positionings, and cultural authority itself rely on the impression of narrative stability, and not the other way around.

In connecting social and generic conformity, however, critics open a new way of reading the narratives that works against their efforts to articulate a "classic" social or textual pattern. If narrative conformity directs social hierarchy, then narrative dissent may well shape social conflict, resistance, and reinscription. At stake in the discrepancy between narratives told by white women captives and the accounts of those narratives by critics and editors is thus not "truth" (who told the most accurate story about the lived experience of captivity), but rather the totalizing discourse of power itself: whose voice has cultural authority, how stories frame social identity and relationships, and to what degree narratives become allegories of aggressive nationalism. This chapter begins to examine some of the "atypical" captivity narratives in which differences of style and content suggest the variety of historical inscriptions of race, gender, and nation made by white women in America.

Captivity accounts occasionally resemble the "typical" account traced above, representing savage Indian tormentors and women captives who rely for rescue on masculine financial or military agency. In other narratives, however, diverging details or narrative patterns question the structures the stories elsewhere support, signaling discursive conflicts *within* white culture. In a large number of narratives, the captive either fights the Indians in order to avoid capture, or, once captured, uses her own strengths to escape. The captives in still other narratives either refuse to return to Anglo-American culture or make clear that their lives among the Indians were no worse than among whites. In yet another type of narrative, the captive sides entirely with neither Indian nor white culture, but uses her position between societies to criticize both. This type of narrative usually involves strong identification by the captive with her female captors. Each of these narratives challenges gender expectations, representing women as cunning, physically fit, often aggressive or violent, and willing to revise their racial, gender, and national identifications. Above all, these narratives make visible the connection between white women's manipulation of language and their survival in a hostile environment, a connection at work not only in confronting Indian captivity but in composing accounts for their home cultures as well. Whatever their narrative structures, then, captivity accounts almost invariably challenge stereotypes of women as frail and contented innocents, and differ only in the manner of challenge and in the degree to which they simultaneously question stereotypes of Indian depravity and white moral, physical, or intellectual superiority.[4]

While often gruesome and pathetic, the captivity narratives also depict captives possessing strengths not usually attributed to white women. While Mrs. Cunningham, taken captive by Delawares in 1785, in no way explicitly questions cultural assumptions about women's essential helplessness, her narrative nevertheless suggests that she could fend for herself:

> For ten days her only sustenance consisted of the head of a wild turkey and three papaws, and from the circumstance that the skin and nails of her feet, scalded by frequent wading of the water, came with her stockings, when upon their arrival at a village of the Delawares, she was permitted to draw them off. (Withers 1895, 371)

While on the one hand Mrs. Cunningham fills the expected role of the suffering and tormented victim, on the other hand her endurance gives the lie to cultural images of women as the "weaker sex." Often, editors maintain a rhetoric of frail and helpless womanhood even as they document acts of extraordinary prowess and endurance. Olive Oatman, captured by Apaches in 1851, marches 250 miles in eighty hours, even though she has been presented earlier by the narrator of her story, Reverend Stratton, as physically unfit. A seventy-year-old captive who for seven years has been "too infirm" to walk the streets nonetheless makes the journey from Albany to Canada "with ease" (How 1745, 8). Several captives note such narrative discrepancies, commenting on the fact that they experience strengths in captivity that no cultural story had prepared them to possess. Mary Kinnan, held by Shawnees between 1791 and 1794, describes her time among the Indians as "a captivity, worse than death" (VanDerBeets 1973, 328). Yet she also notes

> In happier times, I should have thought that my heart would cease to beat, and my pulse forget to throb under such an accumulated weight of misery. But the soul often acquires vigor from misfortune, and by adversity is led to the exertion of faculties, which till then were not possessed, or at least lay dormant. Thus it was with me. I have supported *in reality* what, *in idea,* had appeared impossible. (322)

Kinnan's narrative allows her a "vigor" and "exertion" that the "idea" of women endorsed by her home culture rendered unthinkable. Kinnan echoes Elizabeth Hanson, held captive from 1724 to

1725, who wrote that "none knows what they can undergo till they are tried" (Vaughan and Clark 1981, 238).

While examples of captives enduring terrible hardships are common—and very well publicized, then and now—often, in fact, the tales are less centered on, and even undermine the narrative centrality of, suffering and hardship. When Mercy Harbison, a captive in 1792, decides to kill herself by throwing away the powder horn her captors have told her to carry, the story has an ironic outcome. Both times she throws the horn away, an Indian retrieves it for her. The third time she carries out her suicidal action her master comes and says, " 'Well done; you did right and are a good squaw, and the other is a lazy son-of-a-gun; he may carry it himself' " (Kephart 1915, 225). In the story of Molly Finney, the narrator attempts to make the captive's sufferings seem horrible beyond words: "Miss Finney was graciously provided with a blanket to shield her somewhat from the night air, but her feet were left entirely unprotected. The torture experienced from being forced along over brush and briars in this condition can scarcely be realized" (Finney n.d., 112). Yet this depiction of Finney's heinous treatment at the hands of her captors is soon challenged:

> As day after day rolled by, and she became more used to the Indian character, Miss Finney became more independent. She would occasionally taunt her captors, calling them cowards for keeping a "squaw" in captivity. . . . Such boldness really amused some of the warriors. The Indian never fails to admire courage, wherever seen. This, our beautiful captive maiden possessed in a high degree. (113)

A tension arises in this passage between Finney's independent "boldness" and the "beautiful captive maiden" insisted on by her editor who, unlike the Indians, seems incapable of acknowledging courage "wherever seen."

Women's captivity narratives may be read both as "straightforward" documents upholding religious and social hegemony and as subversive documents of female strength because, as Finney's narrative demonstrates, there is often a gap between what the narratives purport to say and what the anecdotes relate. The most remarkable example of the discrepancy between the rhetoric of submission and patient suffering and the articulation of female agency and adventure may be found in the narrative of Rachel Plummer, taken captive by Comanches in 1836. Plummer frames her narrative in the traditional language of barbarous savagery, as she looks "back at the place where I was one hour before, happy and free, and now in the hands of a ruthless, savage enemy" (1839, 337). "To undertake to narrate their barbarous treatment," Plummer asserts, "would only add to my present distress, for it is with feelings of deepest mortification that I think of it, much less to speak or write of it" (337–38). Plummer certainly had cause to feel herself ill-treated: four months pregnant when taken captive, Plummer gives birth to a boy, whom the Comanches kill by dragging through prickly bushes.

Plummer nevertheless soon changes the tone of her narrative, focusing on her gains as well as on her losses. "Not withstanding my sufferings," she writes, "I could not but admire the country" (339). She in fact proves a keen observer of the landscape, providing a detailed account of the terrain and of the local fauna (ending each of her descriptions with a mention of the relative culinary value of each animal). She learns the Comanche language and in the face of hostile opposition insists on witnessing their councils, a privilege forbidden to women. Her relation of a confrontation between herself and her mistresses suggests that Plummer enjoyed more prominence among her captors than she acknowledges. When her younger mistress orders her back to the village for some forgotten tool, Plummer, like Mercy Harbison, decides to aggravate the Indian into killing her. Instead they begin to fight, and Plummer gets the better of her mistress. When she helps the defeated woman up and cleans her wounds, the chief commends her for being a fair and skilled fighter. Her older mistress is angered, however, and throws burning straw at Plummer, who gathers up more straw, sets it on fire, and throws it back at the Indian. Again Plummer is involved in a brutal fight, in which she knocks down the wall of the hut. In the subsequent trial, the old woman "told the whole story without the least embellishment" (354), a fact Plummer reports without comment. The council rules that Plummer must merely replace the pole for the wall she has knocked down; when she insists that the two Indian women help her, the council agrees. Far from a tormented victim, then, Plummer represents herself as an active and respected

participant in Comanche society. Her participation is characterized, moreover, by her physical strength, her daring resistance,
and her effective powers of speech, traits not often noted and even
more rarely praised in women by white society.

Not all of Plummer's demonstrations of independence are in
opposition to the Indians, moreover. In an extraordinary passage,
Plummer tells of her discovery of a cave, which she convinces her
mistress to allow her to explore in company with a young Indian
woman. Just inside the cave her escort loses her nerve and tries to
force Plummer out. The captive beats her down, however, and
"firmly told her that if she attempted again to force me to return
until I was ready, I would kill her" (349). She delights in narrating
her discoveries in the cave, including a chamber composed entirely
of translucent crystal. Finally leaving the cave, Plummer writes,

> I retraced my steps. I found the distance much greater, on re-
> turning, (or it appeared so,) than I thought. On reaching the
> place where my young mistress turned back, I found that the In-
> dians had been in the cave looking for me. I reached the camp
> just as the sun was setting, and was astonished to learn that I
> had spent two days and one night in the cave. I never, in my life,
> had a more interesting adventure, and although I am now in the
> city of Houston, surrounded by friends and all the comforts of
> life, to sit alone, and in memory, retrace my steps in the cave,
> gives me more pleasurable feelings than all the gaudy show and
> pleasing gaity with which I am surrounded. (351)

29

Critics looking for a "traditional" captivity pattern would find
ample evidence in the Plummer narrative, which in many ways reasserts stereotypes of savage Indians and helpless white women. Even
though she has taken great pains to describe the Comanche rituals,
especially the trial in which she shows how fairly she is treated,
Plummer also asserts that "the manners and customs of the Indians
. . . are so ridiculous that [they] would be of but little interest to
any" (355). Even more surprising is Plummer's self-representation
once rescue is near. In marked contrast to the independence and
bravery she demonstrates in the cave, Plummer suddenly represents
herself as frail and helpless: "Hope instantly mounted the throne
from whence it had long been banished. My tottering frame re-

ceived fresh life and courage, as I saw [rescue] approaching the habitation of sorrow and grief where I dwelt" (360).

The last line of Plummer's description of her adventure in the cave tells another story, however. Her assertion that she never in her life "had a more interesting adventure" may explain why, for all her purported agony, she takes certain briars with her from a tree and, when after her ransom she is offered five dollars for one of them, she refuses, claiming, "They often bring to recollection the distant country where I obtained them" (358). It may also explain why, when the Comanches have concluded that she left the cave, and she knows they are about to move on, she nonetheless returns to camp instead of hiding in the cave and attempting an escape. What the narratives of women like Rachel Plummer imply is that, notwithstanding all the pain and suffering captivity brought into their lives, they also discovered a strength and daring, a sense of adventure, that their prior lives had rarely allowed.

Other narratives fall farther outside the paradigmatic narrative traced at the outset of this chapter and pose a more direct challenge to notions of female helplessness and vulnerability. Narratives of physical resistance and escape also display extraordinary courage and endurance, although they are usually considerably more racist than the accounts of women who endured captivity. The aptly named Experience Bozarth (1779) knocks out an Indian's brains with an ax, then "relieves" another of his "entrails," and finally kills a third as he comes in her door. Similarly, Mrs. Merrill (1791) kills five Indians with an ax; when a few more attempt to enter the house through the chimney, she sets several featherbeds on fire beneath them.

No less popular were the stories of escape. In 1763, Mrs. Clendennin, who reviled the Indians even as they threatened to scalp her, hands her baby to another woman and makes her escape. When the Creek master of Eunice Barber (1818) goes to war with another tribe, he arms the captive with a tomahawk. He is soon wounded and begs Barber for aid; instead, she uses the tomahawk to dispatch him and makes her escape. Hannah Dennis (1761) gains great prestige among the Indians by pretending witchcraft; nevertheless she escapes, traveling three hundred miles with a badly hurt foot and hiding in a hollow log midriver for three days. Frances Scott (1786) so convincingly pretends to adopt Indian ways that she is left alone with only one old chief; when he falls asleep she escapes, wandering through the wilderness for a month, even after she is bitten by a venomous snake. Mrs. Durham (1779) escapes even after she is scalped, while Lavina Eastlick (1862) escapes from a scene of slaughter by pretending to be dead. Although she has been shot through the back (the bullet emerges through her side and her arm) and has been beaten in the head with a rifle butt, she drags herself through woods, swamp, and hot, mosquito-ridden grasses, enduring for fifteen days, sometimes with nothing to drink but the dew she squeezes from her dress, and crawling the last distance on her hands and knees. When Mercy Harbison's one guard falls asleep, she escapes, barefooted and having eaten nothing since her capture. Hardly able to move, she carries her baby in a coat held in her teeth. She outwits rattlesnakes and sleeps in pouring, cold rain, until she is finally discovered and taken to a fort, where the surgeon removes 150 thorns from her feet and legs. Mary Smith, taken captive for sixty days in 1814 by Kickapoos, is about to be tortured to death when an old sachem saves her life. When he then claims her as his wife, Smith "was reduced to the necessity of becoming a prostitute in order to prevent the most cruel death" (1815, 13). Feigning desire for the old Indian, Smith is taken back to his wigwam but pretends to be ill and is left alone. She secures a scalping knife, and after the old sachem falls asleep,

> I took my knife and creeping with as little noise as possible to where the savage lay, plunged it into his bosom; he attempted to rise, and at that instant snatching his tomahawk from his belt, I gave him a severe blow on his head, which I repeated until I was sure he was dead. (14)

Smith's story echoes that of the most famous escaped captive, Hannah Duston, who kills her captors in their sleep, returning to Boston, scalps in hand, to receive the bounty.

Narratives of resistance and escape on one level became the propagandists' dream. Demonstrating a complete refusal of acculturation and justifying the use of violence in the cause of "racial purity," these narratives were deployed by anti-Indian spokesmen from Cotton Mather to John Frost.[5] The more ideally the stories of women such as Hannah Duston and Experience Bozarth express the violently racist assumptions of their white readers, however, the more forcefully they question gender stereotypes. While these women are disgusted by the Indians, they are decidedly not James Fenimore Cooper's Alice, who faints in fright at her first sight of the red man. The challenge presented to the stereotype of white women as helpless victims (a characterization still held by the critics discussed at the outset of this chapter) is evident in the difficulty ministers and editors faced in endorsing the rejection of Indian culture demonstrated by women who resisted or escaped captivity, while also denouncing the active agency women took in their own deliverance. The discrepancy between Hannah Duston's tale of self-delivery and Cotton Mather's description of her as *Judea capta*—the patiently suffering Israel awaiting divine deliverance—apparently was evident even to Mather.[6] In his sermon based on Duston's narrative, delivered while she sat in the congregation, Mather warns, " 'You are not now the slaves of Indians, as you were a few days ago, but if you continue Unhumbled in your Sins, you will be the Slaves of Devils' " (Ulrich 1980, 234). Mather's insistence on Duston's humility implies that he recognized and feared the agency she demonstrates in carrying out her own rescue, which showed, as Tara Fitzpatrick writes, that Duston was exempt "from the communal need for repentance or, perhaps, from the particularly feminine duty of submission" (1991, 15).

More obvious still are the contortions undergone by John Frost, the nineteenth-century editor of several volumes of captivity narratives. Frost's ambivalence about women's agency is evident in his gloss on Mrs. Merrill's story.

> Woman, as an Amazon, does not appear to advantage. Something seems to be wanting in such a character; or, perhaps, it has something too much. Yet, occasionally, circumstances render it necessary for the gentler sex to fight or die; and then, though the record may be bloody and revolting, we experience a kind of pleasure at the heroine's triumph. (1854, 43–44)

Yet elsewhere Frost has more difficulty justifying such "Amazonian" conduct. When Molly Pritchard's husband is killed at a fort in New Jersey, she takes up his gun "to the astonishment of the soldiers." "She fought so *manfully*," Frost reports, "that half pay was granted to her for life by Congress. She wore a soldier's epaulette, and was known by the name of 'Captain Molly' ever after" (1854, 76). Her official recognition notwithstanding, Frost concludes, "We do not see much to admire in the unfortunate character of 'Captain Molly'" (80). For Frost, female agency is forgivable only in the absence of male protection. If a woman chooses to protect herself in defiance of masculine agency, however, she loses all virtue. Ironically, for all his avowed hatred of the Indians, Frost uses them as his stand-in in a confrontation with a gutsy captive. When Mrs. Porter grabs her husband's sword and splits the skulls of two Indians, then runs upstairs and shoots a third, thereby making her escape, Frost speculates that the Indians come back the next day and burn the Porter house "partly to conceal the evidence of their discomfiture by a woman" (1859, 21). Since they leave the bones of the slain Indians behind, however, it appears the Indians were less concerned than Frost in concealing the "evidence" of their unmanly defeat.

Frost prefers the courage of women like Mrs. Rowan, who hands hatchets to all the men near her, letting them defend her, and then manages not to scream as Indians approach. Frost praises this "display of cool courage by a woman, in a degree rarely witnessed, even in the west" (1859, 65). "That mother of the west should have a monument," Frost concludes. "It would remind her descendants who are accustomed to hearing females designated to the 'weaker sex,' that upon trying occasions, the strength of soul, which is beyond that of sinew and muscle, has appeared in women, and may appear again" (67). In valorizing "strength of soul" over that of "sinew and muscle," Frost reasserts the dominant notion of women as spiritually stronger than men but physically weaker. If women must display courage, Frosts wants them to be brave enough to let their men protect them. Better still, Frost would apparently like to forget the women altogether, as he does in praising fifteen-year-old Isaac Bradley, who escapes his captors and wanders for nine days before reaching a fort. *This,* writes Frost, who narrates the stories of Mrs. Durham and Mrs. Davis without comment, much less praise, "is undoubtably one of the most extraordinary escapes from Indians that we have on record" (1854, 234).

At the other end of the spectrum from the stories of those who resist or escape Indian captivity is a third set of narratives, in which women acculturate and refuse to leave their captors. Of 723 captives documented by Emma Coleman, sixty stayed with their Indian captors—they "became Indians outright" (Slotkin 1973, 98), as Slotkin comments—while 150 converted to Roman Catholicism, a "substantial number" becoming nuns (97–98). Ironically, large numbers of captives may have converted to Roman Catholicism, even becoming nuns, due to their Protestant upbringing. Taught that participation in the church was the worthiest occupation, Protestant women were simultaneously denied a place in the hierarchy of the church. Forbidden entry into the ministry, women were forced into the relatively passive role of congregants. Catholicism, while refusing women the priesthood, did accommodate women with "a calling" by allowing them to become nuns. Many Puritan women found in convents the formalized religious life they had heard praised at home but had themselves been denied. The convents were also, as Laurel Thatcher Ulrich notes, women-centered, women-controlled spheres, where inhabitants were freed from the direct authority of fathers and husbands (1980, 210–13). This freedom might explain why some captives, such as Submit Phipps or Frances Noble, could only be removed from the convents by physical force.

The histories of women who remained among the Indians are rarely documented; yet the narratives of three such captives—Mary Jemison, Frances Slocum, and Eunice Williams—became well-known in their day. These stories, like most captivity accounts, survive in the texts of male editors (Jemison's account is told by James Seaver, Slocum's by George Ewing, and Williams' by her father, Reverend John Williams); yet they tell remarkable tales of determination and independence in reimagining cultural identification. Mary Jemison's narrative—and the context it offers for interpreting the cultural prejudices of her editor—is representative.[7] James Seaver casts Jemison's life among the Delawares as a brutal ordeal, survived only with the help of her residual whiteness. Seaver writes, "a strange and wondrous gentleness of spirit, perhaps imbued by her early home training, had persisted in Mary Jemison for three-quarters of a century—despite the cruelties and savagery to which she was continually exposed and the unjust fate that had pushed her into a different world" (1758, 77). Apart from her initial capture, however, Jemison tells of no such cruelty or savagery, at least not at the hands of the Delawares. After her family is killed in a 1758 raid, two Delaware women adopt Jemison in the place of their brother, a slain warrior. She is eagerly accepted in this family of women, who pledge to "guard her from trouble" and to see that she is "happy till her spirit shall leave us" (68). The women make good on their promise: assigned the lightest duties, Jemison later "admitted she suffered no hardships" (68).

Eventually Jemison marries a Delaware warrior.

> Sheninjee, she said later, "was a noble man: large in stature, elegant in his appearance: generous in his conduct; courageous in war; a friend to peace, and a great lover of justice." Gradually "his good nature, generosity, tenderness, and friendship towards me, soon gained my affection; and, strange as it may seem, I loved him! To me he was ever kind in sickness, and always treated me with gentleness; in fact, he was an agreeable husband, and a comfortable companion." (70)

The only injustice Jemison records arrives at the hands of whites. When Sheninjee dies, Jemison marries a great Seneca warrior named Hiokatoo. They live peacefully through the revolution, declaring themselves neutral. When the British convince the Senecas to fight, however, Jemison and the other women are forced to flee, and she supports her family by hiring herself out to escaped slaves as a fieldhand. After Hiokatoo dies, Jemison chooses to settle on the Seneca Reservation, where she resolutely refuses to convert to Christianity, the religion of her "home training."

Rather than supplying the narrative of victimization and brutalization promised by Seaver, Jemison, like other acculturated captives, uses her story to reimagine women's "proper" spaces. To begin with, acculturated captives frequently describe matrimonial patterns unusual in eighteenth- or nineteenth-century white society. Eunice Williams' Mohawk husband, François Xavier Arosen, takes his wife's name, and when Frances Slocum and her Delaware husband find they have nothing in common, they peaceably separate. None of these women makes marriage the conclusion of her story; rather, each goes on to describe the large degree of economic self-

35

governance she achieves among the Indians. Jemison possesses eighteen hundred acres in New York, part of which she farms with her two daughters. Frances Slocum also manages a large tract of land. The only threats to the economic self-sufficiency of these women come from whites. In 1831, uncomfortable among the growing number of white settlers in the region, Jemison sells her land and moves to the Seneca reservation. When the American government forces Indians off their land, Frances Slocum petitions as a white woman and receives ownership of hers. Like Jemison, however, Slocum soon finds herself crowded by whites, experiences the theft of her livestock, and is forced to invite her nephew George, a white missionary, to come and look after her affairs.

Describing life among the Indians as offering white women physical, matrimonial, and economic space, appropriatively "crowded" by the white culture that purportedly helps the captives survive, the narratives of acculturation reverse the values Seaver seeks to impose on Jemison's story. Far from yearning for their home cultures, Jemison, Slocum, and Williams repeatedly relate

their unwillingness to return to white society, explicitly resisting white "protection" or "rescue." When fur trader George Ewing boards with Slocum, he writes a letter to a newspaper to alert the Slocum family of her whereabouts; when it is eventually published (the editor delays its appearance for a year), Slocum's two brothers and her sister find their "lost" sibling, now sixty-two, who receives them coolly. Eventually she accepts their company, but when they ask her to leave, she responds, " 'I cannot. I cannot. I am an old tree. I cannot move about. I was a sapling when they took me away. It is all gone past. I am afraid I should die and never come back. I am happy here' " (1778, 126). Even when her rescuers console themselves with bringing Slocum's image back to white society, she resists complete return; Ewing, who records Slocum's story, includes her claim, "She had been happy with the Indians and distrusted the whites" (124). When Slocum's brother brings a painter to render her portrait, he reports of Slocum: " 'There was indication of no unwanted cares upon her countenance, beyond time's influence which peculiarly marks the decline of life. She bore the impress of old age, without its extreme feebleness' " (128). Several attempts to redeem Eunice Williams over the years fail, including her refusal of an offer of land in exchange for her willing return to Boston.[8] When Williams refuses to leave the Indians with one potential rescuer, he reported, "She looked very poor in body, bashful in the face but proved harder than steel in her breast" (1704, 45). Despite the claim of John Williams, after he visited with Eunice for an hour in Canada, that she "wanted to leave with her father, naturally" (41), "nature" apparently proved less of a determinant in captives' cultural identifications than did the increased possibility for healthy and independent lives.

Representing the Indians as kind and considerate hosts, parents, spouses, and leaders, narratives of acculturation diminish the need for women to live in perpetual fear, requiring the constant protection of white men. As Glenda Riley demonstrates in her study of women and Indians on the frontier, the maintenance of stereotypes about each group relied on fixed ideas about the other. Stories of helpless white women victimized by heartless savages were used to justify the extermination of native populations, Riley argues, while the image of the ruthless, blood-thirsty Indian was deployed to keep white women close to home. Stereotypes thus enabled white men to maintain authority over both women and Indians. While narratives of resistance and escape challenged stereotypes of frail and helpless women, they reinforced images of devilish Indians, and in so doing inadvertently contributed to keeping women in the subordinated positions the captives themselves seem to escape. The narratives of acculturation take the opposite tack, challenging colonizing representations of both women and Indians. Far from resulting in the transformation of women into savages, "masculinized" females, or helpless victims, the acculturation of women captives enabled them to alter their racial, national, and gender identities, and in so doing to achieve extraordinary strength of body (all three captives live well beyond the life expectancy of women in their time: Jemison dies in 1833 at the age of ninety; Slocum dies of pneumonia in 1847, at the age of seventy-four; and Williams dies in 1785, almost ninety years old) and a large degree of economic and social control.[9]

While most captives did eventually return to white culture, not all returned happily. Several "redeemed" captives used their narratives to represent white men as the hellish tormentors Indians were purported to be. Isabella M'Coy (1747) does not want to return to her abusive husband (in fact, she allows him to escape captivity so she may be taken alone), but finally returns for the sake of her children. Jemima Howe, redeemed by a French gentleman, soon has to endure the unwanted affections of both her master and his son, who one day finds her alone and "forcibly seized her hand, and solemnly declared that he would now satiate the passion which she had so long refused to indulge" (1859, 13). When Howe employs the "entreaties, struggles, and tears, those prevalent female weapons which the distraction of danger not less than the promptness of genius is wont to supply" (the narrator is, of course, John Frost), the young man grabs a dagger and threatens to kill her. In his finest Richardsonian prose, Frost relates that "Mrs. Howe, assuming the dignity of conscious virtue, told him it was what she most ardently wished, and bade him plunge the weapon through her heart, since the mutual importunities and jealousies of such rivals had rendered her life, though innocent, more irksome and insupportable than death itself" (14). The Canadian governor finally intercedes and has the son shipped off to war, while an Englishman rescues Howe from the father.[10]

American men, too, often become villains in narratives that continue past the captivity proper. Sarah Horn, for instance, is bought from the Indians by Benjamin Hill, but, rather than attributing his actions to Christian charity, she reports that "the withering spirit of sordid avarice was the god, at whose shrine he devoutly humbled himself—and a bill of human rights, drawn in the chancery of heaven, bearing the seal of the angel of mercy, and presented by the hand of suffering humanity, was by him protested!" (1839, 173–74). She works for him as a domestic servant and makes him linen shirts. Despite this, he forces her to buy her provisions from him and sells her damaged goods to boot. Although Hill knows there are other Americans about, he does not tell Horn (175). When she is rescued from Hill, he continues to send her more linens from which to make him shirts, which she does, although she is never paid. The stories of Isabella M'Coy, Jemima Howe, and Sarah Horn—documents of attempted rape, physical and emotional abuse, economic exploitation, and narrative overdetermination performed on the bodies of women not by Indians, but by white men—contextualize and render more comprehensible the decision of captives such as Jemison, Slocum, and Williams to stay with their captors.

At the same time as captives challenged the dominant discourses of their cultures, often in explicit and daring ways, their challenges were never complete. As David R. Sewell has argued, the very act of narration implicated captives in the ideologies of colonialism, since the Indian captors, who maintain bodily and discursive control over whites in the content of the narrative, become, in the speech act of white narration, "captured and tamed once and for all in the written language" of Anglo-America (1993, 42). Sewell describes captivity as a battle between grammars: white language attempts "rationally" to render the Indian "categorized, comprehended, or condemned" (45), while Indian language relies on jokes, ironies, and falsehoods to subvert the mimetic expectations of white linguistic rationalism. Ultimately, the captivity narrative attests to the superiority of English, making "literacy the foundation of civilized identity" (43). However challenging the content of captives' narratives, then, the very language of the texts reinforces Anglo-American identities and ideologies.[11] Nor were the images captives deployed ever entirely distinct from imperialist representations. Indians frequently appear as depraved or noble savages, both images drawn from the stock literature of Anglo-American imperialism, or are homogenized into a generic "Indian," devoid of tribal or individual specificity. The challenge offered by these narratives is never total, therefore; subjectivity itself is unimaginable "outside" or "innocent" of the languages and hence the ideologies of dominant culture.

Yet neither is any cultural discourse solely effective in its constitutive enterprise: discourses remain in conflict, and where the conflict becomes explicit, there the totalizing desire of language is revealed and opened to challenge. In composing divergent and unpredictable stories that challenge the gender expectations as well as the assumptions of narrative sequence held by their home cultures, captives show their active reimaginings of women's strengths and desires. Whether white women suffered their captivities patiently, resisted or escaped capture, or remained with the Indians, their stories are consistent documents of strength and determination. That, however, is the only "consistency" these narratives demonstrate.

Adopting divergent attitudes toward their captors, variously defining agency, and ending their stories differently (some refusing to close until they had condemned the behavior of their white "rescuers"), women captives produced a rich and heterogeneous body of literature. The chapters that follow will situate the narrative varieties outlined above in three specific periods—the late seventeenth, the mid-nineteenth, and the late twentieth centuries—to trace the changing cultural discourses informing and informed by these textual variations.

TWO *Her Tortures Were Turned into Frolick: Captivity and Liminal Critique, 1682–1862*

IN 1690, INDIANS INVADED SALMON FALLS and took one of the largest groups of captives in New England's history. Two years later one of those captives, Mercy Short, now redeemed, began showing signs of demonic possession, and Cotton Mather came from Boston to serve as her spiritual protector. Not surprisingly, given her experiences among the Indians or his as the minister to many redeemed hostages, Short and Mather combined to create a narrative of diabolic possession couched in the rhetoric of Indian captivity.[1] Mather's description of a tawny-skinned devil would be as appropriate to Hannah Duston's narrative as it was to Mercy Short's: "There exhibited himself unto her a Divel having the Figure of A Short and a Black Man; . . . hee was a wretch no taller than an ordinary Walking-Staff; hee was not of a Negro, but of a Tawney, or an Indian colour; hee wore an high-crowned Hat with strait Hair; and had one Cloven Foot" (Mather 1914, 261).

If Mercy Short's devil is an Indian, however, he is dressed as a Puritan. Her possession seems less a way of exorcising unresolved hostility toward her former captors, as Richard Slotkin suggests, than of indicting all men—Puritan and Indian—who are alike to Mercy Short in their interchangeable hellishness. One can understand this assessment from a seventeen-year-old girl just passed from the control of Indian captors to that of the formidable Reverend Mather. In neither world does Short have *self*-control; she is "possessed" in whatever society she lives. Mercy Short thus indicates the continuum of possession between white and Indian, demonic and sanctified society: when, for instance, the devil offers Short a mate, she responds with a curt conflation of matrimony and possession: "An Husband! What! A Divel!" (269). Mather himself feels the sting of Satan's agents, among whose tactics were "Railing and Slander" (267) against the minister.

By dramatizing her "ownership" by several agents, Short reveals Puritan authority's investment in attaching meanings to her body, few of which grant her physical or discursive agency. As an Indian captive, Short was made to represent cultural anxieties over racial purity and contamination; in the spiritual struggle between Satan and Mather, Short is made to articulate orthodoxy's truthfulness in the face of demonic inconsistency, innuendo, and deceit. The "successful" resolution of Short's trials, according to Mather, bespeaks the impermeability of her bodily boundaries and therefore of the "proper" spiritual and social subjectivity that body represents. Short's interactions with Cotton Mather reveal, finally, that Puritan theocrats ultimately generated their authority not through their uses of the body to discipline the soul (as was claimed, for instance, in the trial of Anne Hutchinson), but through the use of spirituality to discipline the body and its articulations of subjectivity.

The dispossessed identities of the possessed body threaten to disrupt spiritual authority, however, as becomes clear in the remainder of Mather's account. Through her "possession," Short allows herself to occupy the role of either captive or captor, and hence to identify, if only in fantasy, with the subjects as well as the objects of bodily and cultural exchange. In identifying with her captors, Short takes her extravagant pleasure and becomes an agent of difference within Puritan society. In a later passage in his account of the possession, Mather writes:

> Her Tortures were turned into Frolick and Shee became as extravagant as a Wild-cat. She now had her Imagination so strangely disordered, that shee must not Acknowledge any of

her Friends; but tho' shee Retained a Secret Notion, Who wee were, yett shee might by no means confess it. Shee would sometimes have diverse of these Fitts in a Day, and shee was always excessively Witty in them, never downright Profane, but yett sufficiently Insolent and Abusive to such as were about her. And in these Fitts also shee took an extraordinary Liberty (which I have likewise noted in some other possessed Persons) to animadvert upon People, that had any thing in their Apparrel that savoured of Curiosity or Ornament. Her Apprehension, Understanding, and Memory, were now Riper than ever in her Life; and yett, when shee was herself, Shee could Remember the other Accidents of her Afflictions but Forgot almost everything that passed in these Ludicrous Intervals. (271–72)

Mather's description suggests that Short, in her extravagant "Frolick," identified with her mischievous demons, seeming to take as much delight in slanderous wit as they did. In her moments of "extraordinary Liberty," Short distances herself momentarily from control by Puritan authority and in so doing shows that one "becomes" oneself by acquiescing to the cultural discourses that define "proper" behavior. She shows, moreover, how few people successfully "become" orthodox Puritans, foregrounding instead the discrepancies between the sanctioned "self" and its divergent manifestations in numerous sartorial "Curiosities." In her play with the boundaries necessary to Puritan identity—between whites and Indians, pleasure and pain, captivity and liberty—Mercy Short exemplifies the strategies of a number of captives who used their culturally liminal position and their identifications with their captors to destabilize dominant constructions of identity—constructions that, ironically, these stories were intended to support—and to challenge the treatment of women in both societies.[2]

"Liminality," the defining feature of this type of narrative, is described by anthropologist Victor Turner as the state of individuals who move from fixed social positions into a "primitive" state of nature where the laws of culture no longer hold (1974, 232). In this "natural" state, the liminar experiences *communitas,* which Turner describes as a feeling of equality and camaraderie (240), shared especially with others alienated from dominant social structures

(250). Though *communitas* is often produced through a prescribed ritual, Turner notes that it may also occur spontaneously as a "reaction against too rigid a structuring of human life in status and role-playing activities" (254); *communitas* is especially likely to arise, according to Turner, from too strict a definition of gender roles (247).

In *communitas* the liminar sees—and therefore may criticize and posit alternatives to—previously invisible social structures (248). *Communitas* therefore challenges those in power (245), who frequently defuse its threat by turning *communitas* into "an ethical or ritual paradigm" (249); that is, if *communitas* has not been brought about by a prescribed ritual, which institutionally limits its challenge, then it is soon subsumed by a structured ritual, and thereby made part of a hegemonic cultural "system." While the absorption of *communitas* limits the critical power of the liminar, it may also compensate him or her with "a sacred power, the power of the weak derived on the one hand from resurgent nature and on the other from the reception of sacred knowledge" (159). The experience of "comradeship and communion" is thus rendered "sacred": exceptional, revered, but again placed outside the sphere of daily experience.

Turner distinguishes, however, between liminars and a second group, marginals. His distinction is useful for understanding the differences between the racial and the gender critiques offered by the captivity narratives, as well as the different manner in which these critiques were either rendered "safe" or suppressed by ministers and other editors. Marginals, according to Turner, are "simultaneously members (by ascription, optation, self-definition, or achievement) of two or more groups whose social definitions and cultural norms are distinct from, and often even opposed to, one another" (233). The most interesting characteristic of marginals, among whom Turner includes women in changed, nontraditional roles, "is that they often look to their group of origin, the so-called inferior group, for *communitas,* and to the more prestigious group in which they mainly live and in which they aspire to higher status as their structural reference group. Sometimes they become radical critics of structure from the perspective of *communitas,* sometimes they tend to deny the affectually warmer and more egalitarian bond

44

of *communitas*" (233). Unlike liminars, who occupy a similar position between cultures, marginals have "no cultural assurance of a final stable resolution of their ambiguity" (233).

Were captive women liminars, then, or marginals? From the perspective of the ministers and editors who framed their narratives, they were liminars, entering into the "natural" world of the Indians, perhaps experiencing a temporary bond with their captors, but finally returning to the structures of white culture. Yet their narratives also tell the story of their marginality as women. Here they distinguish, in their identities as women, between the "structural reference" (the traditional definition of "woman") provided by their home society and the *communitas* found with their captors. In short, white women captives represent themselves as liminars of race but marginals of gender. Rituals were created to account for their temporary "Indianization," rendering their knowledge of the wilderness "sacred" (part of a divinely ordained pattern) but also evil, exceptional but undesirable.[3] No pattern is created, however, to stabilize the systems of gender asymmetry that emerge through captivity, particularly through the *communitas* white women claim to experience with their captors. The critique posed to white culture and to the policy of colonization is (to a degree) neutralized by the ritual frame of the "trial in the wilderness"; the radical challenge to systems of male domination, among Indians as well as among whites, remains unresolved. The resultant tension within the captivity narrative thus becomes a site at which to explore both the cultural forces exerted on the captive (internalized forces inscribed by the captive herself and those imposed from without by editors) and the resistances enabled by temporary exposure to alternative social models and divergent definitions of "race," "gender," and "identity." 45

Anglo-America's first captivity narrative, published in 1682, commences a long tradition of exploration by white female captives of the relationships between racial and gender identities and hierarchies. In February 1675, Narragansett Indians attacked Lancaster, Massachusetts, and took Mary White Rowlandson, wife of the town minister and daughter of its wealthiest landowner, captive for eleven weeks. Rowlandson later related her ordeal to "Ter Amicam" who in 1682 published the text (divided into twenty sections, labeled "removes," that measure her physical journey) along with his preface and a sermon by Rowlandson's husband, Joseph. Insofar as her story diverges from its stated intention of showing God's providence in saving a helpless sinner from the barbarians, Rowlandson's narrative challenges several central assumptions of her home culture. Rowlandson develops, in contrast to her monovocal theological frame, a more complex perspective that allows her to see the Indians as more than stock characters in the drama of her religious salvation.[4]

At the outset of her narrative, Rowlandson expresses her culture's view of the Indians as "hell-hounds" (1682, 35), possessed of a "savageness and brutishness" (36) beyond description. By characterizing her captors as animals and heathens, Rowlandson affirms the Puritans as human and spiritual, the proper subjects of culture. In keeping with her vision of the irredeemable evil of the Indians, Rowlandson attributes to God any kindness shown her in the first part of her narrative. In the third remove, for instance, when a Narragansett woman brings Rowlandson's son for a visit, or later when a man gives Rowlandson a Bible to read, she attributes both acts to Providence. Similarly, when in the fifth remove the Narragansetts lay some brush on the bottom of a raft so Rowlandson's feet remain dry, she attributes the act to God's mercy.

Later in the fifth remove, however, Rowlandson describes a different sort of divine intervention: namely, "the strange providence of God in preserving the heathen" (44). Pursued by the colonial army, hundreds of Indians, mostly women, many sick or carrying babies, convey their entire settlement across a river that the English cannot cross. With her observation of Narragansett mobility and of English ineptness, Rowlandson, even while she justifies her captors' success by claiming that God preserved the Indians so they could continue to "try" the whites (68), begins to soften Puritan orthodoxy's extreme opposition between the divinely favored whites and the hellish Indians. Consequently, in the eighth remove when Rowlandson receives food and assurances of her captors' kindly intentions toward her, while she does not explicitly comment on the humane behavior of the Indians, neither does she attribute their kindness to God.

Significantly, the eighth remove also describes Rowlandson's "adoption" into the tribe. When she is asked to sew a shirt for King Philip, he pays her a shilling, with which Rowlandson buys some horse meat. For the remainder of the narrative, Rowlandson barters her sewing skills for food and shelter, assuming her place in the tribe's economy. Rowlandson's new economic role alters her views not only of her captors but of her home society as well. Teresa Toulouse discusses the crisis engendered in Rowlandson's narrative by her lost sense of fair "exchange" within Puritan discourses of value. Having "paid her debt," as a wife, mother, citizen, and Christian, both to society and to God, Rowlandson voices a complaint, according to Toulouse, that she is not "paid back" her fair market value in earthly or spiritual satisfaction (664). Given this analysis, it is not surprising that Rowlandson notes when the Indians recognize and, more importantly, compensate, her worth as a producer in their economy. When an Indian fails to pay Rowlandson her price, she records the fact with bitterness. Yet she also notes that she is always paid for her labor, even if the debtor is sometimes late in making payment. In the ninth remove, for example, she writes of making a shirt for a "sorry Indian" (48) who refuses to pay her. "But he living by the riverside where I often went to fetch water," Rowlandson continues, "I would often be putting of him in mind and calling for my pay; at last he told me if I would make another shirt for a papoose not yet born, he would give me a knife, which he did when I had done it" (48). Her sense of divine and secular swindle in white culture is apparently countered by fair trade in Narragansett society, and her captors restore the "worth," as Toulouse discusses it, that her nominal "protectors" have stolen. **47**

In entering the Indian economy, Rowlandson transforms herself from an object of exchange in a trade conducted between men (the Indians and the British haggle over Rowlandson's "worth" in terms of tobacco and firearms) to an agent of exchange. Her new economic role seems to allow Rowlandson more physical agency; when she finds herself hungry toward the conclusion of the ninth remove, Rowlandson for the first time sets out to remedy her own dilemma ("I was fain to go and look after something to satisfy my hunger" [49], she states) rather than waiting, as she had done previously, for someone else to bring her relief. With this change in her economic status, Rowlandson demonstrates a consequent shift in her allegiances: later in the ninth remove, when she receives three tokens of the Indians' favor (her master shows her the way to her son, a squaw cooks her dinner, and another gives her a place to sleep), Rowlandson attributes none to God, even going so far as to note that the Indians show her great kindness even though she is a stranger to them (50).

While she never appears to recognize her captors' strategic behavior toward her, then, Rowlandson, following her economic participation, does acknowledge her random treatment, thereby contradicting her earlier notion that all Indian action was intended for her trial, while all kindness came from God alone. "Sometimes I met with favor," Rowlandson concludes the tenth remove, "and sometimes with nothing but frowns" (50). Continuing this note of arbitrariness, Rowlandson, in the final removes of her narrative, sometimes thanks God for her captors' kindnesses (as in removes twelve, fourteen, and seventeen) and sometimes does not (as in removes fifteen and eighteen). In the nineteenth remove, Rowlandson even thanks the Narragansetts themselves. When her master helps her to bathe, she acknowledges the favor shown her, not by God, but by the Indian. She similarly notes the hospitality of an old woman who gives her food and bedding. Finally, at the conclusion of the nineteenth remove, when strangers feed Rowlandson, she notes how little "we prize common mercies when we have them to the full" (64). The move from God's mercy to "common" mercies marks a change in Rowlandson's spiritual security and in the impermeable selfhood that, at the beginning of her narrative, that security requires her to inscribe.

The arbitrariness that enters Rowlandson's account indicates the degree to which her "wilderness" experience destabilized the rigid hierarchies of Puritan orthodoxy, hierarchies based on firmly held binarisms (white/Indian, society/wilderness, male/female, divine/evil) that Rowlandson clearly articulates at the outset of her narrative. Perhaps, as Tara Fitzpatrick suggests, Rowlandson's narrative shows that Puritanism itself was a divided ideology— divided, for example, between a strong faith in community and an emergent individualism, or between the belief that the "wilderness" was Satan's domain and the belief that it was a realm promising providential knowledge. Whether generative or reflective of discursive conflict, Rowlandson's text refuses to produce coherence, a refusal that challenges not only narrative conventions but the framing assertion of functional Puritan social order as well.

Rowlandson's challenge to the binaries undergirding Puritan ideology is tied to her implicit critique of the notion of fixed and innate identity. In calling some of her captors "insolent," Toulouse argues, Rowlandson acknowledges that there are, among the Indians, differences in "character" (if some Indians are "insolent," others are presumably "polite") that result in social hierarchy and hence social structure. As Annette Kolodny notes, furthermore, Rowlandson's acceptance by the Indians—rather than *of* the Indians—may have served to destabilize her cultural faith in fixed identities. For "native peoples," Kolodny writes, "acceptance into the group was determined solely by acculturation, while for Euro-Americans there was always a racial requirement" (1993, 29). By making the captive part of the tribe (often adopting the captive as a member of the family), the Indians show that "identity" is not the result of preordained essence but of acquired language and behavior.[5] In thus distinguishing between Indians and showing them as socially constructed beings rather than as the innately devilish villains of Puritan sermons, Rowlandson demonstrates "the relativity of social arrangements" and challenges the notion of "fixed status" (Toulouse 1992, 658) with which she begins her narrative.

Rowlandson's articulation of destabilized "status" is not limited to her captors, furthermore. In the course of her narrative, Rowlandson also comes to act less in accordance with what she identifies as "white" values, particularly compassion. In the thirteenth remove, when the papoose of Rowlandson's mistress dies, she callously remarks that "there was more room" in the wigwam without the baby (55). When, in the eighteenth remove, a woman gives Rowlandson and an English child horse's feet to eat, she reports, "Being very hungry, I had quickly eat up mine, but the child could not bite it, it was so tough and sinewy but lay sucking, gnawing, chewing, and slabbering of it in the mouth and hand. Then I took it of the child and ate it myself and savory it was to my taste" (60). Rowlandson eats foods she had previously considered inedible (a standard "turning point" in the captivity narratives), and one can

49

gather from the scene in which her master brings Rowlandson water with which to bathe that she gave up some former standards of cleanliness and grooming (Gherman 1975, 59–60). As Rowlandson begins to seem less "white" by her own definition, the Indians become less alien, and the racial oppositions structuring her earlier notions of identity momentarily collapse.

Rowlandson most disturbingly demonstrates the discursive construction of naturalized "identity" when, at the conclusion of her narrative, she returns to her home culture, where most Puritans would not accept her "sociological" view of the Indians. At that point in her tale, Rowlandson again deploys her initial, predictable stereotypes about Indians. In the twentieth remove, when on her redemption the Indians warmly wish her well, Rowlandson again attributes their kindness to God's intervention. Rowlandson also returns to a picture of the Indians as nothing more than "roaring lions and savage bears" (70). The closure she (or perhaps her ministerial editor) provides in order to align her experiences with the typological image of the passively suffering, captive Israel contradicts the understanding and grudging appreciation Rowlandson has demonstrated for the Indian culture and her lessened security in English "superiority." The very contradiction demonstrates the power investments in different conceptions of identity, however, and destabilizes the absolute and naturalized "us vs. them" opposition that begins the narrative.

Rowlandson's resistance to the power investments of white society is notable as well in her "failed" return to Puritan society. On Rowlandson's redemption, the Boston council orders a day of public thanksgiving, but Rowlandson declines to participate. Stating, "I thought I had still cause of mourning" (72), Rowlandson expresses her resistance to offering a "thanksgiving" that would confirm her successful return by and to divine Providence. Her home culture attempts, as did the Indians, to prescribe Rowlandson's behaviors and even her reactions, but she refuses to comply, hence making her Indian captors and her Puritan rescuers analogous (an association she also makes when, after her redemption, she comments, "I was not so much hemmed in with the merciless and cruel heathen but now as much with pitiful, tender-hearted, and compassionate Christians" [71]), while marking her difference from both. Mitchell

Breitwieser has documented Rowlandson's use of mourning (remembering the individual characteristics of the lost object or person, rather than allowing loss to be subsumed into a discourse of "exemplification" that turns every lost object or person into a "type" or representative of some cultural ideal) to prevent her complete return to white society. Breitwieser seems to assume that Rowlandson's subversion is an innocent by-product of her grief; I am suggesting, however, that her refusal results from her newfound agency. There are moments in her text when Rowlandson chooses *not* to mourn. In the thirteenth remove, for example, when her son tells her he "was as much grieved for his father as for himself," Rowlandson responds, "I wondered at his speech, for I thought I had enough upon my spirit in reference to myself to make me mindless of my husband and everyone else" (54). Her moments of grief are selective and well-chosen, serving to distance Rowlandson from her husband (and the Puritan order that he, as minister, represents), and to prevent her complete reintegration into his world.[6]

Rowlandson's challenge to Puritanism arises due to her position, in Tara Fitzpatrick's words, at an "intersection in the contest of cultures" (1991, 12). The shifting of her racial identity, as I have argued, seems closely related to her changed notion of acceptable gender activities. On the one hand, Rowlandson remains fiercely traditional in her gender identity, as one sees in her great affection for her master and her equally strong hostility to his wife. Accustomed to having a "master" whose pleasure she serves, Rowlandson easily adapts to her subordinate role under Indian men. She chafes, however, under the orders of an Indian woman, who displaces Rowlandson from her traditional role as mistress of the house (Ulrich 1980, 228). Yet Rowlandson's acceptance of Indian life seems to begin precisely at the moment when she assumes an economic position in the community. That position gives her an agency among the Indians that she would not necessarily have had in her own culture where, as Breitwieser notes, her dealings "would always have been subaltern, in the name of her husband, putatively if not really subordinate to his vision and direction" (1990, 147). Allowed a mobility, an economic status, and a political centrality she would not have enjoyed in Lancaster, even given the social prominence of her husband and father, Rowlandson seems more

51

willing to reevaluate the notion of social roles in general. Rowlandson's narrative makes clear that the Puritans, as much as the Indians, have a stake in "possessing" her body and its meanings. Yet even while she reveals the efforts of religion to police the borders of identity by requiring that the Puritan subject be "properly" gendered and racialized, Rowlandson, by assuming agency over the dispossession of her identity, ultimately refuses orthodoxy's selfhoods.

John and Sarah Wakefield were among the settlers who swelled the white population in the Minnesota territory from six thousand in 1850 to over two hundred thousand in 1856. The Wakefields, like many white settlers, lived among the seven thousand Santee Sioux who had farmed the land since signing an 1851 treaty that deeded twenty-four million acres to the United States in return for $445,000 and reserved land in western Minnesota. The Sioux lived peaceably with whites until August of 1862; in that month, while the United States Treasury Department debated whether to pay the $71,000 it owed the Sioux in paper money or in gold that might be better used in the war with the Confederacy, and while food rotted in the warehouses of the agency, withheld from the Indians in part to raise the market value of the traders' already overpriced merchandise, the Sioux starved. Finally, on August 4, eight hundred warriors attacked the storehouse of the Upper Agency in Yellow Medicine, and war resulted. The Sioux underestimated the number of troops the government could spare from its other war, however, and years of "individualization," produced by American-sponsored incentive plans that promoted private ownership and competition between Indian farmers, made it nearly impossible for the Sioux to unite and organize for battle. The American troops, led by Henry Sibley, defeated Little Crow's army, resulting in the apprehension, trial, and conviction of 307 Sioux warriors and the utter dispossession of the Minnesota Sioux.[7]

Sarah Wakefield was taken captive during the battle between Sibley and Little Crow, and lived for six weeks among the Sioux. Published in 1864, her narrative tells a remarkably different story from Mary Rowlandson's. Moving to the Minnesota frontier when her husband becomes physician to the Sioux, Wakefield is initially less than flattering to her Indian neighbors, calling them "filthy, nasty, greasy" (1864, 3). Soon, however, Wakefield notes that the white traders ruthlessly cheat the Sioux and marvels that the Indians do not retaliate (7). She also begins to hire Indian women, coming "to love and respect them as well as if they were whites" (7). Through these experiences, Wakefield learns that all whites are not morally superior and all Indians are not detestable savages; consequently, she adopts a more sympathetic attitude toward the Sioux. She goes as far as to blame the subsequent attack on the settlement entirely on her white countrymen, both because the agency is starving the Sioux and because the agent fails "to understand the nature of the people he had in his charge" (10), an understanding Wakefield herself gains through her interaction with the Sioux women. Many people, she reports, think her "insane" for sympathizing with the Sioux (10), who, when they finally attack, kill the traders and stuff their mouths and ears with gold (11).

When the Sioux first threaten the settlement, Wakefield's husband ships her off to another fort; Wakefield senses the dangers in this plan, but when she tells her apprehensions to her driver, he dismisses her as "hysterical" (12). Soon, however, their wagon is attacked and the driver killed. Wakefield, now a captive, momentarily returns to her initial vilification of the Indians and insists on her commonality with all whites (16–17). Yet, just as she had done at home, Wakefield befriends the Indian women, whose hard labor she reports with sympathy (26); one woman in particular she comes "to look upon . . . as I would upon a mother" (26). Wakefield also befriends a Sioux brave, Chaska, who preserves her chastity by marrying her when she is threatened by another Indian. Very few men, Wakefield states, *"even white men,"* would have treated her with so much respect (many whites, she reports, call her a liar when she notes this fact) (28). Forming friendships with the Sioux again leads Wakefield to revise her belief in the innate superiority—or commonality—of all whites.

When word arrives that the American army is advancing, causing the Sioux chief to retreat, a group of Wakefield's Sioux friends decide to wait with the captives until the army arrives. The American soldiers are moving inexplicably slowly, however, and the small group finds itself caught between the two warring armies (48). When Wakefield finally sees the Americans advancing, therefore, "instead of joy, I felt feelings of anger enter my breast, . . . for I felt that part at least might have come to our rescue before that late hour" (49). The soldiers convey Wakefield to Camp Release, where she becomes such a spectacle that she is "nearly suffocated": "I was a vast deal more comfortable with the Indians in every respect," Wakefield admits, "than I was during my stay in that soldiers' camp, and was treated more respectfully by those savages, than I was by those in that camp" (51). To Wakefield's horror, the army sets up a military court to try the Sioux who waited with the white captives rather than fleeing with Little Crow. When Chaska comes to trial, Wakefield testifies on his behalf. The soldiers "thought it very strange I had no complaints to make, and did not appear to believe me," urging her to tell "anything more of a private matter" (52). Rather than bearing false witness by claiming to have been raped (the obvious desire of the court), Wakefield responds by threatening to shoot Captain Grant if he hangs Chaska (53).[8] The army nevertheless does hang him, Wakefield dismissing the claim that he was executed accidentally. She appeals to heaven to judge the soldiers' guilt, adding that their actions "caused me to feel unkindly towards my own people" (59).

At the same time that Chaska is being tried, another Indian, who saved the life of a white man, is "lauded to the skies" (54) by the soldiers. Wakefield recognizes in this double standard, in which an Indian who saves a white man is praised while one who saves a white woman is condemned, that the army considers neither her testimony nor her life of value (54). As a woman, Wakefield is valuable to the army only as a "victim." Without a raped or tortured female, the army has more difficulty justifying a war that few were willing to admit was waged over land. Wakefield watches as others relate accounts of their captivities she knows to be untrue, yielding to the pressures she has resisted and reshaping their "testimony" so as "to excite the sympathies of the soldiers" (60). Telling a different story, Wakefield articulates the stakes involved in the army's "rescue" of female captives. "My object," she states, "was to excite sympathy for the Indians and in so doing, the soldiers lost all respect for me, and abused me shamefully; but I had rather have my own conscience than that of those persons who turned against their protectors, those that were so kind to them in their great time of peril" (60). In Wakefield's account, to be "abused" comes to mean to be raped *or* to be disbelieved, as she recognizes that her text and her body must become one, and must become "vulnerable" to white male vision and revision, in order to "excite" sympathy.[9] By the end of Wakefield's narrative, the United States Army has entirely dispossessed the Sioux, who are living in exile. When she sees any of her former captors, Wakefield concludes, she brings food to their camp, for which she "was rejoiced" (65).

Both Wakefield and Rowlandson move in their narratives from a dehumanizing and totalizing account of the Indians to a more sympathetic description alert to the humanity, the diversity, and the social organization of their captors. Because of their altered perspective, both Wakefield and Rowlandson gain some distance from their home cultures and begin to criticize the inadequacies of the "protection" those cultures purportedly provide. With less faith in either the innate superiority of whites or the natural barbarism of Indians, both captives return to their homes with difficulty, experiencing their difference from other whites and, arguably, some longing for the Indian society they have left behind.

The two narratives differ in important ways, however. The thematic and stylistic shifts between Rowlandson's text and Wakefield's reflect changes in the social status of female captives, differences related to changing social discourses of class, race, and gender. While Rowlandson begins to soften her individual sense of the Indians as "hell hounds," she does not explicitly challenge her culture's xenophobic drive to vilify—and physically conquer—the native populations. Nor does Rowlandson make an explicit connection between her culture's views of Indians and how she, as a woman, is treated in Puritan society. Wakefield, however, expresses explicit anger at the nationalistic rhetoric encouraging westward settlement. Wakefield connects the discourse of "manifest destiny"—aimed at middle-class men with a desire for cheap, profitable land—with its very human outcome: starved and dispossessed Indians and vulnerable, discredited women. Representing both groups as the victims of a class-inflected rhetoric of national expansion, Wakefield blames neither for staging resistance. Beyond her identification with Indians in general, Wakefield, who notes the unfair burden placed on Sioux women and who befriends her Indian "mother," experiences a particular attachment to her female captors. Wakefield's sympathy with Indian women—a sympathy Rowlandson never articulates—indicates the wide acceptance of the middle-class gender ideology that claimed that all white women share a common "nature" that links them temperamentally with all others of their sex.[10] Captives such as Wakefield, like many female abolition advocates, extended across racial lines their culture's notion of a common female identity, encompassing Indian women in the shared "sisterhood."

While she participates, on one level, in her culture's gender ideology, Wakefield also challenges some of its most cherished preconceptions. She accomplishes this challenge most emphatically by continuing her narrative beyond its supposed ending on her rescue. While both Rowlandson and Wakefield experience incomplete reintegration into white society, Wakefield uses that "failed" return to express some of her most damning insights. Wakefield's critique seems bound up in the ironically named "Camp Release," which soon becomes a site of more tribulation and despair than her Indian captivity had ever been (represented, for instance, by the literalization and reversal of the Puritan belief that Indians existed to "try" innocent Christians; in the nineteenth century, white Christians try innocent Indians). As her experiences in the fort reveal, the project of westward expansion relies not only on an unquestioned discourse of white superiority; it requires as well a carefully policed system of gender roles in which women are sexually vulnerable, unalterably xenophobic, and physically helpless, requiring the protection and support of white men, which the latter skillfully and unflaggingly provide. Wakefield, by "writing beyond the ending"[11] of her captivity, shows the great investment white men have in those roles and how far they are willing to go to enforce them. "Release," far from bringing its promised "freedom" or "liberty," then, brings the captive increased confinement and coercion. Wakefield's narrative demonstrates that women never experience "freedom," not even in white society, where she is dismissed both before and after her captivity as an hysteric and a liar.

In both its textual strategies and its content, Sarah Wakefield's narrative resembles numerous captivity accounts authored by women throughout the late eighteenth and nineteenth centuries.

These narratives are not the "classic" captivity stories in which passive women wait patiently for rescue from savage captors. Nor are they the sensationalized nineteenth-century "penny dreadfuls" dismissed by critics such as Roy Harvey Pearce and Richard VanDer-Beets.[12] Rather, these innovative stories reveal much about how white women received and reshaped cultural discourses disseminated and manifested on the shifting American frontiers. They further reveal that captives such as Sarah Wakefield resisted the binarisms—of white and Indian, civilized and savage, masculine and feminine, captivity and liberty—on which white, middle-class ideologies of class, race, and gender rested.

Unlike Rowlandson, who as the daughter of a wealthy landowner and wife of the town minister was part of the Lancaster elite, most nineteenth-century captives belonged to the upwardly aspiring, often immigrant, middle class, brought to the western frontiers by fathers and husbands in search of land and more profitable incomes. Like Sarah Horn, whose husband is led by "inducements" (1839, 3) in the newspaper to settle in Texas, where they soon find that all they have read proves "unfounded in fact" (8), captives frequently situate their ordeals in the unfortunate collision of the greed or gullibility of husbands and fathers with the highly fictional rhetoric designed to lure settlers into the dangerous frontier territories. Abbie Gardner (1885), noting the widespread, competitive machismo fostered by promotion literature, blames her captivity on the rhetorically induced heroics of her father, who was like "thousands of others who seem to think that because it is best for some to go west, it is best for each one to go further west of all" (10). Having "been made the dupe of others" (1838, 6), Clarissa Plummer's husband, who despite his wife's objections sells their farm and moves to Texas, is forced at the time of her capture by Comanches to beg her "forgiveness, in thus subjecting me, so much against my will, to the privations and hardships which I was then enduring" (9). As Plummer suggests, women settlers were captives to the wills of their husbands and fathers—themselves the "dupes" of expansionist propaganda—as much as they were to Indians.

Anger often surfaces in the narratives when the captive realizes that she is the price paid for, and not the recipient of, the benefits of western expansion. While the opening of Abbie Gardner's 1885 narrative is marked by praise for modern civilization, by its conclusion Gardner bemoans her culture's glorification of war (210–11), at the same time introducing a nostalgic longing for the "innocence" of the landscape, lost to the capitalist "civilization" she earlier praised. Gardner's position on the westward march of civilization changes when, due to her captivity, she finds herself in the position of the dispossessed Indians. After her redemption, Gardner describes herself as "a free girl, tenderly cared for, in a rich and populous city" (265–66). In the great financial crisis of 1857, however, her St. Paul bank crashes, putting Gardner in the position of her former captors, forced to beg for compensation for her family's property from the white man who has appropriated it in her absence. Like her captors, Gardner receives only a "*small* amount" (280) for the stolen land. Following this transaction, when Gardner tells of developers planning to turn the former farm into a resort, she claims that history, which she herself inscribes, will prevent the full possession of the land: "When the hand of art shall have done its utmost to develop and enhance the claims of nature, it will still be found that the weird traditions of the dusky race that once haunted these shores, and the story of the dark tragedies enacted here, have laid over all a more powerful spirit than beauty" (304–5). The histories of the Indians, written by their white female captives, constitute a persistent and "uncanny" cultural trace that, while covered over by the "art" of the conquering race, emerges to disrupt the seamless narrative and exert its disquieting influence.

While captives like Gardner occasionally challenged westward development directly, captives more frequently dismantle the rhetoric of manifest destiny by confronting its twinned assumptions about gender and race. The most significant oversight in the newspaper accounts luring settlers to the west was the fact that increasingly armed and angry populations already occupied and were prepared to defend that land. When addressed at all, the Indians were presented as either "noble savages," eager to befriend the bearers of civilization, or as incompetent bunglers, armed with rudimentary and ineffective weaponry and therefore easily overpowered.[13] The female captive quickly learns the falsehood of both portraits. When Pawnees attack the group of settlers with which she travels, Gertrude Morgan (1866) is surprised that the men cannot dispatch the Indians, as happens so easily in the accounts she has read. She then recalls that those accounts fail to mention that the Indians have guns. Discovering "that a long Missouri rifle, in the hands of an Indian warrior, makes him entirely the equal, nay, often times his superior" (20), she also recognizes that her belief in white male superiority depends on seeing life mediated through white men's texts. Captivity equally gives the lie, in the minds of the captives, to the image of the "noble savage." Sarah Larimer had read many accounts of "the noble character of the red man, of his lofty bearing, scorn, pride, etc., all of which our acquaintance . . . failed to confirm" (1871, 34). More vitriolic, Emeline Fuller writes,

> Let those who have never suffered as I have pity the fate of the noble red man of the forest. My pity all goes out for their poor unfortunate victims, and I can never look even upon one of our poor, degraded, harmless Winnebagoes, without such feelings as I do not like to entertain towards any of God's created beings, and I almost doubt if they are a part of our great Master's work. (1892, 29)

59

Fuller's insistence on the innate evil of her former captors is more frequently softened by attributing the "barbarism" of the Indians to the systematic appropriation of their land. Abbie Gardner at first sees the Indian as "a savage monster in human shape" (1885, 57), but attributes her captors' behavior to their "protestation against civilization's irresistible march across the American continent" (57). Helen Tarble (1904) calls the Minnesota massacre in which she is taken captive "the most appalling exhibition of Indian treachery and ferocity ever perpetrated," but adds that the "terrible affair was one of the strongest evidences of the deadly hate engendered among the savages by the white man's taking possession of their hunting grounds and attempting to force them into what we call civilization" (3). Feeling entrapped by the rhetoric of western expansion, nineteenth-century captives were willing not only to show the Indians to be, like themselves, victims—not causes—of the rhetoric of manifest destiny, they also made explicit the relative construction ("what we call") of "civilization" itself.

Rejecting these caricatures of their captors, nineteenth-century captives, once among the Indians, develop significantly more diverse and sympathetic (although often critical) portraits. The captive often moves, as Wakefield does, from early claims of "savagery" to open recognition of Indian kindness, generosity, and honor. "I shall ever remember this young Indian with affection," Susannah Johnson writes of one of her captors; "he had a high sense of honor and good behavior, he was affable, good natured and polite" (1907, 133). The narrative of Sarah Larimer, who soon after her captivity "was forming a more favorable opinion of Indian gallantry" (1871, 69), becomes a virtual compendium of Indian kindnesses. Larimer reports the story of Mrs. Morton, "kindly received as an adopted child, . . . receiving the kindest treatment, and not being compelled to perform any hard labor" (130). Larimer also relates her efforts to redeem another white woman, who is unimpressed with the man Larimer sends to escort her and sends him back with a message from her Indian master: " 'I will not let the white woman go with you. A man of honor shall come for her, or I will wait until the snows have left the ground, and then carry her to the fort myself' " (132). Finally, Larimer writes of Mrs. Ewbanks, whose former captor, Black Bear, is caught, tried, and convicted: "Before the execution, Black Bear sent a few dollars in money to Mrs. Ewbanks, with the message that he had no further use for it, and it might be made useful to her and her child" (135).

The more sympathetic understanding of her captors often enabled the captive to survive her isolated life on the frontier, offering her much-needed companionship, courage, and survival skills. When Helen Tarble and her husband camp on the land of a white man and his Indian wife, Helen cannot bring herself to cook her dinner in the Indian woman's home, admitting, "I did not get over my fear of that squaw. To me then she was the most repulsive looking woman I ever beheld" (1904, 17). However, when her husband becomes the carpenter on the Sioux reservation, leaving her alone for weeks at a time, Tarble learns to appreciate her neighbors. She writes that "during those long absences of my husband, I became well acquainted with the Indians, who were very kind and friendly to me" (18). "When I could talk with them in their own language," Tarble reports, "they seemed to think I belonged to them. They would at any time give me a share of what they had to eat, and often I would go to their camp and listen to their war adventures" (19).

"Belonging," for Tarble, comes to mean, not proprietary possession, but being admitted to the communal sharing of food and language. Tarble is in particular a "ready and willing pupil" (20) of the
medicine man, who teaches her skills that twice save the lives of her
children. Anticipating the skeptical white audience that dismissed
Wakefield, Tarble apologizes for her friendship with the Sioux, re-
minding her readers, "I was there in the wilderness without books,
papers or even people of my own race" (20). Her text nevertheless
shows that, without the support and training she receives from the
Sioux, for whom she ultimately declares affection, Tarble could not
have survived her otherwise lonely life on the frontier.

The nineteenth-century captive, who learned the customs, rituals, and language of her Indian neighbors rather than holding on
to doctrinal concepts of ethnic "purity," thus struggled with contemporary discourses of "race" and "civilization" more explicitly
than her Puritan precursors would have dared. The more complex
treatment of race is possibly due, as I have suggested, to a general
disillusionment with the middle-class "American Dream" of easily
gained land and prosperity. Soon realizing that they were the price   **61**
paid—the object of exchange—in the struggle to wrestle that land
from its present inhabitants, female captives noted that the newspaper rhetoric created two groups of victims, an understanding that
seems, as in Wakefield's experience, to have moved women on the
frontiers to sympathize more readily with their Indian neighbors.
Their sympathy is perhaps also owing to the fact that many
nineteenth-century captivities occur in the context of the Civil War,
in which captives often had husbands or family members fighting
for the Union.[14] Through both abolition rhetoric and physical
proximity in frontier settlements, many nineteenth-century women
saw people of color as diverse humans, not as the mysterious, savage
demons of Puritan sermons, or as the "noble" bunglers who
peopled contemporary newspaper accounts.

As Wakefield's text demonstrates, however, frontier representations of race were never far removed from discourses of gender.[15]
Captives therefore also contended with middle-class gender roles,
which stressed cleanliness, bodily and spiritual purity, and domesticity as attributes of white womanhood. Since the captive could not
maintain these standards, as defined by her culture, during her cap-

tivity, her sense of "womanhood" necessarily became more at issue in the nineteenth century than in earlier periods. The captives' anxious self-distancing from other white women suggests both the fixity of their cultural constructions of "womanhood" and how far their narratives took them beyond those definitions. Female captives seldom credit other white women with possessing bravery or physical strength, imagining themselves as unique exceptions to the "norm" of femininity. Eunice Barber (1818), who "was often subjected to hardships seemingly intolerable to one of so delicate a frame" (18), states that she endured what "would have been impossible for many females to sustain!" (8). Ann Coleson (1866) asks, " 'Was ever a woman so singularly situated before?' I asked myself over and over again" (33). Mary Barber (1873) tells of her "astonishing adventures such as probably no woman, and few men, have ever experienced" (19). Even Wakefield mocks other white women, whose "greatest terror seemed to be the loss of her feather beds" (1864, 15).

Seeing themselves as different from other white women, captives do not therefore depict themselves as failures; rather, they relish how far they exceed the "true woman's" purported abilities. In her life prior to captivity, Gertrude Morgan was nineteenth-century America's model of white, middle-class femininity, "a delicate, puny girl, shrinking from airs too chilly, or sunshine too warm" (1866, 36). Captivity reveals her uncultivated strengths and abilities, however, and allows Morgan to re-present herself in the language of masculine wilderness adventure: "I, who trembled at the slightest peril; [sic] was now dashing fearlessly through a fearful tempest, over a mighty prairie, with the blazing bolts of Heaven falling at my very feet, the wind howling in my ears, and torrents of rain drenching me through and through" (36). When Abbie Gardner is captured, she believes herself possessed of the "naturally sensitive nature" (1885, 70) supposedly shared by all women in her culture. Consequently, as every story she has ever read of Indian cruelty "now arose in horrid vividness before me" (69), Gardner can only imagine herself "plunged into hopeless, helpless servitude to these inhuman, fiendish monsters" (79). Yet the Indians recognize when a captive surrenders her former model of femininity and ritually reward the reinscription of a "womanhood" Gardner's home culture claimed was immutable: on Gardner's release, her captors present her with their highest honor—a war cap—"as a token of respect for the fortitude and bravery I had manifested" (259). Gardner is obviously proud of her ability to impress her captors with her bravery, "a quality which they highly appreciate but which they did not suppose the white woman to possess" (79).

Cultural definitions of "womanhood" thus made captives, who survive outside the home using physical and intellectual as well as emotional prowess, distinct in their own eyes from the women of their home culture, who, "delicate of frame," were fit only for captivity in the parlor. Ironically, however, the same gender ideology may have heightened captives' sympathy with their female captors (a process discussed in greater detail in the following section). The increasing popularity after the late eighteenth century of the notion of shared "femaleness" may explain why nineteenth-century captives quickly developed sympathetic bonds with their female captors, while Puritan captives such as Rowlandson were more likely to seek connections with their male captors. Such sympathetic connections allowed female captives to enjoy the "sisterhood" prevalent in their home culture without surrendering the strengths and abilities developed in the "wilderness." Working both within and against rhetorics that defined middle-class, white womanhood, captives are able to distinguish between hostile captors and those Indian women whom, in Abbie Gardner's words, "a fellow feeling makes . . . wondrous kind." "How often it is thus in life," Gardner writes, echoing the sentiments of many nineteenth-century captives, "we do not know our friends from our enemies" (1885, 248).

The bonds they establish with Indian women not only enabled female captives to survive—even, occasionally, to enjoy—their time among the Indians, but challenged white women to overcome their culturally enforced "weaknesses" and develop more self-sufficiency. The "mentorship" Indian women provided their white "sisters" becomes evident in the story of Ann Coleson who, taken captive by Minnesota Sioux in 1863, one day escapes with a man named Webb. The escaped captives soon meet an Indian woman, Sunny Eye, who takes them to her hut, where she lives "happy and contented" among comforts "all the product of her own industry" (1864, 59). Sunny Eye's autonomous self-sufficiency offsets Coleson's perceived "need" of a companion like Webb, and the Indian woman teaches Coleson to insist on her own abilities, even in the face of explicit masculine prejudice. At one point, when a wounded man they encounter refuses to be pulled on a sledge by women, Sunny Eye, as usual, has her own way, binding the protesting man and pulling the sledge herself. Another evening, when they hear wolves chasing a rider, Webb has one plan for rescue and Sunny Eye another, and hers succeeds. Coleson's subjectivity becomes bound even on a narrative level to Sunny Eye, whose entrance into the story moves Coleson from the traditional "woman's position" (she is the narrative object in an unnamed narrator's third-person account) to one offering more agency (when Sunny Eye arrives, Coleson becomes the narrative subject of her own first-person journal).

The self-sufficiency Sunny Eye offers Coleson would stand many captives in good stead since, as most learn, the protection on which they more traditionally depend—represented in Coleson's story by Webb—proves highly unreliable, even dangerous. Just as Rowlandson's entrance into the life of her captors provides her the distance to criticize her home society, so most nineteenth-century captives quickly move from a sympathetic bond with the Indians to a challenge to their home cultures' values and supposed strengths. Those challenges, like the bonds that enable them, are gender inflected, aimed almost exclusively at men. Feeling less aligned with the white men who previously defined their identities, captives detail the unwillingness of men to sympathize with their legitimate anxieties about life on the frontier. Helen Tarble, who at thirteen marries her twenty-six-year-old husband, writes that he "seemed to have little patience with my fears." She cries all night in the covered wagon, and resolves "at all hazards to return on the morrow alone, if my husband would not go with me" (1904, 16–17). Captivity apparently awakens Tarble's powers of dissent: "After my capture by the Indians," Tarble writes, "there was discord between me and my husband, and at St. Paul we 'agreed to disagree'" (49). Once those anxieties prove well-grounded, male "protectors" are unwilling to save their female relations from the dangers of frontier life. When her home is attacked by Indians late one night, Ann Coleson cannot rally her sons to protect her; one son is aware of the attack but, afraid of ridicule, refuses to awaken his brothers. A captive named

Mrs. Wright even applies to the legislature for a bill of divorcement from her husband, "urging, as her reason, his cruelty in leaving her and their child in jeopardy when the Indians came upon them" (Larimer 1871, 146).

Often, captives are the victims not only of male ineptness and neglect but of actively directed abuse. Elizabeth Hicks' Indian captivity almost vanishes in her tale of the coercion, endangerment, and immobility forced on her by white men. When her father and brother abandon Hicks at a fort (her father travels for years at a time and her brother, left as her protector, wishes to see the countryside), the new abode quickly becomes a "prison" to the young girl. She resolves to return alone to the family farm, to which her "tormentor," Captain Gilmore, with "sentiments widely different from the fraternal" (1902, 22), insists on accompanying her. When Gilmore pressures Hicks to sign an agreement that she will marry him at seventeen, Hicks refuses until she can sign her own name, thereby convincing Gilmore to teach her to write. Her only moments of happiness prior to her captivity come with her friend Peggy, a purchased Indian servant. Following her captivity, her Indian "uncle" begins to woo her as well, and Hicks only keeps him at a distance by purporting to love Gilmore, all the while describing the Indian in the very language she had previously used to vilify Gilmore (49). Finally Hicks meets Captain Bird, who sends her gifts and promises to help her return home if she will put herself "under his protection" (55). When Hicks tells another officer that she cannot marry Bird (who has ordered the raid that killed her biological father) because she loves another, he counsels: "'You must not be so romantic, you never will be able to get back again; there are many now in this town who would give anything to go home, but cannot; and how is it possible for a poor, helpless girl, without friend or money, to accomplish such an undertaking?" (77). As Bird gets even more insistent, Hicks reports, "I was much distressed by his being so pressing for me to give up my freedom" (83). One morning he shows up with a priest and several witnesses, slips a ring on her finger, and marries her. Bird tells his new bride, "the surest way to victory is a surprise" (86). White men become the most disturbing agents of "torment" in Hicks' Indian captivity, forcing her to surrender her "freedom" (referring here to her life among the Indians).

Hicks, like many nineteenth-century captives, thus learns a disturb-ing lesson: in order to go home, she must first pay a price—the only price she can pay, that of her own body—to the very masculine "protection" that has endangered her in the first place. Hicks can carve a small space for herself only by strategically deploying the language of "romance," a rhetoric that also renders her "vulner-able" and hence "available." Little wonder that she prefers the soci-ety of Indian women who, like Hicks, are threatened by the surprise attacks launched by men like Bird.

Earlier captives also blamed husbands and male family mem-bers for their ordeals, telling of a door left unbolted or a husband who flees on attack. Nineteenth-century captives are unique in their explicit condemnation of institutional "protection," seeing collec-tives like the Indian agencies and the army as extensions of the indi-vidual men who put them in jeopardy. Connecting the failures of individual men with perceived institutional inadequacy, nineteenth-century captives thus launch a thorough critique of the patriarchal prerogatives of their home cultures. When Helen Tarble and her children escape captivity and reach an American fort, having trav-eled sixty miles in eight days with almost no food, the soldiers give them a huge feast, making them all extremely ill and almost killing one of the children (1904, 43). Sarah Horn writes that the incompe-tent pursuit of the United States Army "only made our situation more terrible" (1839, 163). Sarah Larimer quickly learns to distrust the army commanders, who assure the group with which she travels that it has nothing to fear from the Indians, urging the travelers to move into Indian territory where they are soon attacked by 250 Sioux. On the trail to Oregon, Emeline Fuller's family requests an escort, which the army captain refuses when the women and girls decline to attend a ball with his soldiers (1892, 11). Susannah John-son expresses the skepticism of many captives regarding the values and efficacy of white men, especially in contrast to those of their supposedly inferior Indian counterparts:

> As they are aptly called the children of nature, those who have profited by refinement and education, ought to abate part of the prejudice, which prompts them to look with an eye of censure on this untutored race. Can it be said of civilized conquerors,

that they, in the main, are willing to share with their prisoners, the last ration of food, when famine stares them in the face? Do they ever adopt an enemy, and salute him by the tender name of brother? (1907, 76–77)

Lack of confidence in masculine agency—individual and institutional—renders difficult the captive's return to a world in which men are the standards of courage, virtue, and efficiency. Far from depicting the home culture as a haven of liberty, happiness, and ease, captives like Wakefield often represent "rescue" as the beginning of even greater trials. Often, these dramatic experiences of failed "return" leave captives nostalgic for their lives among the Indians and attempting, as Susannah Johnson does, to recreate the liberties of the "wilderness" in the midst of an irksome and constraining "civilization." Toward the conclusion of her narrative, Johnson's husband urges his captive wife to persuade the Indians to take her to Montreal, where he and their children have been redeemed. When Johnson arrives, her husband leaves for New England to raise money for her redemption. "The fond idea of liberty, held forth its dazzling pleasures," Johnson writes with confidence, admitting, however, that only "the ignorance of future calamities, precluded every cloud, that could obscure its effulgence" (1907, 76). Those clouds soon arrive in the form of the Massachusetts General Assembly, which refuses Johnson's husband the money for her redemption. He finally attains the sum from the New Hampshire Assembly, but the governor of Massachusetts detains him so long that he violates his parole and loses his letter of credit, leaving his wife to "roam the streets, without a prospect of relief from the cloud of misfortune that hung over me" (84–88). The "faithful Indians" bring her a great deal of silver, but a French man confiscates the whole amount (88). Johnson finally reunites with her husband, but he enlists in the army and is killed at Ticonderoga. She settles for a short while with her son-in-law, whose treatment she "found almost as painful to be borne, as my savage captivity" (142). "During the time of my widowhood," Johnson laments,

67

misfortune and disappointment were my intimate companions. In the settlement of my husband's estate, the delay and perplexity was distressing. I made three journeys to Portsmouth, fourteen to Boston, and three to Springfield, to effect the settlement. Whether my captivity had taught me to be ungrateful, or whether imagination formed a catalogue of evils, I will not pretend to say; but from the year 1754 to the present day, greater misfortunes have apparently fallen to my share than to mankind in general, and the meteor happiness has eluded my grasp. (136)

Johnson's only pleasures come from telling her story to "numerous progeny" (140), and from the life she finally makes with her daughter, Captive (149).

That Johnson can only find contentment with Captive is ironic, since her youngest daughter bears the traces of Johnson's captivity, during which Captive was born. Like the Indians and the Quebecois with whom they became associated during the French and Indian War, Captive grew up speaking only French and, being "lawless," roamed about Montreal at will, exchanging "very rough language" with sentinels (115). More importantly, Captive denaturalizes Anglo-American values and behaviors, attributing the failure of the English-speaking Americans to understand her French to "their ignorance and impertinence" (116). Captive thus proves a companion who can validate Johnson's "ungrateful" attitude toward whites, her sense of loss for the "faithful Indians," and her newly developed cultural relativism, through which she notes that "the passions of men are as various as their complexions" (135).

Captivity frequently placed women like Johnson at odds with cultural discourses that trivialized the contributions and abilities of Indians and of white women. Denied "authority" over those discourses, captives such as Theresa Delaney came to feel inadequate to the task of writing even their own stories, apologizing for coming into public with so little talent and claiming that their stories "would require the pen of a Fenimore Cooper" (Gowanlock 1885, 82). Captivity also provided women with alternative cultural models through which to define race, class, and gender by offering a story of strong, humane, and exploited Indians and of capable, brave white women able to survive in a wilderness for which they were supposedly unsuited. Expanding their stories beyond their generic endings, female captives show that return to the home culture presented the captives with less "freedom" and happiness than they had expected. Returning from captivity with altered definitions and a sense of the possibilities offered by different identifications and alliances, nineteenth-century white women, armed with the skill of writing Elizabeth Hicks worked so hard to achieve, were able to inscribe more empowering subjectivities.[16]

Fanny Kelly's *My Captivity among the Sioux Indians* (1871) is undoubtedly one of the most detailed and complex accounts authored by a nineteenth-century captive. Like other captive women of the period, Kelly explores and revises the boundaries of identity established through contemporary discourses of race and class. Kelly's narrative is unusual, however, in the degree to which it articulates the complicated impact of gender on the captive's experiences. Mary Rowlandson, like many early captives, underwent an adoption into Indian life. Separated from other whites, the captive is alternately shown cruelty and kindness by her captors, and finally undergoes ritual initiation.[17] Kelly participates in a similar process, but almost entirely in the context of female community: separated from white female companionship, Kelly is shown cruelty by Indian men but comforted by Indian women, and is finally ritually adopted as a mother and a daughter. Kelly's narrative thereby maps more astutely than other nineteenth-century accounts the captive's move from an identity defined primarily in terms of a "whiteness" that alienates her from her captors and unites her with the men of her home culture, to one focused on her gender, a change Kelly is able to imagine due to her identification with her female captors.

69

Like other nineteenth-century captives, Fanny Wiggins Kelly, born in Orillia, Canada, in 1845, comes to the American frontier during the period when "the 'Western Fever' became almost epidemic." Among the infected was Kelly's father, James Wiggins, who in 1856 purchased a farm in Kansas. While en route with his family from New York, Wiggins contracted cholera and died, but not before extracting from his wife a promise that she would continue west with her family. Kelly clothes her mother's predicament in characteristically romantic terms, but her city-bred mother was forced to face very real economic and social obstacles with little expertise. Due perhaps to these difficulties, Fanny married the sickly

Josiah Kelly, who in 1864 moved his wife and their adopted daughter, Mary, farther into the unsettled territories. Giving themselves wholeheartedly to the glamorized rhetoric of westward settlement, the Kellys joined a wagon train of settlers "with high-wrought hopes and pleasant anticipations of a romantic and delightful journey across the plains, and a confident expectation of a future prosperity among the golden hills of Idaho" (12–13). Yet Kelly soon learned, as had many of her countrywomen, the folly of basing "pleasant anticipations" on newspaper rhetoric. On July 12, 1864, Sioux attacked the train in Montana; Josiah Kelly fled, while Fanny and Mary were taken captive. Kelly remained among the Sioux for five months before being redeemed at Fort Sully, after which the reunited Kellys opened a hotel in Ellsworth, Kansas, where Fanny was the first female settler. Soon, however, Kelly's husband, like her father, died of cholera, leaving her alone with two children. Moving back to her mother's farm, Kelly was supported by congressional compensation and by the sales of her narrative, published in 1871.

My Captivity among the Sioux Indians most resembles Rowlandson's narrative in its author's ambivalence toward the Indians. Kelly begins fairly traditionally, feeling fear, anger, and disgust for her captors. Her identity as a white Christian is as secure at the time of her capture as was Rowlandson's. Midway through her narrative, however, with the Indians at war with the American army, Kelly seems to take the side of her captors. When the American General Sully, close to victory, stops to destroy Indian property, Kelly reports that he gave "us an opportunity to escape, which saved us from falling into his hands, as otherwise we inevitably would have done" (103). Her apparent relief in escaping from recapture by the American general is later echoed in Kelly's choice of pronouns: "As soon as we were safe, and General Sully no longer pursued us, the warriors returned home" (106). Kelly indicates a change of loyalties, identifying with the defeated Indians rather than with the victorious Americans. The attachment indicated by these statements is borne out by Kelly's future actions. Despite her professed "misery" among the Indians, in whom "cruelty is inherent" (188), after a period spent in the custody of Blackfeet Indians, Kelly listens with satisfaction on her return to the Ogalalla Sioux when the chief's wife tells her the entire tribe "mourned my absence, and grieved for my presence" (193). When a brave of a rival tribe attempts to kidnap Kelly, she alerts a Sioux woman and frustrates her kidnapper, even though she knows he wants a reward, the collection of which would necessitate her safe return to the Americans.

Kelly further indicates her growing sympathy with the Sioux by the increased number of pages she gives over to their complaints against the whites. Kelly quotes at length the angry speech of the Sioux chief.

> "The pale faces, our eternal persecutors, pursue and harass us without intermission, forcing us to abandon to them, one by one, our best hunting grounds, and we are compelled to seek a refuge in the depths of these Bad Lands, like timid deer. Many of them even dare to come into prairies which belong to us, to trap beaver, and hunt elk and buffalo, which are our property. Those faithless creatures, the outcasts of their own people, rob and kill us when they can. Is it just that we should suffer these wrongs without complaining?" (168)

Kelly repeats many of the same charges herself.   **71**

> [War] is their last hope; if they yield and give up, they will have to die or ever after be governed by the white man's laws; consequently they lose no opportunity to kill or steal from and harass the whites when they can do so. The game still clings to its favorite haunts, and the Indian must press upon the steps of the white man or lose all hope of independence. (97)

Throughout her narrative, Kelly freely acknowledges the ruthless cheating of Indians by American traders, and refers to the "character faults" of the Indian—especially drunkenness and profanity—as "the benefits white men confer on their savage brethren when brought into close contact," concluding, "when the weapons we furnish are turned against ourselves, their edge is keen indeed" (59–60).

Kelly appears to identify with the Indians more readily than earlier captives in part because the abolitionist rhetoric of racial injustice had made people of color seem less completely "other," especially for women like Kelly whose husbands had fought against the "rank rebels" (206). When Mr. Kelly and the other escaped men return to the wagon train, they find Franklin, one of the Kelly's "colored" servants, among the dead. The men prepare a common grave for their murdered kin, while

> the question of color . . . occasioned much discussion, and controversy ran high as to the propriety of allowing the colored people the privilege of sitting besides their white brethren. Poor Franklin had shared death with our companions, and was not deemed unworthy to share the common grave of his fellow victims. (33)

Kelly's xenophobia, when it does appear, seems more the result of literary convention than of sincere dread of the "hostile sons of the forest" (72). Early in the narrative Kelly, in reassuring her daughter, admits to feeling no particular dislike of the Indians.

> Poor little Mary! from the first she had entertained an ungovernable dread of the Indians, a repugnance that could not be overcome, although in her intercourse with friendly savages, I had endeavored to show how unfounded it was, and persuade her that they were civil and harmless, but all in vain. (21)

Rather, her anti-Indian sentiments are generically induced: she expresses fear of the Indians because past captivity narratives tell her she should.[18]

> All the horrors of Indian captivity that we had ever heard crowded on our minds with a new and fearful meaning—the slow fires, the pitiless knife, the poisoned arrows, the torture of famine, and a thousand nameless phantoms of agony passed before our troubled souls, filling us with fears so harrowing that the pangs of dissolution compared to them must have been relief. (40)

Kelly's insistence on writing what she perceives to be a traditional captivity narrative leads her to conclude, "Hunger and thirst, long days of privation and suffering, had been mine. No friendly voices cheered me on; all was silence and despair" (212–13). This rhetorical flourish contradicts, however, what the reader has seen—and what Kelly has declared—to be her experience among the Indians: "These savages proved very kind to me. Though their nation is regarded by the whites as very vindictive and hostile, they showed me nothing but civility and respect" (191). "[I] was treated with almost affectionate kindness," she admits, "by every member of the little community" (169).

Kelly's entrance into "the little community" seems connected to her changed role as a woman. When she first comes into the Sioux village, the Indians make Kelly into a domestic servant. Her status soon changes, however, and rather than serving those around her, she is treated like a prominent member of the community. Kelly feels for the first time in her captivity (and perhaps in her life) relatively free of domestic burdens. However, her release from domestic servitude, far from freeing Kelly from any sense of obligation to other women still in a servile position, sharpens her loyalty to enslaved white and Indian women and initiates her critique of gender imbalances in both cultures. Kelly's becomes a uniquely woman-centered narrative, focused on women's subjugation by men rather than on white women's victimization by Indians. It traces her growing identification with a community of women that, to her thinking, bridges racial difference.

73

Kelly begins her narrative with a clear preference for the company of women, yet with the very traditional notions about female triviality and weakness shared by other nineteenth-century captives. She writes that the "addition of one of my own sex to our little company [in the wagon train] was cause of much rejoicing to me" (13); when the Sioux threaten to separate the female captives, Kelly reports that a "dread of being separated from the only white woman in that wilderness filled me with horror" (43). At the same time as Kelly identifies with white women, however, she admits to being "surprised" by the number of women on the wagon train and at their ability to adjust to the hardships of "wilderness" travel. Rather than perceiving women as fellow adventurers, Kelly creates a romantic picture of female activity more reminiscent of the pages of Louisa May Alcott than of James Fenimore Cooper.

The hours of noon and evening rest were spent in preparing our frugal meals, gathering flowers with our children, picking berries, hunting curiosities, or gazing in rapt wonder and admiration at the beauties of this strange bewildering country.

Our amusements were varied. Singing, reading, writing to friends at home, or pleasant conversation, occupied our leisure hours. So passed these first few happy days of our emigration to the land of sunshine and flowers. (13)

The greatest inconvenience Kelly records is having to cook over a fire fueled by buffalo chips—until, that is, her husband buys her timber by the pound. If such are the "hardships experienced in a journey across the plains" (16), Kelly is understandably shocked by what Indian women endure.

Once her captivity separates Kelly from other white women, she hopes for a new female community among the Sioux.

They had traveled nearly three hundred miles, and, despite my fears, I began to rejoice in the prospect of arriving among women, even though they were savages; and a dawning hope that I might find pity and companionship with beings of my own sex, however separated their lives and customs might be, took possession of me. (77)

Kelly engages in a complicated effort to separate her stereotypes of Indians from her stereotypes of women. The Indians of romances, she writes, are depicted as noble savages, which her experiences have shown her they are not. While she challenges fictional images of Indian men, however, about the "dusky maidens of romance" (77) she is more willing to suspend her disbelief.

Notwithstanding all I had seen and experienced, I remembered much that was gentle and faithful in the character ascribed to Indian women. Perhaps I might be able to find one whose sympathy and companionship could be wrought upon to the extent of aiding me in some way to escape. I became hopeful with the thought, and almost forgot my terror of the threats of my captors, in my desire to see the friendly faces of Indian women. (78)

Kelly is initially disappointed by the Sioux women, however. After observing their dispute over the spoils of the Indian raid, in which the chief's wife grabs a knife and threatens to kill whoever touches her share of the treasure, Kelly states that "terrible as [the Chief] and his men had been, the women seemed still more formidable, and I feared to be left alone with them" (84). Yet once the dispute is ended, Kelly finds the female succor she hoped for. The women of the tribe, who bring her food and dress her wounds, "showed great evidence of compassion, and tried to express their sympathy in signs, because I had been torn from my own people, and compelled to come such a long fatiguing journey" (85). Slowly Kelly begins to "rejoice in the dawning kindness that seemed to soften their swarthy faces" (86). To mark her adoption into this world of women, the chief gives Kelly one of his own daughters, Yellow Bird, a loving and faithful companion; Kelly in turn becomes the daughter of the chief's maternal and hard-working wife. A comic passage marks Kelly's transformation from fearful captive of ruthless tormentors to the contented inhabitant of a world of female compassion. Seeing an Indian woman driving a stake into the ground and preparing to set it on fire, Kelly imagines that she is to be burned to death. Instead, the woman brews Kelly a cup of tea. Realizing the folly of her fears, Kelly gives herself over to the comforts offered by her adopted mother and daughter: "Yellow Bird was told to share my couch with me, and from this time on she was my constant attendant. I laid down, and the wife of the chief tenderly removed my moccasins, and I slept sweetly—the first true sleep I had enjoyed in many weary nights" (87).   **75**

Kelly's adoption, like Rowlandson's, creates a liminal space from which to criticize both the white and the Indian cultures. Kelly's critique, like those launched by other women captives of the period, is inflected by gender. While she is slow to criticize the Indian-as-captor, Kelly is quick to do so with the Indian-as-husband. Indian men, Kelly notes, may marry as many wives as they wish, but Indian women are forced to be monogamous (185). Marriage itself, Kelly implies, is an enforced state among Indian women. "Although no woman's life is made less slavish by the marriage connection," she reports, "and no one is treated with respect, it is scarcely known in Indian life that a girl has remained unmarried even to middle age" (184). Above all, Kelly's sympathy is aroused by watching the women's domestic labor, performed before relatively leisured male spectators.[19] "All drudgery of this kind is performed by the squaws," Kelly reports, "an Indian brave scorning as degrading all kinds of labor not incident to the chase or the war path" (175). Kelly's entrance into the tribe is marked by her strong identification with the Indian women's domestic and social exploitation.

> I sympathized with the poor wife of the chief, who was the only woman, besides myself, in the tent, and to whose labor all the feasts were due. She was obliged to dress the meat, make fires, carry water, and wait upon strangers, besides setting the lodge in order. These unceasing toils she performed alone—the commands of the chief forbidding me to aid her. (196)

Kelly refuses to allow Indian kindness toward her, a white woman, to blind her to the misery inflicted on her Indian "sisters."

> That night, as if in preparation for the work he had planned, the gracious chief beat his poor tired squaw unmercifully, because she murmured at her never-ending labor and heavy tasks.
>
> His deportment to me was as courteous as though he had been educated in civilized life; indeed, had he not betrayed so much ignorance of the extent and power of the American nation, in his address to his band, I should have thought him an educated Indian, who has traveled among the whites. Yet in his brutal treatment of his squaw, his savage nature asserted itself, and reminded me that, although better served than formerly, I was still among savages. (203)

In the end, Kelly measures savagery not in terms of Indian misbehavior toward white captives but in terms of husbands' behavior toward wives.

Kelly's sympathy with the Indian women at moments seems tempered by her pride at outdoing the squaws in subservience, recognizing in her submissiveness the secret to her survival.

> While with the Ogalallas, I had never crossed their will or offered resistance to my tasks, however heavy, having learned that obedience and cheerful industry were greatly prized; and it was, doubtless, my conciliating policy that at last won the Indians, and made them bewail my loss so deeply.
>
> The squaws are very rebellious, often displaying ungovernable and violent temper. They consider their life a servitude, and being beaten at times like animals, and receiving no sort of sympathy, it acts upon them accordingly.

The contrast between them and my patient submission had its effect upon the Indians, and caused them to miss me when separated from them. (196–97)

At the same time that she endorses a "conciliating policy," however, Kelly also explains and justifies the squaws' tempers, not in terms of a "natural" tendency toward disruption but in terms of their treatment by their husbands. She in fact uses the same justification for women's rebellion against domestic servitude as she does to excuse the Indians' armed resistance to American colonization. If one substitutes "husbands" for "white men" in her defense of Indian warfare—"if they yield and give up, they will have to die or ever after be governed by the white men's laws"—one sees the parallels between Kelly's analyses of gender and racial injustice. Far from gloating over her freedom from the domestic slavery forced on the chief's wife, Kelly sees her "conciliatory policy" as part of the burden piled on her already overtaxed "mother." In its juxtaposing of paragraphs, Kelly's text registers the tensions between the necessity of subservience as a captive and of self-assertion as a mistreated woman.   **77**

Americans fare no better in Kelly's analysis of the transcultural abuse of women by men. Kelly notes that war is used to excuse white men's physical abuse of Indian women. At one point she accuses an American general of making "his name famous by an indiscriminate massacre" (18) of Indian women and their children. Kelly has special scorn for American soldiers who take Indian "brides" and father children, only to abandon them when their white wives come west. The treatment of those white wives by their husbands is also criticized by Kelly, mainly in her contrasting of the health and abilities of Indian and white women. Indian women, Kelly notes, are heartier of body and, due perhaps to their explicit demonstrations of anger, of mind. Indian men, like their white counterparts, may be brutal and ignorant, but their wives are far from madwomen in the attic. Rather, their lives seem to Kelly "a most efficacious means of imparting strength and vigor to the constitution, and it is certain that Indian women are less subject to what are termed female complaints than white women" (180). In short, while Kelly pays lip service to a "conciliating policy," the cure for hysteria is "ungovernable and violent temper" and a life lived not in the home but in nature.

Given her growing disillusionment with "civilized" life, it is little wonder that Kelly's return, like that of most female captives, is troubled:

> The reader naturally supposes that here my narrative ought to end; that, restored to husband, mother, and friends, my season of sorrow must be over. But not so. Other trials were in store for me, and even fortified as I was by past tribulation, I sank almost despairingly under their affliction. (233)

By continuing her narrative beyond its expected conclusion, Kelly joins other nineteenth-century captives in deconstructing the traditional oppositions of the captivity narrative, in which life among the Indians represents tribulation and misery while redemption signals a return to peace and freedom. Kelly's return brings her further trials—the death of her husband, the theft and unauthorized publication of her narrative, social disapproval that prevents her from operating a business. Kelly's narrative, in fact, is one long tale of disappointment: in the "romantic" West, in the protection of her father and husband, even in the conventions of her own narrative.

Once again, the only fulfilling aspect of Kelly's redemption arises from her return to female community. Just as Kelly finds her place in the tribe in relations with her adopted mother and daughter, so too does she regain her place in her home culture. Beginning as an adoptive parent, with no real appreciation for her own mother (Kelly expresses the same regrets over her former complacency about her mother that Rowlandson does about God), Kelly ends by returning to the home of her mother with a newfound respect for the older woman's strength and determination. In turn, Kelly becomes for the first time in the narrative a biological mother herself. While this might seem to fix her in a traditional role, in fact motherhood places her firmly in the generational line of women from which she has drawn strength throughout her narrative. Among both Indians and whites, then, Kelly, like numerous nineteenth-century captives, used gender as a way to turn isolation and despair into community and comfort. That her "sisterhood" is made among the Sioux attests to the ability of nineteenth-century captives to adapt to new conditions and to use those conditions to create more complex configurations of the female "self."

Captivity narratives contain many paradoxes: through their servility, captive women gain a position of relative eminence among their captors; attempting a condemnation of people perceived as radically "other," they end by criticizing the inadequacies of their own culture; in the experience of captivity, seemingly the most helpless and effacing of conditions, captives generate speaking voices, female subjectivities, they would have found nearly impossible to claim in their home cultures. The final paradox of the captivity narratives lies in the fact that once the captive escaped, apparently regaining her independence and creating a speaking subject, her voice was again taken hostage, this time by editors of various sorts. The publishing history of women's captivity narratives not only further complicates notions of "freedom" but problematizes the very terms I have used to discuss the achievement of the narratives: "subject," "author," "self."

The paradoxical situation of the captive in the hands of her editors is best encapsulated by Jemima Howe, who tells her story to Reverend Bunker Gay. He, in turn, passes the narrative on to Dr. Belknap, writing:

> It was from the mouth of this woman that I lately received the foregoing account. She also gave me, I doubt not, a true, though, to be sure, a very brief and imperfect history of her captivity, which I here insert for your perusal. It may perhaps afford you some amusement, and can do no harm, if, after it has undergone your critical inspection, you should not think it (or an abbreviation of it) worthy to be preserved among the records you are about to publish. (Drake 1851, 157)

Just as Howe is passed within her narrative from one group of men to another, from the Indians who hold her captive to the French gentleman and his son who threaten her with rape, and finally to the English army, so too is her narrative circulated "between men."[20] Her authorship is deemed "imperfect," open to and in need of expert (male) critical "inspection." The captive's narrative no longer serves, as those of earlier captives purportedly did, for moral edification; rather, the body of her text—like her body within the text—exists solely for the pleasure and "amusement" of the men who traffic in it.

Since every captive discussed so far has, like Howe, received editorial "assistance" of some sort, how can one speak of the "captive's voice" in the narratives? Where does that voice appear, distinct from editorial tampering? Howe's narrative is again instructive. The captive's voice does emerge in her critique of her treatment by both white and Indian men, in her story of survival in the wilderness, and in the very act of narrating her experiences. Her situation is summed up in the first sentence of her narrative as related by Gay: "The Indians (she says) having plundered and put fire to the fort, we marched, as near as I could judge, a mile and a half into the woods, where we camped that night" (Drake 1851, 157). The parenthetical construction Gay employs to indicate the transformation of his voice into Howe's makes clear her position as the object of his discourse—a "she"—rather than as the subject of her own. But it also represents her liminal position, not entirely with the Indians any longer but not assimilated into her editor's culture either. Within her separate space—a space figured by the parentheses—Howe gains the distance from the discourse of two cultures which grants her a critical insight and also, therefore, a voice. I would argue that in many narratives one hears the captive's voice in those moments when the text speaks, as does Howe's, against the grain of the interpretive frame created for it. In the remainder of this chapter I will examine efforts made by male ministers and editors to turn the captivity narratives of women into documents supportive of the social status quo—efforts, as the foregoing discussion makes clear, that the narratives themselves resist.

The history of appropriation and resistance begins with the first captivity narrative—Mary Rowlandson's—and the "Preface to the Reader" provided by the pseudonymous "Ter Amicam," possibly Increase Mather.[21] Creating from Rowlandson's story a parable of the captive Israel delivered from heathen bondage by God, Ter Amicam must simultaneously assure his congregants of their hopes for salvation, calm their racial anxieties in the midst of a destructive war with the Indians, and excuse the extraordinary fact of a Puritan woman telling her own story while discouraging other women from doing the same. Rowlandson's editor undertakes the task by making her narration a sign not of her articulateness and daring resilience, but of her continuing subservience and obligation to her divine protector.

> This Narrative was penned by the Gentlewoman herself, to be to her a memorandum of Gods dealing with her, that she might never forget, but remember the same, and the severall circumstances thereof, all the dayes of her life. A pious scope which deserves both communication and imitation. Some friends having obtained a sight of it, could not but be so much affected with the many passages of working providence discovered therein, as to judge it worthy of publick view, and altogether unmeet that such works of God should be hid from present and future Generations: And therefore though this Gentlewomans modesty would not thrust it into the Press, yet her gratitude unto God made her not hardly perswadable to let it pass, that God might have his due glory, and others benefit by it as well as her self. I hope by this time none will cast any reflection upon the Gentlewoman, on the score of this publication of her affliction and deliverance. (Lincoln 1913, 115)

Rowlandson did not *wish* to speak, Ter Amicam assures his congregants, knowing her proper place as a (silent) woman, but felt compelled to do so, to warn others of the savageries of the heathen Indians and to praise the mercies of God in overcoming them. "Excuse her," Ter Amicam requests of his readers, "if she come thus into publick, to pay those vows, come and hear what she hath to say" (116). Given the frame of reference her editor provides—in which women only by extraordinary acts of God can be persuaded to come into public—one wonders how her readers *could* have heard "what she hath to say," since her content deals largely with women's adaptability and fitness to exist not only in public but in the wilderness itself. In the editor's hands Rowlandson's narrative reinforces prevailing stereotypes, thereby justifying fear and hatred of the Indians and ensuring women's submission. Yet a tension remains between the narrative as described by the minister—featuring female modesty, Indian depravity, and English superiority—and the evidence that emerges from the narrative itself, which represents female endurance and cunning, Indian kindness and social complexity, and English ineptness and brutality.

Increase Mather's son, Cotton, found a more effective way to use the captivity narratives to reinforce prejudices. Operating by omission and suggestion, Mather's narrative ensures the reader's participation in embellishing the captive's tale. His strategy of suggestion ultimately serves to exploit and reinforce his audience's prejudices, since the reader, filling in the blanks Mather creates in the narrative, will bring his or her cultural preconceptions without the detailed accounts that might serve, as they do in Rowlandson's narrative, to mitigate stereotypes. In his narration of the captivity of Sarah Gerish, for example, Mather asks, "Who can enumerate the frights she endured before the end of her journey?" (Drake 1851, 69). Describing the Indians, Mather reports, "unlike cultivated people, they have no restraints upon their mischievous and savage propensities, which they indulge in cruelties surpassing any examples here related" (69). The minister luridly suggests atrocities far worse than those he names, and in doing so opens the way for the imagination—and hence the prejudices—of the reader. The tortures possible at the hands of the Indians are rendered always already worse than any he describes, thus achieving the exact opposite effect to that of Rowlandson's narrative, where an increased observation and detailed description of what happens among the Indians serves to challenge, not reinforce, stereotypes.[22]

In the anthologies that throughout the nineteenth century kept the captivity accounts before the public eye,[23] editors such as Samuel Gardiner Drake and John Frost assumed the role of secular ministers, adopting their clerical predecessors' strategies for turning potentially subversive narratives into documents of racial depravity and, more immediately, of female helplessness and modesty. In dazzling displays of rhetorical manipulation, these editors propagandize westward expansion and Indian extermination while turning the captive in the wilderness into the nineteenth-century Angel in the House.

Samuel Drake represents himself as an even-handed editor; not only does he present a wider variety of stories, he explicitly refrains from tampering with the narratives or offering editorial comment (1842, iii). Drake seems to have recognized a female readership, as

suggested by the change he made in the title of his anthology. Originally called *Tragedies of the Wilderness* (1842), the anthology was
later rechristened *Indian Captivities; or, Life in the Wigwam*
(1851), moving the tales from the outdoors ("the wilderness") to
the indoors ("the wigwam"), and thereby reflecting the growing
popularity of domestic fiction among women readers. While Drake
may have adapted himself to his female readers and scrupulously
endeavored to maintain a light editorial hand, his anthology nevertheless reflects the relatively small cultural space allotted women.
Of the thirty narratives contained in the Drake anthology, thirteen
are by women. Despite this apparent gender parity, however, only
three of the women's narratives (those of Mary Rowlandson, Elizabeth Hanson, and Jemima Howe) are told in the first person, while
only three of the men's narratives are told in the third person. Of the
360 pages of text, moreover, the women's narratives take up only 97
pages, with over half of those used by Rowlandson's and Hanson's
narratives; the remaining eleven women's narratives occupy only 43
pages. Drake's anthology does nothing, therefore, to challenge either the prominence accorded men's stories or the cultural refusal
to have a woman speak as an authoritative "I."

John Frost, as I have already suggested, was vehement in enforc-
ing norms of proper feminine behavior, condemning the actions of
"Amazons" who reject masculine rescue in order to take care of
themselves. Frost piously condemns Winona, an Indian woman
who chooses to kill herself rather than marry the man her parents
have selected to be her husband: "Winona was an uncivilized Indian; she had never been taught the word of the Master of Life,
'thou shalt not kill'—she had never heard that 'the patient in spirit
is better than the proud in spirit'" (1854, 62). The virtues of patience are lost on Frost when he narrates men's violence directed
against the Indians; when he describes a woman's attempts to control her own destiny, however, Frost has a different set of standards.

Frost's commentary reinforces gender stereotypes even as it appears to be championing the cause of women. His tribute to the Indian women who suffer under their husbands' laziness is a case in
point.

The life of an Indian woman, even though she may be the favorite wife of a great chief, is always frought with toil and drudgery. The men will go through great fatigue in war or in hunting, but any thing like regular work they scorn. Scooping out canoes, building their huts, dressing the skins of animals, and cultivating the earth, are labours which fall to the lot of the squaw; but, what is still worse, they are obliged to carry all the heavy burdens without any assistance from their husbands. (1854, 318–19)

Fanny Kelly also found appalling the amount of labor expected of Indian women, as did female captives such as Rachel Plummer, who observes:

The women do all the work, except killing the meat. They herd the horses, saddle and pack them, build the houses, dress the skins, meat, &c. The men dance every night, during which, the women wait on them with water. No woman is admitted into any of their Councils; nor is she allowed to enquire what their councils have been. When they move, the women do not know where they are going. They are no more than servants, and are looked upon and treated as such. (1839, 355)

The difference between Frost and a female captive like Plummer, however, is that the latter sees the traditional "women's work" performed by the squaws as part and parcel of the unjust burden placed on women and admires their strength in carrying out their duties. Frost's outrage is directed not at the fact that women work hard (he never mentions their domestic labor), but at the fact that they do men's work, thus challenging the notion that men are "naturally" better suited to certain tasks. That Frost objects not to unjust labor but to the confusing of gender-specific tasks is indicated by the fact that he is bothered by what women themselves apparently did not mind. In fact, as Frost suggests, the more rugged labor made Indian women healthier, as the stories of Slocum, Williams, and Jemison, as well as the explicit observations of Kelly, suggest. "We may believe," Frost concludes, "that women so trained are not very delicate, or easily daunted by any difficulties that may befall them" (1854, 320).

When white women do act nontraditionally, Frost finds a traditional cause, as in the case of the "War-Woman," who, after a tribe of Indians attacks her cabin and kills her children, trails them and murders them in their sleep. "This instance of intrepidity in a woman," Frost concludes,

> furnishes a remarkable proof that the heroism of woman, to whatever excesses of daring and even ferocious courage it may lead her, has its foundation in love. It was this "War-Woman's" love for her children, that made her exhaust the last energy of a life, which had lost its motive and its charm, in taking vengeance on their murderers. Under such circumstances, it is difficult to imagine the extent to which a woman's outraged affections will not carry her. (1854, 35–36)

Women, whose only "motive" and "charm" in life (according to Frost) are found in their children, take up nontraditional actions in support of—not in opposition to—their "proper" roles as nurturing mothers. Frost makes the connection between women's unconventional actions and their paradoxical desire to maintain a traditional role even more clear in his introduction to *Pioneer Mothers of the West*.

> The heroism of woman is the heroism of the heart. Her deeds of daring and endurance are prompted by affection. While her husband, her children, and all the other objects of tenderness are safe, her heroic capabilities repose in peace, and external troubles have little power to disturb her serenity. But when danger threatens the household, when the lurking savage is seen near the dwelling, or the war-whoop is heard in the surrounding woods, the matron becomes a heroine, and is ready to peril life, without a moment's hesitation, in the approaching conflict. (1859, iii)

Frost assures his male reader that if he will "bear in mind, as he peruses these thrilling histories of women's noble deeds, that affection prompts her daring, this volume will afford him much instruction as to the true character of woman" (1859, iii–iv). Using the popular rhetoric of sentimentalism, Frost reassures male readers that women's single "true character" does not include—as the narratives suggest —physical strength and mental cunning, but a selfless, even suicidal devotion to hearth and home. Frost has a message for female readers as well: "Our women of the present age may be heroines, no doubt, in another way; and the occasions for self-sacrifice and noble generosity will still present themselves and still be heroically met" (9). Frost urges women to emulate the motives of the women he describes—especially their overwhelming desire to remain mothers and wives within traditional families—but not their actions. Divorcing the captives' motives from their actions, Frost can assert that gender identity (women's "true character") is—and *should* be—absolute.[24]

Despite editorial claims that captivity is a tale composed of Indian depravity and female conventionality, however, the narratives themselves tell a different story. Whether women resist or escape their captivities, endure captivity until redemption, or choose to live their lives among their captors, their narratives attest to the continued ability of women from Mary Rowlandson to Fanny Kelly to survive—even occasionally to prosper—outside their traditional sphere, beyond their accepted roles, and in defiance of prevalent notions of innate ethnicity. Richard Slotkin, attempting like his editorial predecessors to "domesticate" the captive's voice, speculates that the captivity narrative "speaks for an inward turn: . . . the 'garden' of the captivity is a small cultivated plot, protected from the encroaching wilderness by a stiff 'hedge' of religious dogma and rigorous government" (1973, 99). As the narratives discussed in this chapter demonstrate, exactly the opposite seems true.

Far from representing a turn "inward," the narratives of women captives describe an unprecedented move outward. That move beyond the "hedge" is literal, providing an important corrective to our cultural myth that only men have explored the physical terrain of America. More subtly, however, the narratives represent a willingness to go beyond what Slotkin calls "dogma," in particular to reevaluate one's cultural preconceptions of class, race, and gender—in short, of identity itself. Defying not only the editorial frames attached to their narratives but the very underpinnings of cultural authority, captives envisioned different social arrangements, different definitions of community, and hence different articulations of white womanhood.

THREE *That Was Not My Idea of*
Independence: The Captivity
of Patty Hearst

I sat down and then they talked to me and said, "Can you read for us a
little bit?" And I went, "Yeah, I can read." But I had only just read
through the script once, and I just went for it, and it was horrible. Actually John [Waters] said that because I didn't, you know, say, "Oh, I need
time to get into my character" and do all these prima donna things, he
knew I wouldn't be any trouble . . . within a few months, I was in Baltimore shooting.

> Patty Hearst on "Good Morning, America"
> discussing her audition for *Cry Baby*

ON DECEMBER 26, 1973, *The Exorcist* opened in twenty-two
American cities. In its first two weeks, the film played to more than
four million people and grossed over ten million dollars, creating a
wave of hysterical fascination that led one reviewer to quip, "all hell
has broken loose" (*Newsweek,* January 11, 1974, 60). The film, in
which an innocent white girl is possessed by the dark forces of evil,
owes much of its success to the anxieties of the early 1970s. News
journal stories of the day express fears that a lack of "strong" leadership, following President Richard Nixon's duplicitous dealings in
Watergate, had resulted in a breakdown of American society. Having lived through the tumultuous sixties, in which role models were
discredited and social conventions flouted, America was looking
once again for strong leadership to rescue it from chaos. Moving
"Beyond the Sexual Revolution" (*Newsweek,* September 29, 1975)
that purportedly left the country vulnerable, the press heralded that

America was "Ready for the Right" (March 24, 1975) that would soon put "family values" back on the map. According to the press, the most dramatic result of America's weakened state was the oil crisis, in which America's economic liberty was "held hostage" by terrorist Arabs.[1]

The Exorcist craze becomes more understandable in the context of this rhetoric. Like the American children reportedly left by the sexual revolution in broken homes, without strong, paternal "role models" (the film is set, significantly, in Washington, D.C.), sweet, twelve-year-old Regan (Linda Blair), living in a single-parent household, is not offered sufficient spiritual protection by her independent, divorced mother (Ellen Burstyn). In that vulnerable state, she is possessed by the dark forces of evil, just as America was held hostage by the "dark forces" of the Middle East (soon to be recast as the Dark Star of *Star Wars*). Only the entrance of a strong male figure—represented by the Roman Catholic Church, which conveniently supplies an endless series of Fathers—can return Regan (her name is prophetic) to the innocence that is, paradoxically, her strength.

In staging national apprehension through the drama of demonic possession, *The Exorcist* hearkens back to the experiences of girls such as Mercy Short in 1693 Salem. As Richard Slotkin has argued, the witchcraft mania of the late seventeenth century offered a microcosm for confronting the period's anxieties over race, capital, and leadership, concerns similar to those of the early 1970s.[2] The social tensions embodied in the witchcraft trials also found expression in the captivity narrative, however, in which innocent females are more tangibly possessed by the dark forces of evil. The metaphoric parallel between captivity and satanic possession emerges again in the early 1970s, when the most famous captive of the late twentieth century pushed even Watergate off the front pages.[3] Patty Hearst's 1974 kidnapping provided a useful metaphor for the struggles of the mid-1970s over oil, power, and gender. In the popular media, she became the central figure in an allegorical war over innocence, in which the "good guys" (the police and the wealthy) battle with the "bad guys" (the poor, the black, the sexually "liberated") over the body of a young, white woman.

Like earlier captives, however, Hearst, who saw the battle in different terms, had another story to tell. Regan's tale, authored and directed by white men, ends predictably with the paternalistic return of white femininity from the hell of iconoclastic disruption to the tranquillity of religious ritual and social order.[4] Hearst's autobiography, *Every Secret Thing*, foregrounds the constraints of gender inscribed in that male-authored fantasy of rescue and restored hierarchy, demonstrating the ultimate impossibility for women of "freedom" in any patriarchal context. In so doing, Hearst helped redefine the contest between her kidnappers and her home culture as a struggle for control not only over her body, but over her story as well; in fact she asserts that the two had always been the same. *Every Secret Thing* explicitly demonstrates what I have been arguing was more implicitly the case in earlier narratives: in captivity, white women generate social accounts that feature people of color in roles other than irrational and savage tormentors and white women who are not simply voiceless and frail items of exchange. In so doing, captives recognize that the dominant narratives of their home cultures are neither natural nor universal and turn a critical eye on the ways white Anglo-America normalizes and circulates its values. Discursive "crossing," occasioned by the experience of capture, thus enabled captives to challenge the enforcement of "proper" gender, racial, and class behavior. Like earlier captives, Hearst moves quickly from her entrance into the life of her captors to a critique of American normalcy, which she ultimately represents not as a realm inhabited by free citizens but as a police state brutally maintained by governmental sanction.

89

On February 4, 1974, Patricia Campbell Hearst, the twenty-year-old granddaughter of millionaire newspaper tycoon William Randolph Hearst, was preparing for bed in the Berkeley, California, apartment she shared with her fiancé, Steven Weed. When Weed answered a knock at the door, what appeared to be two black men and a white woman armed with machine guns burst into the apartment, beat Weed, and dragged Hearst away, locking her in the trunk of a waiting car.[5] Hearst was now the prisoner of the Symbionese Liberation Army (SLA), a group comprised of a black ex-convict named Donald DeFreeze (Cinque Maume) and his eight disciples, six women and two men, all white. Hearst was kept for weeks in a small closet, blindfolded and often gagged, while the SLA "soldiers" read to her from various revolutionary tracts. Despite a number of efforts to ransom their daughter, on April 3 the Hearsts received a tape in which Patty announced her decision to "stay and fight" with her kidnappers. Two weeks later the SLA held up the Hibernia Bank, and security cameras photographed Hearst, now rechristened Tania, machine gun in hand, participating in the robbery. On April 21, the FBI issued a "wanted" poster that named Hearst as a voluntary member of the SLA. Hearst again found herself wanted by the FBI in May when, during a holdup in which store security guards arrested SLA member Bill Harris, Hearst, unsupervised, took up a machine gun and rescued him. On May 17, police and FBI agents fire-bombed the SLA safe house, killing all but Hearst, Bill Harris, and Emily Harris, who were lodged elsewhere. Hearst and the Harrises then disappeared for a year. On September 15, 1975, FBI agents arrested Hearst and her companion, Wendy Yoshimura, in San Francisco, apprehending the Harrises in a separate arrest. Hearst stood trial and was convicted for the Hibernia robbery; her sentence was commuted in 1979 by Jimmy Carter and she was pardoned a decade later by Ronald Reagan.

Hearst's autobiography, *Every Secret Thing* (1982), bears remarkable similarities to Indian captivity narratives. Like earlier captives, Hearst at first associates her captors with pure evil. When she hears the SLA leader, Cinque Maume, called "Cin," Hearst responds, "New fear struck my heart as I thought: Sin—these people must be evil incarnate" (37). Far from seeing a political purpose in her kidnapping, Hearst can only attribute the actions of her abductors to inherent depravity, and, like her Puritan predecessors, she looks for divine rescue: "I found myself praying to God for deliverance. I did not know how He would accomplish this. But I prayed in blind faith" (59).

Once she realizes that she will not be ransomed or killed, however, Hearst begins to participate in the lives of her captors. At first Hearst simply follows her captors' commands, but like earlier captives she becomes increasingly more enthusiastic about her participation as she finds her position within the group. In a passage that echoes Kelly's identification with the Indians fleeing from the American army, Hearst, sharing the SLA's claustrophobic sense of being surrounded by the FBI, remarks that "we were all closed in, together" (93). Far from resenting this enforced camaraderie, Hearst experiences a liberation through her entrance into an "us." "In trying to convince them," Hearst writes, "I convinced myself. I felt that I had truly joined them; my past life seemed to have slipped away. The FBI, the police, and all the authorities in the world might be searching for us in their great manhunt, but I felt somehow free" (103). "My new comrades," Hearst admits, "did not seem quite as strange as they did before" (109).

Before long Hearst thoroughly blurs the line between what she tells the SLA in order to survive and what she purports genuinely to believe. Like earlier captives, Hearst's openness to her captors begins when they successfully question her racial stereotypes. The political focus of the SLA was racial inequality, particularly the mistreatment of blacks in the prison system. Its goal was the complete "symbiosis" of white and black cultures. Hearst therefore begins her initiation into radical politics with lessons on the situation of people of color in America and throughout the Third World. When the stereotypes fostered by her conservative upbringing begin to fail her, Hearst's general ideological security falls away as well.   91

> I thought I was merely humoring them. After all, I was in no
> position to argue. And yet they did read me news items they
> clipped from the newspapers almost every day, reporting horror
> stories from dictatorships around the world as well as revolu-
> tionary "actions" in Puerto Rico, Mozambique, the
> Philippines, and various other countries in the Third World.
> Some of their stories were indisputable, sometimes I did not
> know what to believe. It was all very confusing. (69–70)

No longer blaming her captors' "rants" on deranged politics or inherent evil, Hearst begins to question her own naive and over-protected upbringing: "I realized that my life prior to my kidnapping had indeed been very sheltered; I had taken little or no interest in foreign affairs, politics, or economics" (70).

Hearst recognizes that underlying her "sheltered" upbringing was the assumption that upper-class girls were not supposed to take an interest in the public world of politics and economics. In this way, Hearst, like many nineteenth-century captives, moves from a challenge to her racial stereotypes and the politics they support to an examination of class-defined systems of gender socialization and inequality. Hearst's examination of gender, arising from the assault on her racial privilege, is furthered by and renders more comfortable her membership in a community of women. Hearst's indoctrination into the SLA begins when one of its women, Gabi (Camilla Hall), shows her kindness. "If Cin played the heavy and roused utter fear in my heart," Hearst reports, "this girl, among all the others, played the light part, the one who seemed to want to be friendly" (44). As Hearst takes her first bath since the kidnapping, Zoya (Patricia Solysik) tells her about "the woman's role in the people's revolution, . . . sexual equality in the utopia of the future, and similar favorite topics. As she droned on, I washed and scrubbed, feeling new and rejuvenated and clean again" (52). Although Hearst's choice of the verb "droned" indicates her dismissal of Zoya and her radical feminism, her linkage of women's liberation and ritual renewal becomes increasingly important in Hearst's narrative.

Hearst herself soon deploys her newly learned feminism to rethink her status as a woman within patriarchal domesticity and thereby to sever her ties with her former life. When Weed publishes a letter in several newspapers calling for her release, Hearst seems in perfect agreement with the analysis offered by the SLA women.

92

> It was not difficult to agree with "my sisters" that Steve Weed's attitude toward me, as revealed in his open letter, was chauvinistic, sexist, and bourgeois. Zoya fumed, saying that Steve acted as though he owned me and that he wanted me back, as though I were a piece of property. All of the SLA women insisted that the trouble with Steve and with the bourgeois men was that, in the final analysis, they could not abide the thought that women could think and choose for themselves. It was easy to agree with Cin as he condemned the whole bourgeois world for accusing me of being brainwashed because I no longer agreed with their middle-class values. (158)

Hearst seems less cynical, even enthusiastic, when her lessons center on a feminist principle. After the Harrises, Hearst, and Yoshimura are separated from the rest of the SLA, Yoshimura challenges Bill Harris' right to teach the women how to use weapons, insisting that Hearst do so instead. In the face of Harris' violent objections,

Hearst assumes authority and leads the class. "For once I was not the know-nothing idiot in the group," Hearst reports, with apparent satisfaction; "for once I was contributing something; for once I was receiving praise from my sisters. They, in turn, declared that it was a real victory for the revolution to receive instruction from another woman" (339). Finding agency by engaging with the SLA women, Hearst no longer distances herself by putting quotation marks around the phrase "my sisters." Hearst goes so far in her feminist training that she criticizes her female comrades for their participation in patriarchal structures: "It was ironic that all of the SLA sisters believed in the liberation of women, and yet the men in this cell acted as though the women were there to serve them sexually. It was even more peculiar that none of the other women appeared able to see what I could see" (159). Far from remaining immune to their feminist "droning," then, Hearst is soon able to out-SLA the SLA.

Despite her acknowledged satisfaction in being included in the sisterhood of the SLA, Hearst, like Mary Rowlandson, undergoes a representational reversal once return is inevitable; her disavowal at the conclusion of her autobiography of any sympathy with her kidnappers is explicit and absolute: "The tangled and perplexing truth for me was that I was relieved that they were all dead and now out of my life" (259). Surrounded by ministers—Hearst reports that her "best moments in that jail, perhaps the only times I enjoyed a sense of normalcy in those surroundings, came with the regular pastoral visits" (380)—and doctors "who kept trying to explain the necessity for me to repent" (420), Hearst, like earlier captives surrounded by cultural agents framing her story in terms of sin and pathology, reenters the bourgeois society she had days earlier vehemently condemned.

Such a disavowal is not surprising in the autobiography of a woman who, at the time of its composition, was still seeking pardon for a criminal conviction that had tarnished her family's prestigious name. Less predictable, however, is Hearst's refusal in *Every Secret Thing* to represent white America as liberty regained. Rather, Hearst links her autobiography to earlier captivity narratives by insisting that her "return" is necessarily incomplete. "I was different," Hearst reports, "changed and hardened and grown streetwise from my days with the SLA. I had been through too much to revert to the naive, innocent girl I had been as a teenager" (427). When Hearst is arrested by the FBI, she reports, "I knew it was not over; it was just beginning. I was a prisoner again" (366). Hearst describes her time in jail in terms strikingly similar to those she uses to represent her life with Weed, as prison and traditional domesticity become virtually indistinguishable: "I took up crocheting, puttered around the little cell, living in limbo, waiting" (379). Not surprisingly, given the analogous rhetoric of imprisonment that Hearst uses to describe her life during and after her kidnapping, she soon finds the San Mateo County Jail, originally terrifying to her, "familiar as home" (410). Once again, Hearst survives by forming an emotional bond with her jailers; shown kindness by a prison matron, Hearst reports "the start of a rather special friendship between prisoner and guard" (377). Following her release from prison, Hearst again replicates the social model derived from her kidnapping: "I found myself spending more time at home, talking with my sisters and with the bodyguards. These police officers understood the SLA and what had happened to me better than any of my old Hillsborough friends" (430). Rather than reintegrating into the society she left behind, Hearst replicates her captivity, in which she constructs community out of jailers and "sisters." Hearst's autobiography recounts a series of mediated imprisonments rather than a drama that, in framing her kidnapping as anomalous, would normalize the fiction that life in white America is free of coercion and restraint.

Hearst thus joins previous captives in writing "beyond the ending" of her return, using the language of captivity to describe the constraints of white, middle-class femininity, and to mark her distance from the culture that would claim her as its idealized representation. Hearst exceeds earlier captives, however, in describing not only her life after but her life before kidnapping in the language of imprisonment, representing "normal" socialization as a training ground for captivity. Refusing to normalize her privileged upbringing, Hearst insists on depicting her life before and after captivity as extensions of, not alternatives to, her experiences with the SLA. Hearst's father, Randolph, took his daughters fishing and horseback riding, encouraging them to lead active lives in the outdoors

(10). The Hearst girls "were not tomboys, I like to think; we were just three little girls who played as hard as boys did" (3). These outings were strongly condemned, however, by Catharine Hearst, "a poised, gracious Southern lady of the old school" (3). Catharine Hearst, her daughter complains, would "drive us crazy with her overprotectiveness" (3), insisting "that we grow up as proper young ladies. That meant learning that young ladies did this, and that young ladies did not do that; no matter how much we protested" (6). In her descriptions of her childhood, Hearst depicts her mother as a jailer, confining her four daughters in a prison of gender socialization. Often this imprisonment was more than metaphorical; when Anne Hearst was found playing on the roof of the mansion, the next day bars were placed on all the windows (3). Hearst's description of her early education repeats the pattern of rebellion against gender expectations, followed by physical restraint. Hearst finds her Catholic school "so strict, so rigid, so unreasonable in its petty rules and regulations that I soon came to loathe it. I felt like a prisoner in a medieval dungeon" (12). Her parents have Hearst "confined" to the school grounds, believing, Hearst writes, that "I would, in time, learn to acclimate myself to the school's regimen" (12).

If the FBI "rescued" Hearst from the SLA, then, the SLA, with its rhetoric (if not its practice) of sexual equality, rescued her from a naive acceptance of the gender roles that she had been taught from childhood were "natural" and hence inescapable.[6] Nowhere is this more clear than in her descriptions of her life with Steven Weed prior to her kidnapping. Hearst and Weed, who was ten years her senior, became "a happy domestic couple" (16), Hearst reports. "I delighted in putting some order into 'our home,'" Hearst writes, "and I began buying cookbooks to help me in preparing special meals and desserts. We did everything together, like a married couple, and I discovered in myself a 'nesting' instinct" (17). Describing herself as "primed for domesticity" (19), Hearst "thought that marriage would satisfy me completely" (17).

Hearst's dream of wedded bliss soon sours, however, owing not to her kidnapping but rather to the roles women are expected to play in traditional heterosexual unions. Although "in the eyes of all our friends, we were the perfect happy couple" (27), Hearst admits, "inwardly, I was not sure" (27). Hearst apparently did not like being forced into the kitchen by her fiancé any more than by her mother.

> Perhaps it was simply that I was growing up and was no longer satisfied to adore him, eagerly absorbing all he could teach. I was wholly aware of women's rights at that time, but I did not realize the unfairness of his making *all* the decisions in the house. I always did what he wanted me to do. I did the cooking and the washing up afterward. He set the times when the meals should be on the table. In a million small things and most large ones, he was the boss. I came to wonder if I had exchanged parental authority for his authority. That was not my idea of independence. It was just the air about him: his role to command and mine to obey. (24)

Feeling locked into her relationship by all the wedding preparations, Hearst becomes depressed: "I felt unusually tired, languid, not so much from overwork . . . but rather as a general malaise" (29). Sensing that "my life was closing in on me" (27), Hearst contemplates escape: "At one point, I considered joining the navy and seeing the world. Literally. It was a way out, but it was not very practical" (27). Little wonder that Hearst admits of her kidnapping, "Strangely enough, as I was being bound, a great sense of relief swept over me" (34).

Hearst adopts the representational strategies of the SLA to link the apparently "individual" values of her parents and her fiancé to the policed enforcement of those values throughout American society. Like nineteenth-century captives who move from criticizing individual men who failed to protect them to a broader condemnation of ideological agents, particularly the military, that circulate the values responsible for their capture, Hearst repeatedly joins the SLA in representing the FBI as collaborating with her parents to generate images of the vulnerable and passive Patty. Hearst had good cause to undermine FBI accounts of her capture. Generating stories that turned Hearst's abduction into sexual titillation, exciting official narratives of possession and control, the FBI's desire to rescue Hearst was contingent on her continued passivity. As long as she remained a helpless—and voiceless—victim, "Patty" was an obsession for the FBI, which launched HERNAP, the largest rescue campaign in its history. But the FBI made clear while still seeking Hearst that the narrative of her desired rescue was not just a simple narrative about helping a poor hostage. It was a sexual narrative as well. The unofficial title for the campaign to find Hearst was HER-SNATCH.[7] Hearst's purported passivity, while gaining the sympathy and cooperation of the federal government, also insured her incorporation in a narrative of sexual chase and possession metonymically centered on her "snatch" (a slang term for vagina), the very spot where she was supposedly most "vulnerable" to her black captor.

Once Hearst became "Tania," however, not only refusing to ask for the help of the FBI but rejecting accounts of her vulnerability, the bureau sought her not as a rescuable victim but as a dangerous criminal. That Hearst's "crime" was the denial of her passivity is demonstrated by the government's prosecution of Hearst for the Hibernia Bank robbery months before its prosecution of her fellow criminals, Bill and Emily Harris, who were not even immediately charged with kidnapping. In the opinion of the government and of the press, Hearst's participation in the robbery was somehow more serious than that of the Harrises, even though they were more active in its planning and execution.[8] The issue was not whether someone other than Hearst should control her life; that she would have no self-control was a foregone conclusion. The issue was *who* was to have control, the good (white) guys or the bad (black) guys. The FBI's search for Patty Hearst, perpetuating images of female helplessness and sexual availability and of the depravity of those on the margins of society, thus proved the accuracy of the SLA's critique.

In waging its dramatic "War for Patty," as one headline labeled it, the FBI was only the most violent contender for control over what Hearst could and could not represent. Throughout her life, as *Every Secret Thing* testifies through its trope of repeated captivity, many joined the struggle to affix "meaning" to the figure of Patty Hearst. The emerging official story of Hearst's kidnapping demonstrates a public anxiety about the possibility of a subject's—particularly a female subject's—ability to alter her cultural identifications and her public meaning. In pursuing "Patty" as the icon of national innocence, America watched her become Tania, the national nightmare, on one hand, of rhetorical overdetermination

97

and, on the other, of the possibilities of change. One *Newsweek* cartoon shows Tania sitting cross-legged on a prison cot, writing a letter to her parents on elaborate stationery. The letter reads, "Dear Mummy and Daddy, Wow! . . . All I can think about now is going home! The very first thing I'm going to do is get myself a great big glass of milk and some chocolate chip cookies and curl up on my own bed with my kittycat and *all* my little stuffed animals. I can't wait!!" The letter is signed with the SLA's slogan, "Death to the fascist insect," followed by Patty's signature and a smiley face. The cartoon's "humor" arises from the tensions introduced by Tania into the readers' belief in girlhood innocence—diminutive, domestic, and inarticulate.

More to the point is another cartoon showing Hearst, half her face "Patty" (smiling, her hair coiffed and clean), half "Tania" (uncombed hair and darker skin, wearing a man's shirt and a patch over one eye, with a cigarette dangling from her snarling lips). "Tania" is thus made to represent a betrayal of the naturalized codes of class, race, and gender, rendered more threatening in that both sets of codes are inscribed on the same body, implying the false "uniformity" of identity itself. These caricatures, which present Hearst, in David Boulton's words, as "a gun-toting Barbie doll" (1975, 149), represent fears that a woman's "character" might not be unified, overdetermined, and unchangeable. Rather, Hearst-followers feared, "good girls" might suddenly snap (a fear often awakened by feminism in the early 1970s) and show that race, gender, and class identities are not biological givens but the result of discourses of power that can be interpreted and interrupted.

The fear that normative American (white, male, middle-class) identity might not be innate is represented most forcefully by the explanations of "brainwashing" or the "Stockholm Syndrome" offered by the media to explain Hearst's crossover. Captives, these accounts argue, replicate the behavior of their captors in order to survive, but the replication is never "real," never truly believed. As I have attempted to show, Hearst's autobiography complicates these explanations by showing that even after she is reportedly "deprogrammed," Hearst continues to express many of the doctrines she adopts from her kidnappers, such as the equality of women. Hearst seems to undergo a shift in ideological paradigms more significant than the "brainwashing" accounts imply. Hearst's story further suggests why the public was so eager to accept the "brainwashing" narrative in the first place. At the time of her trial, the media argued that Hearst "conformed to the model of people most susceptible to something like brainwashing: young, suggestible and passive. 'Because Patty wasn't convinced of anything, the SLA hoped to convince her of the rightness of their cause,' says Paul Chodoff, a Washington psychoanalyst" (*Newsweek,* March 1, 1976, 31). The "brainwashing defense" raises exactly the questions about her upbringing Hearst explicitly asks in her autobiography. Why, for instance, was she "suggestible" and "passive" in the first place? Why, having nearly completed her college education, was she not "convinced of anything"? If brainwashing is a process of "commanding people to behave in a prescribed way" (31), then wasn't Hearst, through her class and gender socialization that taught her to be passive apparently to the point of holding no opinions of her own, already brainwashed? Her story, which casts her upbringing in the exact language that describes her kidnapping, suggests she was. Hearst's experiences suggest that *all* behavior might be "learned," and might therefore also be unlearned and relearned. In the face of that threatening suggestion, "brainwashing" becomes the rhetorical boundary that naturalizes Hearst's "original" personality.

As in the narratives of earlier captives, change does not occur in Hearst's story in the context of freedom or free will. Having "exchanged parental authority for [Weed's] authority," the control of the SLA for that of the FBI, Hearst comprehends her status as a commodity in several dramas, none of which allows women "to think or choose for themselves." "I feel older and wiser now," Hearst states at the beginning of her autobiography, "more disillusioned in my feelings about my fellow man. I am aware of the stark reality that I am vulnerable" (1982, 1). Hearst's vulnerability, as her consistent use of the language of imprisonment and captivity reveals, is not simply to revolutionary kidnappers but also to the restrictive codes of traditional white femininity and the regulatory practices that enforce them at each period of her life. Rather, change occurs in Hearst's narrative in the passage between captivities. If Hearst must return, as Kelly and Rowlandson did, to a patriarchal society in which she has little value except as a passive item of exchange, she also gains a vocabulary with which to articulate and to criticize the constrictions imposed on her. Far from implying that the captive may claim an idealized liberty at the end of "captivity," *Every Secret Thing,* like the narratives discussed in the previous chapter, adopts the language of captivity to explore, critique, and revise white America's grammars of cultural identification and the politicized narratives they engender. In so doing, Hearst tentatively asserts that she came to feel "somehow free" (103).

While the twentieth century has seen a marked increase in women's first-person narratives, female subjects—particularly captive subjects—continue to face editorial appropriation and manipulation. Just as Hearst's narrative most clearly represents the patterns of the liminal captive's autobiography, so does it most strikingly typify the loss of the captive's textual control at the hands of a male editor. In 1988, Paul Schrader adapted Hearst's autobiography for his film, *Patty Hearst.* Not content with the ambiguities of *Every Secret Thing,* Schrader offered the closure that Hearst's own recounting denied. At the conclusion of the film, Hearst (Natasha Richardson) explains to her father that she has become a national icon because she was a vanished body, a vacant screen onto which the public could cast its fantasies without the interference of her own articulated desires or experiences.

> People fantasized about me so long they thought they knew me. When I finally surfaced—a real person, a real story—I was inconvenient. But I'm here, and I'll let them know it too. I made it worse, hiding from the press. I let people keep their fantasies. I hope to let people see the real me, to demystify myself.

Hearst tells her father that her crime was surviving her captivity, as her return rendered her apparently clear-cut story "emotionally messy." "Pardon my french, Dad," Hearst says in the last line of the film, "but fuck 'em, fuck 'em all."

When asked whether she found the film faithful to her autobiography, Hearst said she did, but singled out the last scene, described above, as dishonest. Asked why in the face of Hearst's objections he imposed this ending on her story, Schrader replied

I said, "Patty, I simply cannot make a film where for an hour and a half someone is constantly put upon and never gets a chance to speak their own mind. I know this scene didn't happen, that it's a composite scene. But you were thinking all these things, and you put all these ideas in your book."

But she saw it again and agreed with the scene . . . because she knew it was true—that people can't watch a movie about a character who does nothing and doesn't finally have a chance to turn to the camera and say, "this is what I think." (Mitchell 1988, 160)

Schrader's response represents a stunning misreading of his own film, in which Hearst explicitly states that she became a national obsession and survived the SLA precisely *because* she was passive, silent, and invisible. Schrader's sense that surviving two years of captivity means "doing nothing" is in itself extraordinary, but not unusual; as the nineteenth-century anthologies repeatedly claimed, only those women who resisted or escaped were "heroines." But above all, Schrader's response highlights the continuing difficulty editors have had in letting former captives tell their own stories. While the message that concludes *Patty Hearst* is nominally feminist—an analysis of the cultural use of a woman as a *tabula rasa* on which to inscribe national fantasies of female helplessness and masculine rescue, at once policed and sexual—Schrader, like earlier editors, nevertheless appropriates Hearst's autobiography for his own agenda, "convincing" Hearst that her text conforms to his script and not the other way around.

Hearst's loss of control over her own narrative is signaled both by the poster for Schrader's film and by the cover of her reissued autobiography, which in its reprinting adopts the title and the graphics of Schrader's film. The poster reads, "What actually happened could only have been known by one person. The person who lived it. Now 14 years later her story is about to be told." The passive construction foregrounds the paradox of the entire project. Only one person—Hearst herself—knows her story, yet, the poster implies, *she* is not about to tell it—the story *is . . . to be told*. The cover of the autobiography, too, takes Hearst's narrative away from her through a seemingly innocent phraseology. *Patty Hearst,* the cover reads, *Her*

Own Story. Rather than stating *My Own Story,* as one might expect, the cover implies the mediating presence of an editor who confers Hearst's narrative, divorced from its autobiographical authority, on the reader. The graphic adorning both the movie poster and the autobiography's cover is most telling. It features Hearst's face, with her name across her mouth. On one hand, the graphic bespeaks the articulation, through autobiography, of the author's identity. But the name also becomes a gag, as the re-covering of Patty Hearst is represented as yet another captivity. Readers of Rowlandson's narrative and Ter Amicam's preface to it—or of any of the Mathers' introductions to women's narratives, be they witches, captives, or saints— can hardly be surprised to learn that before he became a filmmaker, Paul Schrader was a Calvinist minister.

As the character Patty Hearst articulates in Schrader's film, the American public maintained its control over the representational value of the captive woman through its prurient detachment of her narrative from her body, thereby denying her any physical agency in shaping or revising either. Schrader's film perpetuates that control by casting another actress in Hearst's role, signaling the captive's completed participation in the creation of her story. In other films, Hearst's body returns, however, to foreground and to subvert her status as an actress in the scripts of white womanhood. While attending a screening of *Patty Hearst* at the Cannes Film Festival, Hearst met another director, John Waters, best known for directing tacky and iconoclastic camp classics such as *Polyester* and *Pink Flamingos.* Waters told Hearst that he would like to cast her in one of his movies, and subsequently Hearst appeared in two Waters films, *Cry Baby* (1990) and *Serial Mom* (1994). In *Cry Baby,* Hearst camps on the traditional domesticity she condemns in her autobiography, playing Meg, the wife of Hector (played by 1960s all-American boy David Nelson) and the mother of Wanda (Traci Lords), a troubled teenager involved with a rowdy youth gang. Attempting to cure their daughter of her unsavory affiliations, Meg and Hector arrange to trade Wanda for a better-behaved Swedish exchange student. "Let's all put on a folk hat and learn something about a foreign culture," the naive Meg tells Wanda, attempting to convince her daughter to participate in the exchange. This scene relies for its humor in part on the audience's familiarity with Hearst's

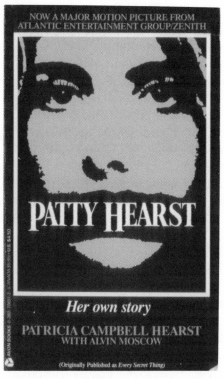

Cover of *Patty Hearst,* by Patricia Campbell Hearst and Alvin Moscow. Reproduced by permission of Avon Books.

own story, in which she accepted exchange with another culture as a way to engage "trouble" and escape her strict upbringing, not as a maternally arranged "cure" for class-crossing waywardness. Although Wanda, unlike Hearst, refuses to be exchanged, she does find herself in court, arrested with the other members of her gang. When Meg and Hector arrive in court to retrieve their daughter, Hearst has her second comic scene.

HECTOR: Hi Wanda, honey.
MEG: You were on the radio!
WANDA: Would you just get me the [bleep] out of here?
MEG: What does [bleep] mean, Hector?
HECTOR: It's just a keen, nonsense word Wanda uses to make herself feel grown up.
MEG: Your honor, could we take Wanda the fuck home?

Hearst is again in court in her second film, *Serial Mom,* in which Kathleen Turner plays a stereotypical housewife, Beverly Sutphin, cheerful, polite, and nurturing, who happens to be making obscene phone calls to her neighbors and killing anyone who breaks what she considers proper suburban decorum. When finally brought to trial, Beverly faces the jury and assures its members that she is just as normal as they are. As she makes this claim, the camera focuses on the face of one juror, played by Hearst. Thanks largely to this juror, the "serial mom" is acquitted (and later kills Hearst's character for wearing white shoes after Labor Day).

Waters' decision to cast Hearst in both roles demonstrates his witty understanding of what was at stake in her kidnapping and subsequent trial. Like Hearst's autobiography, both films depict white, middle-class domesticity as a thin veneer barely concealing violence, frustration, and intolerance. Especially in *Serial Mom* where her character serves as the unstable threshold between the juridical maintenance of convention and its criminal resistance, Hearst again undermines naturalized representations of American "normalcy." The films further insist, in their content as well as in their camp aesthetic, that "identity" be viewed not as the logical outgrowth of innate essence, but as a perpetually revised performance. Prior to *Cry Baby,* Waters' films were known by their star, Divine, a drag queen whose rags-to-riches narratives denaturalized the codes of class and gender and mocked glamorized screen depictions of the American Dream. Camp notoriously upsets established boundaries of taste, treating as art what the mainstream culture considers trash and vice versa. By insisting that value and identity are the result of normalized convention and not self-evident "nature," Waters' films echo Hearst's autobiography. When in *Cry Baby* Meg suggests that entering a culture is as simple as wearing its folk costume, underlying her comic innocence is the captive's staggering conclusion that culture-crossing is a matter not of ethnic impurity and sin, but of trying on a new hat. In setting Hearst's campy reversals in the courtroom, moreover, Waters does more than play on her sensationalized trial. He points to the potentially subversive results of Hearst's strategic performances. In both roles, Hearst's "misreadings" disrupt the operation of justice and hence the regulation of codified behavior. In *Serial Mom,* Hearst's character renders guiltless a series of violent and criminalized actions arising from frustration with the limited sphere offered white, middle-class women. Hearst's characters thus invert the language of "guilt" and "innocence" that were used to convict her and disrupt the social order that they are nominally working to support.

The status of the captive's body as an exchange item in the drama of captivity has repeatedly found its parallel in the "traffic" in her text between male editors, filmmakers, and yes, even literary critics. The history of the captive's text thus underscores one of the most crucial insights offered by these narratives: there is never a space of freedom, of autonomy, where one speaks purely for oneself. Waters chose Hearst to appear in his films, she reports, because he knew she could play a role without being any trouble. In treating Hearst like an obedient participant in any script he put before her, Waters used Hearst much as the SLA or the FBI did, even while his deployment of the figure of Patty Hearst continues the subversive work of her autobiography. Yet as *Every Secret Thing* demonstrates, the captive can speak from a place between cultures, between captivities. Given this insight, it is fitting that America's best-known captive, Patricia Hearst, returned to address the nation in the language of camp. Camp introduces to Hearst's story a final liminality between "truth" and "irony." Appearing to speak on behalf of America's dream of economic mobility and boundless social possibility, camp turns dominant rhetoric against itself from within to articulate less obliging, less patriotic, less "normal" stories of American life. That, too, is the lesson of captivity.

FOUR

The Wilderness of Fiction:

From Captivity Narrative

to Captivity Romance

I made it through the wilderness
Somehow I made it through
Madonna
"Like a Virgin"

The Wilderness provides you with an opportunity to experience a natural environment, to have solitude, and to use your outdoor skills.
Trailhead marker
Roosevelt National Forest

CAPTIVITY NARRATIVES, AS THE PREVIOUS CHAPTERS demonstrate, have repeatedly transgressed boundaries between cultures and identities. As these historical narratives became fictionalized, they allowed white women authors to cross literary boundaries as well, combining conventional genres and challenging distinctions between fact and fiction. As Carter's "Our Lady of the Massacre" and editorial rewritings of the captives' accounts show, captivity narratives from their inception have complicated the apparently transparent overlap of experience and representation. Editorial tampering as well as more subtle restrictions in the available language result in the filtering of captives' experiences through cultural stories circulated in myth, folklore, expansion pamphlets, abolition tracts, and legal, scientific, and liturgical discourse, among other sources. Resisting an easy equation of autobiography and experientially supported "fact," captivity narratives have reproduced dominant constructions of the social world, but they have also imagined new stories—and hence new "realities"—for white women's lives in America.[1]

The captivity narratives' challenge to the illusion of individual discursive invention becomes clear in nominally distinct texts that "borrow" passages from each other. These narratives blur the line between what a captive witnessed and what she added or invented for the sake of narrative convention or the projected prurience of her audience. In "An Affecting Narrative of the Captivity and Sufferings of Mrs. Mary Smith" (1815), for example, the captive relates the torture of three girls:

> [The Indians] pitched them from their knees to their shoulders, with upwards of six hundred of the sharpest splinters above described, which, at every puncture, were attended with screams of distress that echoed and re-echoed [sic] through the wilderness!—and then to complete the infernal tragedy, the splinters, all standing erect on the bleeding victims, were every one set on fire. (11)

The scene of torture, which Smith paradoxically depicts as "beyond the power of speech to describe, or even the imagination to conceive" (11), was so horrible that she was forced to bolster her traumatized imagination by borrowing the above passage, verbatim, from the 1779 narrative of Frederick Manheim. The torture appears again three years later in the 1818 narrative of Eunice Barber (13–14).

In addition to influencing each other's prose, captivity narratives were transformed by the increased popularity of "women's literature," particularly sentimental and domestic fiction. The emergence in late-eighteenth-century America of a female readership, and the subsequent acceptability of female authorship, literally changed the shape of the autobiographical captivity account.[2] After a century of slim accounts such as those featured in the Drake anthology, the sheer bulk of Fanny Kelly's narrative is striking: the text runs an impressive 260 pages, with 28 chapters, a preface and dedication, and 18 pages of appendices. Buoyed by the increasing social and commercial success of American women novelists, by the mid-nineteenth century female captives were producing weighty texts for the first time since Mary Rowlandson and Elizabeth

Hanson. In style as well as form the captivity narratives began to draw on popular literary genres. The death of Kelly's daughter Mary, for instance, is derived from the religious prose of popular domestic novels.

> Of all strange and terrible fates, no one who had seen her gentle face in its loving sweetness, the joy and comfort of our hearts, would have predicted such a barbarous fate for her. But it was only the passage from death into life, from darkness into day-light, from doubt and fear into endless love and joy. Those little ones, whose spirits float upward from their downy pillows, amid the tears and prayers of broken-hearted friends, are best to enter in at heaven's shining gate, which lies as near little Mary's rocky, blood-stained pillow in the desolate waste as the palace of a king, and when she had once gained the great and unspeakable bliss of heaven, it must have blotted out the re-membrance of the pain that won it, and made no price too great for such delights. (1871, 221)

108 One need only compare Mary's death with that of Eva in Harriet Beecher Stowe's *Uncle Tom's Cabin* to discover the fictional roots of Kelly's style.

> The child lay panting on her pillows, as one exhausted,—the large clear eyes rolled up and fixed. And, what said those eyes, that spoke so much of heaven? Earth was past, and earthly pain; but so solemn, so mysterious was the triumphant bright-ness of that face, that it choked even the sobs of sorrow. . . . A bright, a glorious smile passed over her face, and she said, brokenly,—"Oh! love,—joy,—peace!" gave one sigh, and passed from death into life! (1852, 318–19)

As the frontispiece to the Drake anthology demonstrates, with its dancing Indians surrounding a burning woman beneath the cap-tion, "TORTURING A CAPTIVE," by the nineteenth century the hard-ships of captivity no longer signified spiritual trial but had instead become a form of sensationalist literature.

Critics have claimed that former captives introduced fiction into their "autobiographical" accounts first in order more effec-tively to generate hatred of the French and the Indians, and later to

Illustration from Samuel Drake, ed., *Indian Captivities*
(1851). Photo Courtesy of The Newberry Library.

exploit the market created by women novelists and thereby enjoy
greater profits.[3] It is important to recognize, however, that the increased "fictionalization" of the captivity narrative also loosened
the constraints of genre and, in an age when literary forms inscribed

"proper" behavior for men and women, the constraints of gender as well. Nancy K. Miller has argued that women's texts often adopt "implausible" plots because "believable" stories simply replicate naturalized social codes. Since those codes also inscribe gender hierarchies in which women are permitted less agency than men, "plausible" plots therefore reinforce gender constraints for women characters and, by extension, for women readers. Miller argues that women novelists have had to write "implausible" narratives that break with naturalized gender codes in order to provide heroines with opportunities denied to most female readers (1988, 25–46).

The fictionalization of captivity narratives allowed women just such expansive implausibilities, as the narrative of K. White (1809) amply demonstrates. Embellished if not entirely fabricated, White's narrative bears out Miller's analysis and demonstrates the advantageous opportunities women claimed in the wilderness of fiction.[4] White's brief captivity occupies little space in her narrative, ending when a kindly Indian woman returns her to her family (29). At that point, however, White's real troubles begin, as the text becomes a compendium of the hardships faced by sentimental heroines. White consents to marry an American officer, who commits suicide when his fiancée discovers he already has a wife. Resolved that his daughter will not make an embarrassing choice again, White's father chooses for her a new husband, a "hypocrite" with "no sense of honor" (50). When this husband abandons her, leaving both his wife and her chambermaid pregnant (50), White enters business as a merchant in search of an "independency" (54) but is ruined by her husband's creditors. Fleeing to Schenectady, White, who has a "masculine form" and "a robust strong complexion" (62), is mistaken for a man. Permitting this misconception in order to move more freely, White becomes engaged to another woman until a rival suitor forces her to flee.

Up to this point in her narrative, White, despite her independent ambitions, is invariably defeated by the jealousies and passions of men. Soon, however, White demonstrates how an "eccentric" story permits women to flout "plausible" gender conventions and thereby gain economic independence, physical mobility, self-protection, and sexual adventure. When a man accuses White of being a spy, she challenges him to a duel, warning, "You shall not resort to the flimsy pretense of my being a woman to excuse your acceptance of it. I am content to wave [*sic*] the distinction with which society has marked the walks in life of the two sexes" (109). Now facing trial for espionage and threatened violence, White takes the opportunity to demonstrate her independence.

JUSTICE—What occupation do you follow?
ANSWER—Travelling.
JUSTICE—To answer what purpose?
ANSWER—Pleasure. (79)

Assuming male drag, White reverses an earlier conviction: the narrative begins with a melodramatic metaphor in which White is "tried" at the "bar of criticism" where a "timid female, unused to so severe and arduous a task, with a trembling step approaches the threshold of her tale of woe" (9–10). Claiming she "can plead no exemption" from the "weakness" of her sex, White hopes her text may "have some claim on your pity and indulgence" (10). While "femininity" allows the bar of criticism to find her story lacking, by the narrative's conclusion White's play with gender enables her to turn the tables, refusing the court's power to pass judgment on her "occupation." White apologizes, in the narrative's final lines, for its "novel and eccentric parts" (126), adding that "nature and disposition struggle hard" (127). Yet she has shown that her "disposition" and the conventions of narrative have come into conflict as well; only through the "eccentricity" created by fictional license can she resolve her "nature" and her "disposition," her prescribed gender role and her "novel" desires. As White's transformation of genre and of gender demonstrates, fiction allowed white women to turn captivity and harassment into agency and pleasure.

The narratives of Mary Smith, Fanny Kelly, and K. White show how and why white women drew on the world of fiction to compose their autobiographical captivity accounts. In the late eighteenth and early nineteenth centuries the border of fact and fiction was crossed in the opposite direction as well, however, giving rise to a series of novels based on captivity accounts. These novels, among America's first, suggest that the captivity narrative played a central yet largely unrecognized role in literary history. Critics have traditionally credited men such as Charles Brockden Brown and James Fenimore Cooper with bringing captivity—and hence the American "wilderness"—into fiction.[5] Yet in their fascination with the gender critique possible through the captivity narratives, women, not men, popularized the wilderness of fiction. Before Brown's *Edgar Huntly* (1799) there was Ann Eliza Bleecker's *The History of Maria Kittle* (1793). Susanna Haswell Rowson's *Reuben and Rachel* (1798) predates Cooper's novels. Even as the latter published the first of his Leatherstocking tales, *The Pioneers,* in 1823, the market for wilderness romances by women flourished: the following year saw the publication of Eliza Laneford Cushing's *Saratoga,* Lydia Maria Child's *Hobomok,* and Harriet Cheney's *A Peep at the Pilgrims.* Catharine Maria Sedgwick's *Hope Leslie* (1827) established its author as one of the most popular novelists of her day. Historical romances set in seventeenth-century New England, these novels all feature strong, independent women who free themselves from the tyranny of fathers and husbands and, with the exception of Mary Conant who willingly marries an Indian in *Hobomok,* enjoy adventure in the wilderness as the result of an Indian captivity.

Emerging in the period between the American Revolution and the heyday of domestic literature, these novels register the resistance of middle-class white women to domestic identity and demonstrate their power to shape that resistance into cultural myth. The allure of the wilderness for these novelists was arguably the same as for their male contemporaries: it provides an escape from what were perceived as the strangling conventions of an increasingly commercial society with rapidly rigidifying gender expectations.[6] David Leverenz describes the effect of America's increased obsession with profit, rationalism, and competition on male writers such as Hawthorne and Emerson, who suffered from the common perception of artists as economic parasites and, worse, as effeminized men (1989, 14).[7] In their desire to redefine masculinity and thereby escape charges of effeminacy, male authors turned toward the woods. Far from the markets of Boston, New York, and Philadelphia, and associated with preindustrial heroism and "savage" lawlessness, the wilderness proved an ideal metaphorical realm for masculine refashioning. In the wilderness, the hero (and by extension the author), without surrendering his privileges of race, class, and gender, can circumvent cultural expectations of both social behavior and literary convention.[8] The fantasy of life beyond convention (but not without culturally prescribed authority) is best formulated as what Thoreau in *Walden* calls *extra-vagance,* a desire to "wander far enough beyond the narrow limits of my daily experience" so as "to speak somewhere *without* bounds" (1854, 240).

Male writers were described as "effeminate" largely because of a perceived separation of spheres that termed public (commercial, "practical") endeavor "masculine" and private (domestic, "emotional") responsibilities "feminine."[9] Literature, which is read at home and addresses emotions and sentiment—those enemies of rational competitiveness—was considered part of "women's sphere." Men of letters thus became associated, through their art, with the domestic world of women. Women authors did not have to wait until they picked up the pen to find themselves associated with domesticity, however, for they were already assigned to the private sphere by virtue of their gender.[10] The "domestication" of women intensified, as numerous historians have documented, in the period following the Revolutionary War, the same period that saw the emergence of the woman-authored wilderness novel.[11] As women were increasingly presented with depictions of their lives that stressed privacy, domesticity, "sensibility," and a rejection of the world outside the immediate circle of their families, the wilderness tale offered a story set outside the home, requiring not only sensibility but mental shrewdness and physical prowess. The same division of spheres that troubled male romantics, resulting as it did in a culturally enforced consignment to the feminine realm of domesticity, led women authors to invent a literary wilderness where dualisms—public/private, commerce/domesticity, male/female, practical/frivolous—are denaturalized and hence opened for debate.

Because the terms of extra-vagance are gender-inflected, however, women who wrote wilderness romances faced difficulties of authority their male contemporaries would not encounter. "Home" not only bore the symbolic burden of convention, tradition, family history, and obligation, but almost invariably was associated with womanhood itself.[12] Even if a woman author imagined a plot that would send her heroine into the wilderness, risking the erasure of the one cultural identity "believable" for female characters, her heroine could not willingly go. There were few precedents for a female character who picks up and runs off, while the prescriptions against such "flights of fancy," in life or in literature, were ubiquitous. Paradoxically, women authors from Ann Eliza Bleecker to Catharine Maria Sedgwick resolved these difficulties and discovered their textual extra-vagance through stories of captivity. The captivity plot circumvents the dilemma of authority, drawing on the one narrative that, from its inception, not only permitted female authorship but also took place outside the home, foregrounding women's fortitude, cunning, and physical as well as emotional strength. Above all, the captivity story provides a necessary narrative pretext, striking a compromise on the issue of female agency. Because the heroine is a captive, taken against her will, she can enter the wilderness without blame. The captivity romances thereby both express and veil the daring of women authors like Bleecker, Rowson, and Sedgwick, and the extra-vagance of their female characters.

Increasingly, women authors used the trope of captivity to describe not only life among the Indians but the quotidian domestic experiences of the female reader as well, depicting with growing urgency the social conventions from which both author and heroine had to free themselves before exercising their newfound extra-vagance. As the genre developed, authors stripped captivity among the Indians of its associations with violence and destruction. Instead, one finds captivity minimalized (as in Bleecker), turned into a metaphor of restrictive national policy (as in Rowson) or, more frequently, of restrictive domestic and social attitudes toward both white and Indian women (as in Cheney and Sedgwick). In these metaphorical deployments of captivity, the threat is not so much the Indian, often depicted as a fellow sufferer, but rather the white men with whom the women supposedly identify. By the time Catharine Sedgwick writes *Hope Leslie* in 1827, captivity at home is the principal danger, captivity among the Indians a relative reprieve. If male extra-vagance created the fantasy of woman-as-civilization, then, women authors showed that the proponents of domesticity were in fact men with a social and economic stake in keeping women shut away from the world. By equating women's imprisonment within domesticity to their captivity among the Indians, female authors dissociated their heroines from their metaphorical connection with the home. In each of the novels of female extra-vagance, women, far from being "naturally" inclined toward the hearth, are duped into domesticity by men who wield the powerful tools of romance and religion (or their nineteenth-century equivalents, sentiment and virtue).

The captivity romances privilege friendship over romance and spirit over religion, substitutions that can only be accomplished, according to these novels, in the cultural no-man's-land of the wilderness. Harriet Cheney's *A Peep at the Pilgrims,* in which the heroine rushes into her Indian captivity to escape the more dangerous constraints placed on her at home, exemplifies how the captivity narrative allowed women novelists to rewrite the gender codes of their society. At the novel's start, Miriam Grey is pressured by her father to marry the most bigoted and cheerless of the Pilgrims. When Miriam resists, her father, sounding more like a nineteenth-century patriarch than a Pilgrim, lectures her on her "proper" place in society: " 'Women are born to submit, . . . and of the weaker vessel, it is meet they should be guided by those who rule over them' " (1824, 171). Miriam is simultaneously pursued by the more vivacious Edward Atherton, but she discourages his suit as well, urging him to think of her " 'only as a friend, a sister' " (224). When her father and suitors persist, however, Miriam proposes joining her relatives on a dangerous journey to Hartford, commencing "the preparations for her expected departure with an alacrity which surprised her friends" (306). Her defiantly enthusiastic desire to make the journey into the wilderness begins a transformation in Miriam that all around her note; Miles Standish, for instance, is amazed that his " 'little rose-bud, with all her sweetness and smiles, would set up for a will of her own' " (307).

Miriam's transformation is not complete, however, until captivity provides her with a "wilderness" existence and an Indian role model. During her captivity, Miriam is comforted by the chief's wife, Mioma, whom the white girl regarded

> with involuntary admiration. She had scarcely passed the season of youth, and her mature and noble figure, at once dignified and graceful, possessed that vigor and elasticity so peculiar to

the matrons of the forest; while her regular features, her soft and intelligent countenance, expressed a mind susceptible of elevated sentiments. (405)

Mioma, both dignified and vigorous, intelligent and sentimental, combines traits the heroine recognizes as conventionally separated between men and women. Captivity thus denaturalizes the gender constructions of Miriam's culture (which are closer to those of Cheney's nineteenth century), allowing the heroine to reconstruct her life on less restricted terms. "Miriam became more cheerful and contented than she had conceived it possible to be at the commencement of her captivity" (410), Cheney writes, summing up the position of many novels that demonstrate the benefits for women of a wilderness life the heroine could only have through the "accident" of capture.

As Miriam's bond with Mioma demonstrates, the primary aspect of nineteenth-century domestic ideology heroines took with them intact into captivity was the awareness of other women—both as interlocutors and companions within the text, and as a growing female readership of the text—as a source of survival and strength. The typical story of masculine extra-vagance involves not a movement toward but a flight away from community.[13] In the captivity romances, however, a heroine's confinement invariably leads to her adoption into an alternative community of women.

The dialectic of confinement and community central to the captivity romance embodies the process, documented by Nancy Cott and Carroll Smith-Rosenberg, of the "group consciousness" that emerged among late eighteenth and early nineteenth-century American women due to a perceived separation of spheres. Cott describes how, to justify their exclusion from the public sphere of commerce and politics, women were credited with a "natural" aptitude for domestic influence, child nurture, and religious morality. But the attribution of special characteristics that marked each woman as inherently different from all men yet like all others of her sex gave women, along with their domestic confinement, a common ground on which to gather, to sympathize, and to identify. "Women's sphere" became, then, not only a site of exclusion but of identity that, shared with others in the same social category, provided the basis of community.[14] In the fictional topography of the captivity romance, the social transformation of the home from a site of constraint to one of expansion is literalized into two separate locations, the place of the heroine's confinement and that of her newfound community. Between lies the wilderness, the liminal space in which the heroine moves from captivity to community, the change dramatized as a journey—often a jail-break—from one space to another.

By making community contingent on the wilderness, the women-authored captivity romances challenge a literary and critical tradition that more typically opposes the wilderness to society. While masculine extra-vagance seeks to leave behind a stifling community in favor of a romanticized solitude, women's extra-vagance offers escape from a stifling isolation into a community that grants agency to its members. The captivity narratives also resist a nostalgic longing for the white society the heroine has left behind. The captive heroine and the author who creates her use captivity to conceive of new, hybrid communities, and to take women out of the home and into paradoxical and denaturalizing locales.

117

The authors of the captivity romances thus used community to free their heroines from the conservative impulses both of individualism and nostalgia, in contrast to the adaptation of the captivity narrative in some of the first novels written by men. As Nancy Armstrong and Leonard Tennenhouse have argued, Samuel Richardson's *Pamela,* for example, draws its narrative from Mary Rowlandson's captivity narrative: in both texts white women are taken from their home communities and threatened with bodily invasion, which they resist by writing themselves into place as inviolate individuals who maintain their lost homes through language. Armstrong and Tennenhouse contend that both women, in attempting textually to restore a communal "wholeness" that no longer exists (the purely "English," colonial culture in Rowlandson's case, and in Pamela's the aristocracy), forever distinguish themselves from those communities by becoming individuated "authors." While as authors Rowlandson and Pamela never again speak from a collective identity, they continue to articulate the values of those communities that now exist only in their texts. The synthesis of a desired return to fractured "wholeness" and modern individuation thus brings forth fictional communities that are traces of the lost social "real" and which are, according to Armstrong and Tennenhouse, historical accidents that the authors did not intend to create but which nevertheless legitimize their address.[15]

The comparison of Pamela and Rowlandson will not account for the women-authored romances, however, for it assumes masculine reception, transfers that reception onto authorial design or desire, and finally generalizes male reception onto the rise of all early fiction. For Armstrong and Tennenhouse, the recipients of Rowlandson's text are assumed to be male authors like Richardson who profit from resurrecting a fragmented British empire into an integrated textual nation. In reading backwards from Richardson to Rowlandson, the critics make his frustrated nostalgia her desire. Compared to male authors such as Richardson, early American women, who were legally disenfranchised and economically reliant, apparently had difficulty imagining themselves as part of a national "whole." In the captivity romances, therefore, the heroines, like Pamela, are torn from communities and come to speak as individuals in relation to a posited, "fictional" collective. Yet women authors imagined their heroines returning to a reading community based not on nation but on gender. The captive leaves behind a shattered national community defined by the shared assumption of white, male values, and "returns" by conceiving herself as a strong individual supported by a community of women (much as the author addresses a projected "public" of supportive women readers). In short, the captivity romances create not an individual and a national collective in a state of tension but an individual woman and a community of women that interact to disrupt, not resurrect, the assumed values of the cultures they have left behind.

As the captivity narrative entered fiction in America, it shaped not only modern authorship in general, then, but women's authorship in particular. By taking gender into consideration in analyzing the relationship between individualism and collectivity, one can trace a history not of frustrated return and accidental creation but of willed separation and imaginative alternatives. The connection between an emerging wilderness mythology and the female signature prompts such a reconsideration of American literary and social history. The following chapters will participate in that investigation, examining why women wrote wilderness novels and how those texts differed from both the "classic," male-authored romances and the sentimental or domestic genres traditionally considered the proper domain of women authors. Of more central concern to the present chapter, however, is the question of how the captivity narrative, previously considered an "autobiographical" or "factual" account, came to reveal its literary potential, bringing captives like Mary Rowlandson into the wilderness of fiction.

The privileging of female community in white women's fiction occasioned a strikingly different textual closure than that imagined in most autobiographical accounts. In the captivity narratives, the greatest threat to the captive's extra-vagant imagination typically came neither at the moment of capture nor during her trek through a new physical and cultural terrain but on her return. No matter how far a captive went toward joining the lives of her captors or challenging the assumptions of her home culture, such revision usually ceased once return appeared inevitable. Extraordinary exceptions notwithstanding, for captive white women going home meant acquiescing, if only partially and in the eleventh hour, to models of representation that supported the colonialist and patriarchal desires their texts previously resisted.

Typically, the captive's return—both physical and textual—is ensured and enforced by a human agent, a "rescuer," whose duty is not only to convey home the white captive but to supervise the reinscription of conventional narratives of identity on her body. Narratives such as K. White's, in which captives are either self-protected or returned home by other women, are rare; while captives frequently survived captivity with the help of other women, they were ultimately "rescued" only by a white man or a group of white men. Since, as the narratives of captives such as Patty Hearst demonstrate, the captive's body and her text become interchangeable through captivity, her reliance on men for rescue *in* the text determines her anticipation of a masculine readership *of* the text. Male rescuers thus become privileged readers, with equal access to the captive's body and to her text. Forced by historical necessity to anticipate and appeal to a masculine audience, white women frequently conclude their captivity by depicting themselves as passive, vulnerable, and xenophobic—in short, as "rescuable"—in marked contrast to their earlier self-representations.

A brief return to Fanny Kelly's *Narrative of My Captivity among the Sioux Indians* reveals both the historic necessity of anticipating a masculine audience and the disastrous consequences of "rescuability" for white women and their Indian captors. Kelly describes the surprise attack by a war party of Indians on an American wagon train escorted by Captain Fisk, who keeps the braves at bay for three days. The Sioux, waiting for the train to recommence its journey in order to ambush it from behind, urge Kelly to write a letter assuring Fisk of the Indians' friendly intentions. Recognizing that her only chance of rescue lies in keeping Fisk alive, Kelly forms a plan of her own.

> Knowing their malicious design, I set myself to work to circumvent them; and although the wily chief counted every word dictated, and as they were marked on paper, I contrived, by joining them together and condensing the information I gave, to warn the officer of the perfidious intentions of the savages, and tell him briefly of my helpless and unhappy captivity. (1871, 149)

Fisk answers that he has no intention of trusting the Indians, and the Sioux force Kelly to write a more convincing assurance.

> Again I managed to communicate with them, and this time begged them to use their field-glasses, and that I would find an excuse for standing on the hills in the afternoon, that they might see for themselves that I was what I represented myself to be—a white woman held in bondage. (150)

Kelly's strategy proves immediately gratifying both to herself and to the soldiers.

> The opportunity I desired was gained, and to my great delight, I had a chance of standing so as to be seen by the men of the soldier's [*sic*] camp. I had given my own name in every communication. As soon as the soldiers saw that it truly was a woman of their own race, and that I was in the power of their enemies, the excitement of their feeling became so great that they desired immediately to rush to my rescue. (150)

As Kelly's narrative makes clear, to be rescued women must first arouse desire—the desire to rescue—in men, which they accomplish by shaping themselves and their texts so as to be acceptable to the masculine audience on which rescue depends. Desire is awakened in Kelly's audience through the suggestion of a traditional rescue plot, the key elements of which are contained in her phrase, "in the power of their enemies." Manipulating both the Indians and the United States military by presenting herself as helpless, Kelly's self-representation is obviously paradoxical. Yet having survived life in captivity through a combination of fortitude and understanding, Kelly can return to her home culture only by asserting her vulnerability, her powerlessness, and her disdain for her culture's "enemies."

In presenting herself to male spectators, Kelly also becomes what female captives historically have been: an object of exchange in a power struggle between two groups of men. Kelly's objectification and its relation to the desire of the male soldiers become clear when she writes, "As soon as the soldiers saw that it truly was a woman of their own race . . . the excitement of their feeling became so great that they desired immediately to rush to my rescue." The same sentence that relates the arousal of the soldiers' desire witnesses the captive's transformation from an "I" to an "it," her prose registering her change from a subject to an object of both physical and textual exchange.[16] Having stripped herself of agency by representing herself as "helpless and unhappy," Kelly tries to maintain her independence by asserting her signature, noting, "I had given my own name in every communication." Yet Kelly is no longer in control of her text; her "name" is not hers to own. Like other captive white women, Kelly had little choice in anticipating a masculine audience, since the power of physical rescue lies with the strongholds of patriarchal authority: the government and the military. Yet in presenting her text to a masculine audience, Kelly perpetuates a narrative of female dependency and racial depravity, thereby transcribing the social and economic agenda of white men.

The dangerous irony of Kelly's transformed self-representation is that, in seeking "rescue" from Fisk's soldiers, she is threatened by further appropriation and powerlessness: her apparent passivity in relation to her rescuers places Kelly, as it would later place Patty

Hearst, in a narrative of sexual objectification and control as well. The soldiers' "desire" to rescue Kelly on viewing her through their binoculars arises from the scopophilic dynamic of masculine/ active/gaze and feminine/passive/spectacle that Laura Mulvey describes as characteristic of the fetishistic masculine gaze.[17] Kelly's letter fails to receive the "proper" response until her vulnerability is "embodied." Desire awakened by her letter therefore becomes connected to desire awakened by her body, while both are effective only insofar as they represent female powerlessness in the face of masculine vision and agency.

Kelly's transformation into a powerless object of sexualizing surveillance undertaken in the guise of rescue epitomizes the representational crisis encountered by numerous captive white women, who repeatedly resist the objectifying prurience not of their captors but of their countrymen. Mary Rowlandson refused the sexualization of vulnerability in the minds of her readers, asserting

> I have been in the midst of those roaring lions and savage bears that feared neither God nor man nor the devil, by night and day, alone and in company, sleeping all sorts together, and yet not one of them ever offered me the least abuse or unchastity to me in word or action. Though some are ready to say I speak it to my own credit, I speak it in the presence of God and to His glory. (1682, 70)

Two hundred years later Kelly made a similar assertion: "I had never suffered from any of [the Indians] the slightest personal or unchaste insult. Let me bear testimony to this redeeming feature in their treatment of me" (1871, 178). Following her arrest, Patty Hearst complains that the prison psychiatrists are interested in hearing only the sexual details of her kidnapping, despite her insistence that the SLA spent more time planning revolution than fornicating (1982, 376). That Rowlandson, Kelly, and Hearst all needed to refute the suggestion of rape, despite the fact that the Indians reportedly did not rape captives, points to an identification in the minds of their white audiences between captivity, race, and sexual vulnerability.[18] That connection, which perhaps lay behind what Rowlandson's ministerial editor refers to as the "coy phantasies" (Lincoln 1913, 115) of her readers, is articulated in the 1962 introduction to the reprint of Kelly's narrative, where the editor reports, "The female captive, because of her greater potential for pathetic effects and because of the excitement she created as an object of sexual interest, all but crowded the male captive off the scene" (Zanger 1962, vi). The captive's efforts notwithstanding, something about "rescuability" suggests to white, male readers—both then and now—sexual availability, powerlessness, and hence "interest."

White male (super)vision has destructive consequences not only for the captive but for her captors as well. Dominant narratives of manifest destiny, from the colonial era through the present day, have relied for dramatic tension on the threatened sexualization of white women by men of color who possess uncontrollable, violent, and animalistic lusts. The persistent belief in the sexual "tainting" of white women through captivity, which exposes the captive to men of color, is revealed in the etymology of "rape," the root of which is the Latin verb, *rapere,* to seize, to capture, or to carry away. Yet captivity narratives repeatedly show that the depiction of captors as lurid threats to white innocence serves both to disguise white, male control of women's bodies and to justify the extermi- 123 nation of the Indians and the appropriation of their lands. Sarah Wakefield describes the pressure white soldiers put on redeemed captives to produce rape narratives that activated retaliatory "rescue" campaigns, bringing large profits to white men. White women who believe that "rescue" is undertaken on their behalf, and not in the service of imperialism, pay a heavy price for their naïveté. Kelly relates the story of Mrs. Blynn, a captive who sends a letter to her father urging him to have the governor of Kansas sign a peace treaty with the Sioux so she may return home. Instead, Custer's men "came charging with loud huzzahs upon the village" (1871, 248), resulting not only in the murder of Mrs. Blynn by her captors but in the slaughter of the entire Sioux tribe.

Kelly's narrative ends by dramatizing these losses suffered by women and Indians due to "rescuability." After her redemption, Kelly finds herself alone and destitute; her husband has died of cholera, and her narrative appears in a pirated edition before Kelly can enjoy any profits from its publication. Her only means of support is government compensation, promised to her by one of her most avid readers, President Ulysses S. Grant. But Kelly encounters "difficulties" in receiving her money, and while Congress eventually passes a bill granting Kelly five thousand dollars, no one tells her of the proposed bill until after it is passed. Ironically, Kelly's only financial support comes not from the United States government or her white countrymen but from her former captors. Kelly one day encounters on the streets of Washington a group of familiar Sioux who have come to collect money for lands appropriated by the government. Appalled by her financial distress, the Sioux ask Kelly to draw up a bill of losses suffered at their hands, which they immediately present to the Secretary of Indian Affairs, demanding that she be paid from monies owed to the tribe. The final depiction of shared litigation challenges the faith Kelly has placed in a white, male audience and in the rescue it provides. Far from having gained "insider" status by anticipating that audience, Kelly finds herself like her captors relying for definition and sustenance on a government she could not elect and which is interested in her only as a symbol of powerlessness and suffering.

The authors of the captivity romances were as aware of the dangers posed to their heroines by masculine rescue as they were of the adventures offered by captivity in the wilderness. In *A Peep at the Pilgrims,* for example, Edward Atherton launches a campaign to rescue Miriam Grey that results in a bloody war between the Pequods and the Plymouth colony. When Atherton later boasts of rescuing Miriam, Miles Standish responds, "'I cannot learn that she was in any danger, till you provoked the Indians to vengeance'" (1824, 454). Cheney contrasts Atherton's "private and romantic enterprise" (386) with a more peaceful and effective plan: Miriam's Indian "mother," Mioma, works diligently to ensure the captive's release and is near success when Atherton's actions force the chief back into an adversarial role.

Never having been captured themselves, the authors of captivity romances were at greater liberty to reimagine rescue and the modes of self-representation it offers the captive heroine. As Cheney's alternative to masculine rescue suggests, in the wilderness of fiction women rescue other women, bringing the heroine not from Indian captivity to the "freedom" of white society but from isolation in households dominated by fathers to communities imagined through the enabling fiction of shared gender identity.[19] Like their

124

narrative sources, furthermore, captivity romances equate rescue with reading, although again they differ in inscribing a readership of women. In the captivity romances, rescue does not come through the solitary heroics of men like Atherton, leading to alienation or to the loss of agency, as in Kelly's. Rather, rescue arises from a community composed of "sisters" who are in turn invited to share a literary meeting place and a coded indictment of the constraint and coercion in women's daily experiences.

America's first captivity fiction, Ann Eliza Bleecker's *The History of Maria Kittle* (1793), presents an instructive contrast to the rescue depicted in Fanny Kelly's narrative. Bleecker begins her tale by critiquing the masculine agency at the center of conventional rescue plots. Bleecker depicts men as stubborn and rash, motivated by a self-destructive fatality that renders "protection" and desertion at their hands equally calamitous to women. Despite his distrust of the Indians, Mr. Kittle (he never receives a first name) leaves his wife alone with the Indians when they come to warn the Kittles of an imminent raid, and then, believing their warning, again deserts Maria while he travels to Albany to seek a safer house for his family. **125** When Mr. Kittle plans to leave his family alone a third time, Maria expresses her frustration with male adventure, " 'Is it not enough . . . that you have escaped one danger, but must you be so very eager to encounter others?' " (31). Other husbands who, like Mr. Kittle, abandon their wives to captivity have received justification from male authors. When Mr. Duston left his wife Hannah to battle the Indians alone, Hawthorne rose to his defense. In "The Duston Family," Hawthorne writes that Hannah, who rescued herself when she murdered and scalped her Indian captors, will be "remembered as long as the deeds of old times are told" as "the bloody old hag" who should have "drowned in crossing Contocook River," while her husband will be recalled as a "tender-hearted yet valiant man" (1900, 238). Bleecker offers no such defense. When Mr. Kittle cries, "Burst—burst my shrinking heart, and punish a wretch for not having died in the defense of such lovely and innocent beings! Oh! why was I absent in this fatal hour?" (1793, 46), Bleecker meets his question with pointed silence.

The same self-destructive rashness characterizes Mr. Kittle's life after Maria's capture. Rather than attempting to find his wife,

Mr. Kittle throws himself into a suicidal stint in the army; "in hopes of ending a being that grew insupportable under the reflection of past happiness, he tempted death in every action wherein he was engaged, and being disappointed, gave himself up to the blackest melancholy" (85). Other men prove more dramatically destructive in their fatality. When the Indians come to the Kittle home, Maria is in the company of her sister-in-law, Comelia, and Comelia's husband. As the Indians attempt to break down the door, Comelia's " 'rash, rash, unfortunate husband' " opens the door to the attackers, urging his distraught wife to " 'be resigned to the will of God' " (35). The tempering of "rash" with "unfortunate" does not disguise the blame Comelia (or Bleecker) puts on her husband for their imminent deaths. Most disturbing is Comelia's final plea—" 'Have mercy on yourself, on me, on my child' " (35)—made not of the Indians, but of her nominal "protector."

Rather than relying on masculine agency for their rescue, Bleecker's women—represented, in contrast to the men, as rational and courageous—are either aided by other women or are self-delivered. Mrs. Willis makes the difficult journey to Montreal to redeem her husband, "flushed with hope, and with indefatigable industry and painful solitude" (80) (after his friends point out the dangers, Mr. Kittle abandons the very same plan for redeeming Maria). During her captivity Maria never loses her "stoical composure" (52). When the Indians surrender Maria and her brother to the governor of Montreal, he begins questioning them harshly. From the crowd curiously observing the interview emerges Mrs. D——, an Englishwoman "whom humanity more than curiosity had drawn to the place" (63). Mrs. D——, moved by "the soft impulses of nature" (63), intercedes with the governor and is granted permission to take Maria to her home, where she shows her new "sister" so much tenderness that Maria "again melted into tears; but it was a gush of grateful acknowledgment" (66–67). Rescue comes to Maria, finally, not through masculine heroics, but through female sympathy and "sisterly" affection. Even Maria's role as narrator is created through her bond with Mrs. D——. During the governor's questioning, Maria remains petrified and mute. Under the Englishwoman's care, however, the "tempest of [Maria's] soul subsided in a solemn calm; and though she did not regain her vivacity, she became agreeably conversable" (66). Moved not by "curiosity" but "humanity," not prurience but empathy, Mrs. D—— rescues Maria not only from her period of captivity but from a debilitating silence as well.

Just as Maria's story is "redeemed" by a sympathetic female auditor, so Bleecker's new rescue plot is enabled by an equally new, specifically female audience capable of recognizing and drawing strength from the codes of the captivity story. Bleecker inscribes a female readership first through the epistolary form of her text, composed as a letter from the narrator to her sister. Bleecker constructs an even wider female audience within the events of the narrative. When Mrs. D—— arranges a tea in Maria's honor, the women who attend—French and English gentlewomen as well as other American captives—call upon each other to tell their stories, which are heard amid "tears, and pleasing melancholy" (68). Although not all the women assembled at Mrs. D——'s have been abducted, the degree to which *all* female auditors appear to identify with the captives highlights the captivity narrative's particular significance for audiences of women. Sharing their feelings of isolation and power-lessness, the women of Bleecker's text have their less tangible constraints embodied and validated. Women reading Bleecker's text are encouraged to witness the powerful benefits of female community, to sympathize with female suffering, and to admire female strength, endurance, and resolution. They are also offered, through the representation of a female audience, membership in that community. In the end the women declare sisterhood that crosses class and national (although not racial) barriers:[20] "'I now reject (interrupted MRS. BRATT) all prejudices of education. From my infancy have I been taught that the French were a cruel perfidious enemy, but I have found them quite the reverse'" (73). Where Kelly's relationship to her spectators hinges on gender difference, Bleecker's is predicated on an empathy—a faith in shared experience—between speaker and audience.

The women of Bleecker's text arguably form America's first literary consciousness-raising group. Teresa de Lauretis describes consciousness raising as "the process of self-representation which defines 'I' as a woman, or, in other words, en-genders the subject as female" (1984, 159). The political potential of this en-gendering, according to de Lauretis, lies in the critical revision of social reality, undertaken in two stages. In the first, a woman "places [herself] or is placed in social reality, and so perceives and comprehends as subjective (referring to, even originating in, oneself) those relations—material, economic, and interpersonal—which are in fact social and, in a larger perspective, historical" (159). Having found her subjectivity in the "social world," a woman may then share her narrative with others who have had similar experiences, collectively constructing a discourse that at once validates female subjectivity (showing that her interactions with society are not aberrant or neurotic) and enacts "a continual modification of consciousness; that consciousness in turn being the condition of social change" (184). The change brought about by consciousness raising need not be "in 'concrete action,'" de Lauretis notes, "but in a disposition, a readiness (for action), a set of expectations" (178).

The narrators of autobiographical accounts undertake the first stage of consciousness raising, understanding the experience of captivity, enacted on their bodies, to represent social and historical relations. At the point of return, however, they surrender their participation in the second stage, in which female subjectivity is validated and changed. The female community inscribed in Bleecker's text returns the captive to the second stage of consciousness building, thereby transforming both the captivity narrative and its heroine. If her newfound community does not "change" patriarchal discourses of gender, it does enable the heroine to articulate her social experience of constraint in ways that transform her from an object to a subject of interpretation. Put another way, if Kelly's interaction with a masculine audience marks the end of her self-inscriptions, Maria Kittle, in finding a female audience, has just begun to speak. For Maria's audience, her powers of narration are her primary attraction, rendering the captive heroine visible as the subject of discourse and desire, not solely as their object.

Of course, the very community that rescues both captive and author from masculine appropriation simultaneously binds them to dominant representations of "true womanhood" as well. To appeal to an emerging female readership, both the captive and her creator must conform to certain conventions: the former must be emotional and nurturing, temperamentally attached to all other women, while the latter must communicate in the language of senti-ment and triumphant sisterhood. The very concept of "female com-munity," as Nancy Cott and others have argued, emerges from a discursive "separation of spheres" that, while it gave women a com-mon identity that allowed them to come together in imagined com-monality, also represented them as unsuited for the "public sphere" of men and masculinity. Rendering rescue as restrictive as well as liberating, even when it comes at the hands of other women, the captivity romances demonstrate the impossibility of any ultimate "freedom" for women characters. The inescapability of representa-tional overdetermination in the romances thus echoes the continual "captivity" of the autobiographical narrators who, held hostage in their own society by tyrannical fathers and lovers, again become captives in the "wilderness," often in the same way as at home—as surrogate mothers, daughters, and housekeepers.

At the same time, however, the heroine's captivity ends in a cul-tural liminality from which she criticizes the conventions of her own society and explores alternative narratives for women. For example, the captivity romances show the gender conventions apparently po-liced through "female community" to be contradictory construc-tions, capable of leading women into the very discursive "spheres" they were designed to foreclose. Women's domestic and nurturing nature suits them for lives outside the home, free of their families, while the communities borne of "sameness" increasingly permit the heroine to articulate her salutory knowledge of transcultural "dif-ference." In the captivity romance, then, one can never return to the community one has left behind, nor can one enter one's newfound community, without exceeding the representational—and hence the ideological—borders of both. From that excess, however, arises the possibility for what Leigh Gilmore, in reference to women's au-tobiographies, calls "unruly subjects who are unevenly objectified and who represent identity in relation to other values and subjec-tivities" (1994, 12). Unlike the masculine romantic dream of life "without bounds," female extra-vagance, gained through the cap-tivity story, thus resists the utopian impression of "freedom" that, as D. H. Lawrence notes, is the surest sign of one's imprisonment.[21] Rescue leaves women not in a state of antesocial liberty but in the moment of articulation arising between two forms of confinement.

At least one community, however, must grant the female subject permission to experiment, to exceed her objectification and speak. As long as autobiographical narrators could imagine a return only to the patriarchal community they had left behind, no such experimentation was possible. Fanny Kelly at one point in her narrative attempts, like Maria Kittle, an epistolary escape. As she is carried into captivity, Kelly leaves a trail of letters so her rescuers can find her. When after some time she realizes that no rescuer is following her paper trail, Kelly, who dedicates her *Narrative* to Fisk's soldiers, admits, "my great fear was that my letter had not fallen into the right hands" (1871, 205). To ensure that her text fell into the "right" hands, Bleecker advertised for her desired readership, one that could imagine more complex social arrangements and subjective identifications, for whom "rescue" would not mean "return." Within the circle of her captive audience, Maria Kittle is returned neither to a false promise of liberty nor to absolute overdetermination. Rather, she tells a tale that resists the naturalized binaries of white, middle-class America and concludes, if not with freedom, then with a more authorizing mode of rescue.

130

The critique enabled through liminality in the plot is echoed in the captivity romance's liminality of genre. The captivity romance was never entirely distinct from the more "acceptable" female genres of each period. Susanna Rowson, author of America's most renowned sentimental novel, *Charlotte Temple,* cast *Reuben and Rachel* within the Richardsonian tradition. Two authors of captivity romances, Eliza Cushing and Harriet Cheney, were daughters of another well-known sentimental novelist, Hannah Foster, author of *The Coquette,* and drew on their mother's literary style in their novels. Catharine Sedgwick was one of the most successful domestic novelists of the early nineteenth century and used many conventions of that genre in *Hope Leslie.* These authors introduced the captivity narrative into already existing narrative structures, modifying both. Just as the heroine exists in a liminality between cultures that allows us to "read" both of her captivities, so the text exists in a liminality that reveals how certain genres reflect and perpetuate the cultural attitudes the heroine encounters in a more immediate and threatening manner within the events of the narrative.

From its inception, the captivity romance has crossed traditional generic boundaries particularly in order to contrast, and
hence denaturalize, depictions of "womanhood." On one level,
Ann Eliza Bleecker's *The History of Maria Kittle* is a novel of sensibility.[22] Describing Mr. Kittle's actions on finding his home de-
stroyed and his family either murdered or captured, Bleecker
interrupts her narrative to address her female reader: "But doubtless, my dear, your generous sensibility is alarmed by my silence
about Mrs. Kittle" (1793, 48). Within the narrative, one of Maria's
auditors cries, " 'my heart is now sweetly tuned to melancholy. I
love to indulge these divine sensibilities, which your affecting histories are so capable of inspiring' " (73), while Maria, even in the
midst of her captivity, indulges in "the luxury of sorrow" (56). By
introducing "sensibility" as a privileged concern of her captivity
story, Bleecker places the wilderness tale within the realm of
women's authority—emotion—and puts the suffering heroine in a
central and sympathetic position.

Yet Bleecker also contradicts and modifies the expectations
produced by the appearance of "sensibility" in *The History of*
Maria Kittle, thereby avoiding a seeming endorsement of female
suffering.[23] As Mary Poovey argues, the novel of sensibility with its
"emotional indulgence served not only to sublimate frustrated sexual desire but also to inflame emotion and thus keep [the heroine]
hostage to passion" (1984, 54). Carroll Smith-Rosenberg argues
that women writers of the 1790s frequently warned female readers
of the dangers of sentimental romances, not only "because they
taught women sex and passion for men but because they taught
women to renounce their own reason and independence" (1988,
177). Bleecker resists these dangerous renunciations by consistently
contradicting the signifiers of suffering: "the *eloquence* of sorrow,"
"the *luxury* of sorrow," "*sweetly* tuned to melancholy." Suffering is
no longer imposed from without on an unwilling female subject
who lacks all agency in the drama of seduction and/or abandonment; rather, it becomes a relished and cultivated form of expression. Exaggerating their emotional suffering, furthermore, the
women of Bleecker's text make their role as victims apparent *as* role,
thereby denaturalizing their position in oppressive social dramas.

Beyond her play with the content of sensibility, Bleecker com-

131

plicates the sentimental depiction of women as domestic, emotional, and spiritual, juxtaposing the world of feeling and its genre—the novel of sensibility—with the world of action and its genre—the wilderness tale. By contrasting genres, Bleecker foregrounds the ideological contradiction between cultural prescription and resistance experienced within the narrative by Maria herself. The moment of greatest generic conflict in *The History of Maria Kittle* occurs precisely when Maria is faced with the difficult choice between a return to her previous domestic life or a commitment to the adventure and community she has found in the wilderness. During the course of Maria's captivity, from the time of Comelia's death to the entrance of Mrs. D——, Bleecker's language remains measured, the prose mirroring Maria's "stoic" composure. Even in the company of Mrs. D—— and her friends, Maria and her prose remain relatively controlled. Maria becomes a heroine of (overwrought) sensibility only when reunited with her husband. Seeing Mr. Kittle, "The tide of joy and surprise was too strong for the delicacy of her frame; she gave a final exclamation, and stretching out her arms to receive him, dropped senseless at his feet" (1793, 82). The Kittles' reunion effects a representational transformation, as a woman who has survived captivity in the wilderness suddenly becomes delicate of frame. While Maria must be strong to survive captivity and tell her tale, she must be inscribed within the role of a delicate, fainting wife if she is to fit culturally acceptable models of womanhood. In short, Maria is caught in the crossover from the wilderness to the parlor, from her existence as a strong survivor to her reemergence into her "proper sphere." The tension between the two worlds—one of action and the other of feeling—is represented in *The History of Maria Kittle* by a conflict of genres.

Later captivity romances, following Bleecker in her use of the captivity narrative to modify existing literary genres and the cultural ideologies they inscribe, provide one of the most striking enactments in American literature of what M. M. Bakhtin has called "heteroglossia." When a text usually considered "nonliterary" yet also essential to the novel's development (Bakhtin here includes the confession, the diary, the conversion narrative—all forms the captivity narrative has taken at one time or another) enters a more traditionally "literary" genre, the author deploys two languages "to avoid giving himself up wholly to either of them; he makes use of this verbal give-and-take, this dialogue of languages at every point in his work, in order that he himself might remain as it were neutral with regard to language, a third party in a quarrel between two people (although he might be a *biased* third party)" (1981, 314). Bakhtin's description of the conflict between languages and of the author's position as a fought-over subject attempting to free himself (Bakhtin assumes the author is male) from the confines of either, accurately describes the situation of the heroine *within* the captivity romance. Fought over by white and Indian men, in whose economy she serves as metonym for the land and capital at stake, the captive attempts to remain neutral—or to carve out a third subjectivity, identified with neither of the masculine parties—in order to escape domination by either. The social restrictions imposed by either of her captivities (within a domestic or sentimental ideology on one hand, or as a passive item of exchange on the other) battle each other through their respective, representative genres, the result being that both sides begin to lose their definitive claim on "truth," giving rise instead to a cultural relativism in which the heroine can reimagine her status in both worlds.

133

This is the process Bakhtin, moving beyond the plane of the strictly literary, calls "social heteroglossia": a "dialogue of two voices, two world views, two languages" (325). Through the creation of social heteroglossia, the novel deconstructs the illusion of "a sacrosanct, unconditional language" (324)—thereby also questioning the cultural hegemony represented by that language—by "making available points of view that . . . exist outside literary conventionality" (323). Heteroglossia serves in the captivity romances not to replace one view of/from womanhood with another, substituting and universalizing the frontier novel's representation of women in place of that contained in domestic or sentimental literature; rather, it seeks, by putting two often conflicting depictions of women side by side, to question whether "womanhood" can ever be definitively fixed in literature. Through the layering of genre, the authors of the captivity romance therefore introduce difference into the construction of white womanhood as well.

With its combination of the emotion and the female community so central to domestic or sentimental fiction and the extra-vagance that lies at the heart of the wilderness tale, the captivity romance occupies a final liminal space: the uncharted territory between the terrains mapped out by critics of American literature. This final liminality has proven less beneficial, however, for the genre's refusal to follow either a "masculine" or a "feminine" plot has ensured its invisibility in both traditional and revisionist considerations of American literary history. The captivity narratives unfortunately prove Nancy K. Miller's insight that to "depart from the limits of common sense (tautologically, to be extravagant) is to risk exclusion from the canon" (1988, 25).

Traditionally, the wilderness has been the domain of the American Adam. Literary criticism has neglected women writers in general but has been particularly reluctant to consider women in the wilderness. In her groundbreaking "Melodramas of Beset Manhood, or How Theories of American Fiction Exclude Women Authors," Nina Baym exposes the sexism of critics who have made stories of the frontier the central myth of America. Baym's quarrel with traditional literary history is not, however, that it excludes women writers who wrote wilderness tales. Rather, Baym accepts the traditional critical premise that the mobility required for wilderness adventure is "a male prerogative" (1985, 72), placing the entire genre of wilderness fiction beyond the reach of women. Baym's assessment is understandable if one considers only the wilderness tales accounted for in traditional literary history—the novels of Cooper and the tales of Daniel Boone—in which women are indeed rendered as essentially immobile, unfit for life outside "civilization." When one considers the captivity romances, however, a different "wilderness" emerges, and consequently a different configuration of gender outside the home.

The women-authored captivity romances have been overlooked because the central binary of traditional literary history—in which men thrive in the wilderness while women rule at home—has been circulated even in feminist revisions of the American canon.[24] Many recent discussions of women and American literature present domesticity as empowering rather than—or at least at the same time as—confining, but do not challenge the inherited equation of women and the home. Claiming that the "ethic of sentimental fiction, unlike that of writers like Melville, Emerson, and Thoreau, was an ethic of submission," Jane Tompkins, for example, contends that American women "lacked the material means of escape or opposition. They had to stay put and submit" (1985, 161). In response to this "lack," Tompkins concludes, "the domestic novelists made that necessity the basis on which to build a power structure of their own" (161).

Tompkins' analysis, like the novels she discusses, seems to make a virtue of a perceived necessity, rather than challenging the association of women with the home or questioning the "fact" of women's powerlessness in the face of social prescription. Tompkins ignores that several of the novelists whom she claims "had to stay put and submit" also wrote wilderness novels that express both a dissatisfaction with domesticity and an ability to partake in a supposedly "masculine" resistance. Reclaiming domesticity as a site of women's culture and a source of strength has led to valuable reassessments of nineteenth-century women's literature, but it has simultaneously diminished the work of authors who expressed in their wilderness novels a strong dissatisfaction with domesticity, no matter how enabling that realm might be.[25]

A response from within feminist literary criticism has argued the dangers of assuming that women moved without resistance into their domestication, or that domesticity itself was a singular and uncomplicated phenomenon.[26] Karen Sanchez-Eppler, for instance, has noted that a model of literary history that "accepts the notion of domesticity as a separate, enclosed sphere" (1992, 348) perpetuates "the two basic presumptions of the cult of domesticity . . . : not only does the home remain essentially separate from the public realm, but in its adherence to a moral, nurturant, and noncompetitive ethos the domestic sphere is itself construed as inherently undivided" (348). Literary histories that assume generic "purity" based on conceptions of a self-contained, undivided sphere thereby perpetuate gender essentialism, argues Sanchez-Eppler, who favors instead the model of domesticity marked by division or contradiction, the "self-divided and therefore anti-essentialist domestic scene" (353).

A consideration of the captivity romances, which depict a highly complicated "domesticity" and jarringly combine sup-

135

posedly "separate" spheres, provides an ideal opportunity to reconsider not only cultural constructions of gender but the ways in which literary histories inscribe those constructions through their framings of "appropriate" mythologies. In their combination of domestic or sentimental fiction and the wilderness tale, the captivity romances question essentialist constructions of "identity" in terms of both individual characters and cultural mythologies, and thereby open the way for new revisions and reinscriptions of gender and of literary history. Until we recognize women's place in creating the wilderness of fiction, a realm that complicates the very binarisms criticism has unwittingly perpetuated, we have refused women writers their most important form of extra-vagance: "the extravagant wish," as Nancy K. Miller writes, "for a *story* that would turn out differently" (1988, 40).

FIVE

Captives in History: Susanna
Rowson's Reuben and Rachel

Great genius and the people of these states must never be demeaned to romances. As soon as histories are properly told there is no more need of
romances.

Walt Whitman
Preface to *Leaves of Grass*

REPRINTED ONLY ONCE SINCE 1720, Mary Rowlandson's
captivity narrative suddenly appeared in three editions in 1770, followed by three more printings before 1773. Rowlandson's narrative
owes its renewed popularity in the 1770s, as Greg Sieminski demonstrates, to revolutionary politics. As "the colonists began to see
themselves as captives of a tyrant rather than as subjects of a king,"
Sieminski argues, the "image of collective captivity" (1980, 36) at
the core of narratives such as Rowlandson's reflected colonial political rhetoric in crucial ways. The captivity story became effective as
propaganda in part because it offered a model for forming identity
through opposition. While contemporary narratives such as Daniel
Boone's stressed assimilation into a culture perceived as "other" (in
Boone's case, Indian culture), the reprinted Puritan narratives instead valorized resistance to acculturation. When a Puritan survived captivity, the resistance to the captors' culture affirmed his or
her place in a community defined by what the captive—and by extension the entire community—does not believe, what rituals she or
he will not perform (36). So too the colonists defined the new
"American" culture in opposition to the British. The captivity narratives thus provided a vehicle for affirming the essential "same-

ness" of all colonists held in captivity and for defining a national character in opposition to the culture of British captors.

Despite the deployment of her story to espouse antityrannical ideals of inalienable freedom for all Americans, however, Rowlandson's gender would have precluded her from enjoying the liberties her narrative helped attain. Rowlandson is a more fitting figure, then, not for the common American destiny but for the fate of white American women who, despite their active involvement in the war, soon discovered the meaning of "home rule": as a rule, women in the new republic were kept at home. Historians have documented the disappointment women faced in the early federal years, as the situation of women under democracy remained virtually unchanged from what it had been under British rule. Women enjoyed slight improvements in legal and social rights—the British legal principle of coverture was less strictly adhered to, although by no means abandoned; divorce became easier to obtain in some states, although women were still largely denied access to courts—but these were counteracted by an increased insistence on the separation of public and private spheres after the war.[1] No longer having England to define themselves against, American men turned their attention to gender rather than national identity and enforced with renewed vigor the "essential" differences between men and women. Carroll Smith-Rosenberg argues that these asserted gender differences defined women so as to excise from "the feminine character" the very qualities—independence and virtue—necessary for public and civic duty. In the new republic, Smith-Rosenberg notes, "independence" came largely to mean the ability to earn one's living, while "virtue" implied modesty in regard to one's commercial success. Women, forbidden by law to earn their own living, instead were expected to become showcases of their husbands' prosperity. Required thus to be "elegant and nonproductive" (1985, 166), women of the early republic were by definition denied both independence and virtue, and hence access to the public sphere.

Smith-Rosenberg locates the cause of this betrayal in the need of middle-class American men to restore a lost legitimacy through the subjugation of women. Tracing the charges leveled by American men against women, Smith-Rosenberg notes their similarity to those the English gentry used to justify foreign rule. "As the gentry had accused middle-class men of venality and extravagance," she writes, "so middle-class men, depicting themselves as hardworking and frugal, harangued middle-class women for alleged extravagances in dress and household management" (166). Moreover, the English gentry had asserted that commercial men, "living in the fantastical, passionate, and unreal world of paper money, stocks, and credit," were incapable of civic virtue. Smith-Rosenberg notes that middle-class men turned this charge against women by characterizing them as unreliable and impractical "because they lived in another fantastical, passionate, and unreal world of paper—the world of the novel and the romance" (166).

Other historians have argued more generally that the vigorous reassertion of white women's "proper role" was meant to limit the revolutionary zeal threatening the stability of the newly formed United States government.[2] Betsy Erkkila outlines postwar efforts "to silence and disembody women politically by depriving them of citizenship and legal rights under the terms of the Articles of Confederation and the Constitution" (1987, 198). For the founding fathers, Erkkila concludes, "the American Revolution became a kind of Pandora's box, releasing potentially violent and disruptive female energies that would not and could not be controlled once the war was over" (190). Renewed domestic, economic, and legal constraints on women became the mode of control chosen by the new government and were energetically carried out by a society eager to attain prosperity within a stable state of "normalcy." Women, in the meantime, rather than enjoying the new liberties promised by the rhetoric of the revolution, instead found themselves increasingly more confined.

The significance of Susanna Rowson's novel *Reuben and Rachel; or, Tales of Olden Times* (1798) lies in its appropriation of the genres and metaphors of the revolution to resist the forces that excluded women from the liberties promised by that rhetoric. Striking in scope, *Reuben and Rachel* follows ten generations of women, from Christopher Columbus' wife to the colonial women who lived through the American Revolution. Historical accounts such as *Reuben and Rachel* were mainstays of late eighteenth-century American literature. Emory Elliott documents the efforts of federal authors such as Philip Freneau and Timothy Dwight "to give America a vision of herself as a promised, New World utopia" (1986, 11). Like other postrevolutionary writers, Rowson creates in *Reuben and Rachel* an American "past," a fictional tradition that the present nation could live up to and complete.

More than a standard historical novel, however, *Reuben and Rachel* is a chronicle specifically of those most typically excluded from the "official story" of the nation. The denial to women of the privileges attendant on public life in America also involved their removal from the record of that sphere and of its past—in short, women were erased from America's history. While literature that attempted after the war to establish America's heroic past broadcast the courage of white men—Columbus, Washington—it also romanticized the conquering of the native population while ignoring the achievements of colonial women. In contrast to works such as Timothy Dwight's *Conquest of Canaan* or Joel Barlow's *Columbiad,* however, *Reuben and Rachel* brings the courage of white women and Indians back into American history.

To tell her version of American history, Rowson turned to the
captivity narrative.[3] Rowson's use of the captivity story in her generic hybrid of history and romance is logical, since women's personal narratives, as Linda Kerber notes, were the only sanctioned form of history that also contained women heroes (1980, 260). Her choice also reflects the popularity of captivity narratives before and during the revolution. However, unlike deployments of the captivity narrative that furthered a nationalistic zeal ultimately ending in the disempowerment of white women and of people of color, Rowson used the captivity story to imagine for both groups liberties denied by more traditional stories of America's past.

First, the captivity story took Rowson's heroines out of the home. *Reuben and Rachel* depicts white women successfully adapting to the American landscape at a time when they were being separated, in literature if not in reality, from the wilderness where Rowson's heroines prosper and thrive. Second, the captivity narrative allowed Rowson to present a version of American history that centered on the enforced helplessness of white women and the violence directed at Indians but that also celebrated the resistance and fortitude of both groups. As confinement becomes the experience not of a single woman but of ten generations of women, paralleling the development of the nation, captivity comes to be the defining trope of America itself. The new nation, in Rowson's novel, will only do as well as its women, as the strength of the American character becomes measured by the successful resolution of the captivity story. But a successful resolution for Rowson did not mean the massacre of Indians and masculine rescue of helpless white women that would soon fill male-authored frontier fictions. In an inversion of the official tale of the nation's heroic founding, in *Reuben and Rachel* America's prosperity is measured by the ability of its natives to withstand violent colonialization and of its white heroines to endure and escape confinement imposed not only by British tyrants or Indian invaders but by their own husbands, fathers, and brothers.

By Rowson's standards, America's story is not one of increasing democracy and liberty but of growing misogyny and racism. As the American identity grows stronger, white women and Indians become increasingly more isolated and powerless, their captivities harder to escape. Explaining the popularity of the captivity story in revolutionary America, Sieminski notes that the "captivity experience began and ended in freedom" (1980, 44), thereby prefiguring America's ultimate delivery from British tyranny. Rowson's captivity romance never achieves the closure that liberty brings in the conventional captivity narrative. Rather, Indians increasingly lose their lives, their land, and their cultural integrity, while generation after generation of white women must repeat their captivities, released from one tyranny directly into another. *That,* Rowson implies, was the experience of white women and of Indians in America, moving from restriction under British law to restriction under a new "democracy." The economic and social losses of Indians and white women are signified by the generic change *Reuben and Rachel* undergoes toward its conclusion, as Rowson's history approaches the author's own period. From a frontier romance featuring strong and independent Anglo-American, Peruvian, and Indian women, *Reuben and Rachel* becomes a sentimental novel, complete with abandonment by worthless lovers and a lovelorn suicide. The move from a frontier romance to a sentimental novel accurately reflects the experience of many American women, who witnessed their own transformation in the nation's perception from brave and industrious fighters for liberty to frail, housebound sentimental heroines.

While *Reuben and Rachel* suggests that history contains many prisons for women, however, Rowson also casts a critical eye on the roles available to women, offering her readers a history not only of confinement and victimization but also of endurance and even resistance.[4] As in *The History of Maria Kittle,* resistance in Rowson's novel depends on women's ability to create and sustain communities capable of reading and interpreting, rather than simply internalizing, national(ist) fictions. Women gather in *Reuben and Rachel* to read letters and share stories circulated between different ethnicities, nations, and generations. These texts tell the tale not of the great founding of a noble and united land of liberty, but of betrayal, exploitation, and contradiction. Through collective interpretation, the women in the novel render explicit systems of domination concealed in patriotic literature and compose alternative representations of white women and of Indians that allow them to imagine healing the ruptures engendered by dominant national narratives.

The gender communities imagined in Rowson's novel therefore both mirror and resist the larger national communities forming at the same period. Benedict Anderson documents the rise in the eighteenth century of the ontological nation, which he characterizes as the most dominant "imagined community" of the modern age. National identities are set, he argues, through print commodities, especially newspapers and novels, which circulate print vernaculars that diminish the differences between ideolects and create the impression of a perpetual and simultaneous existence common to all literate "citizens." National communities become "imaginable," therefore, primarily through the experience of reading. While reading in (and of) *Reuben and Rachel* allows heroines to participate in the genesis of America, it simultaneously demonstrates their exclusion, as women, from the national fiction. The two communities imagined in *Reuben and Rachel*—of nation and of gender—come into conflict, most particularly so for Indian women who witness the growth of America at the expense of the indigenous cultures. The conflicts that arise in the novel between collective identities prevent the heroines' complete participation in either but also allow them a liminal position from which to communicate the lessons of each community to the other. In so doing, the captive heroine, like her autobiographical prototype, learns the impossibility of freedom from ideological determination at the same time as she discovers the pleasures of community, of interpretation, and of transgressive articulation.[5]

Written in two volumes, *Reuben and Rachel* contains four captivity stories framed by two narratives depicting the figurative and literal rape of a native population by Christian colonialists. The volume begins with Columbus' settlement of Peru, where a native woman, Bruna, is raped by Columbus' deputy and kills herself rather than live as a reminder of Peru's subjection. Rowson's narration of the settlement and victimization of Peru is followed by a series of captivities endured and escaped by Columbus' descendants, beginning with his granddaughter, Isabelle Arundel, and her daughter Columbia. The widow of an executed Puritan, Isabelle is arrested by Sir James Howard, a spy for the Catholic Queen Mary. When Sir James arrives to arrest Lady Arundel, he falls in love with Columbia and consequently convinces Queen Mary to allow him to keep the women jailed in his house, where they remain until their escape shortly after Elizabeth's ascension.

This Richardsonian imprisonment is then translated into an American setting, as New Hampshire Indians capture Rachel and William Dudley, Columbia Arundel's great-great-grandchildren. William gains the favor of the Indian sachem, is named his heir, and marries the sachem's daughter, Oberea, while William's younger sister, Rachel, becomes engaged to an Indian warrior, Yankoo. But during an attack on an English settlement, Yankoo is about to kill an Englishman whom William recognizes to be his long-lost father. Throwing himself between his father and Yankoo's tomahawk, William is killed. Not long thereafter, during a retaliatory attack by the English, Yankoo too dies, and William's widow Oberea returns with her grieving sister-in-law Rachel and Rachel's mother to England.

The reader then follows Rowson's characters back to England, where in the next captivity story Jessy Oliver, best friend of Rachel Dudley (the first Rachel Dudley's niece), is locked up by her father until she agrees to marry the nobleman he has selected for her husband. But Jessy, whose affection belongs to Rachel's brother Reuben, is resolute. On the eve of her arranged wedding, Jessy escapes her father's prison and establishes herself as postmistress in a remote village where she one day encounters her old friend Rachel, and together they set off to America to find Reuben. In the meantime, Reuben has become the subject of Rowson's fourth captivity story, taken hostage by Indians like his grandfather William. With the help of an Indian princess, Eumea, Reuben escapes his captivity and returns to Philadelphia where he is reunited with his sister and marries his beloved Jessy. The novel then ends as it begins, with the suicide of a native woman. Eumea, who loves Reuben desperately, drowns herself on learning of his marriage.

The symmetrical structure of *Reuben and Rachel* makes two important claims about women's lives.[6] First, the balance of English Richardsonian imprisonments with New World Indian captivity narratives dehistoricizes the experience of constriction. Women in all generations, in all nations, Rowson implies, have been captives —of lovers, of warriors, of fathers. Second, the relationship between the central captivity tales and the framing stories of Bruna and Eumea suggests a similarity between the subjection of white women and of Indians. Several captivity romances depict Indian culture as fractured by the gender divisions that marked white culture. Later authors equated the oppression of white and Indian women—both are the victims of abusive husbands—but tended to ignore the violence of white men directed specifically at native women. Rowson is unique among early novelists in depicting Indian women as the objects of a dual subjection, as she implies through the representation of their oppression through rape—an act of violence directed both by a colonialist against a native and by a man against a woman. In so doing, Rowson not only correlates her analysis of racial and gender oppression but subverts the image of native women as the promiscuous sexual objects of white men, a common stereotype in wilderness tales by men.[7] The very structure of the novel suggests its two primary thematic assertions: that captivity is metaphorically expressive of racial and gender subjection under white, male colonialism, and that only through cooperation can white women and Indians of both genders escape their captivity.

The oppositions that the structure of *Reuben and Rachel* seeks to integrate—between whites and people of color, men and women— were particularly troublesome at the time of the novel's composition, as the founding fathers attempted to define the place of women, Indians, and slaves in a republic in which all are nominally created equal. Rowson presents these racial and gender divisions as indigenous to the American character, brought to the continent by the nation's first ancestor: Christopher Columbus. Rather than a benign settler and heroic adventurer, Rowson's Columbus is shown through his letters to be naive and self-serving. When Columbus sees the political havoc his settlement of Peru has brought on the native people, represented by the rape of Bruna, he exclaims, "'I am innocent! I sought not new worlds for conquest, or for power; I felt, forcibly felt, the blessings of Christianity, the comforts resulting from a commercial intercourse with other nations'" (1798, 1:45). That Columbus has found nicer terms to express religious proselytizing and economic exploitation does not keep Rowson from depicting the harsher realities behind the words, exemplified by the turning of his "intercourse" into Bruna's rape. The gloss on Columbus' letter offered by his wife, Beatina, is more to the point: of the European settlers who came with Columbus into the "new world," Beatina asserts that "'their idols were avarice, ambition, luxury, and lawless passion; to them they bend the knee, and on their altar did they sacrifice millions of innocent people'" (1:79).

In her treatment of Columbus, Rowson is also quick to assert—again despite his protestations of innocence—a close relationship between geographic and domestic exploitation. In a letter to Beatina, Columbus writes,

> "Why, why, my beloved, are you not endowed with strength of frame, that your friendship might increase my fortitude in danger, and share the glorious triumph of unexpected success? Yet why should I wish you to lose the sweet feminine softness which first won, and still holds captive my heart?" (1:22)

His rhetoric to the contrary, it is Columbus who holds his wife, shown elsewhere in the novel to be as strong and courageous as her husband, captive in a rhetoric of feminine passivity. Columbus must assert women's weakness, which defines him as the strong, adventuring male and justifies him in leaving his wife and family behind, just as he must believe in the passivity and inferiority of the natives whose land he appropriates.

While Rowson thus presents colonial and domestic subjugation as central features of America's first father, she offers its first daughters as the agents of equality and justice on both fronts. The gender division between Columbus and Beatina is healed by their great-granddaughter, Columbia, whose very name combines her two ancestors and establishes her as representative of the ideally American character. Columbia, who accompanies her mother to what she considers certain death at Sir James' hands and wages verbal battle with Bloody Mary, is a hybrid of the rational and adventurous spirit of her great-grandfather and, in her devotion to her mother and to her girlhood friend Mina, a more traditional "femininity." Columbia escapes her captivity precisely through her combination of gender roles, becoming the ideal "human" Rowson writes of in her textbook, *A Present to Young Girls:* "A woman who to the graces and gentleness of her own sex, adds the knowledge and fortitude of the other, exhibits the most perfect combination of human excellence" (Weil 1976, 37).

Moreover, in her characterization of Columbia, Rowson stresses that the "knowledge and fortitude" needed to create the ideal woman are best instilled by other women. Living in an abandoned castle with her Peruvian maid, Cora, her best friend, Mina, and her mother, Isabelle, Columbia inhabits a world of women.[8] Columbia is particularly strengthened by her relationship to Isabelle, who was to her daughter "mother, sister, friend, every tender connexion combined in one" (1798, 1:14). When, during her captivity in the home of Sir James, Isabelle learns that Elizabeth is on the throne, she prepares Columbia for escape by redefining "femininity":

> "We are women, it is true, and ought never to forget the delicacy of our sex; but real delicacy consists in purity of thought, and chastity of words and actions; not in shuddering at an accidental blast of wind, or increasing the unavoidable evils of life by affected weakness and timidity." (1:189)

Ironically, in Isabelle's lesson to her daughter on the proper feminine character, "delicacy" comes to mean hardiness, assurance, bravery—exactly the opposite of its eighteenth-century definition. In the face of potential rape, Columbia is taught by her mother that

" 'nothing is more pernicious to the health of mind or body, than indolence and inaction' " (1:189). Even when Columbia meets a milder threat to her independence in the form of Sir Egbert, whose affections Columbia returns, Isabelle urges her daughter to see the world before she settles down into romance. Participation in female community offers agency to Rowson's heroines from Columbia Arundel to Jessy Oliver, who, encountering her friend Rachel after years of quiet country life, tells her, " 'I am weary of this dull sameness of scene, and you and I will now set out together in search of adventure . . . we will live together, my dear Rachel, in humble, but contented independence' " (2:278). That Jessy and Rachel reunite in a post office, the literal site of the circulation of letters, points to the central connection of reading and writing between women and the creation of female agency. Rowson's heroines thus reflect the experiences of many women of Rowson's generation who used literature to create strong and empowering friendships with other women as a partial resistance to the prescribed isolation of domesticity.

In addition to integrating the gender roles of her ancestors and remedying her great-grandmother's enforced isolation, Columbia heals the violent split between colonizers and indigenous people represented by Columbus' conquest of Peru. Columbia's grandfather was Columbus' son, Ferdinando, who married a Peruvian princess, Orrabella. Thus Columbia physically combines the colonizer and the colonized. Columbia is also raised by a Peruvian woman, Cora, who teaches her that

> "Avarice had discovered this new world was an inexhaustible mine of wealth; and, not content to share its blessings in common with the natives, came with rapine, war, and devastation in her train! and as she tore open the bowels of the earth to gratify her insatiate thirst for gold, her steps were marked with blood."
> (1:42)

Columbia also learns of the violence of male imperialism from Beatina herself, who indirectly enters the female community surrounding Columbia through a series of letters written to Isabelle in her youth and now read to Columbia by Cora. The word of the mother—Beatina's first-person narrative is longer than that of any other character in the novel—enables and educates the daughter, and in turn brings the mother into the integrated community of women.

The fusions Columbia effects are short-lived, however; as the English colonies grow larger and more secure, granting white men increased power to represent white women and Indians, Rowson's utopian solution to interracial strife becomes harder to maintain. The novel marks this decline through the increased difficulties faced by members of interracial couples. The first interracial marriage— between Columbus' son Ferdinando and the Peruvian princess Orrabella—is relatively successful. Although Orrabella lives to see Peru subjugated by Christian pirates and her family assassinated, Ferdinando shares her pride in Peru's native culture and her anguish at its colonization. The second interracial marriage occurs between William Dudley and Oberea in the New World, through which Rowson appears to suggest that Christians not only can be assimilated to Indian culture but will benefit from the conversion. Although the interracial romances of William and Rachel Dudley end tragically, Rowson unambiguously assigns guilt for those tragedies to white colonial aggression, and shows the enlightening and invigorating effect of "Indianization" on the two English children, particularly on the girl. The first Rachel Dudley, taken captive in the New Hampshire wilderness, is strengthened and cheered by her friendship with her Indian sister-in-law, Oberea. Rowson writes that although Rachel was "naturally more timid" than Oberea, her nerves became "new-strung by affection" (1:25).

When William's grandson, Reuben, is himself taken captive, however, he demonstrates how far he has come from the sympathies of his ancestors. "Often," Rowson reports, "would his thoughts revert to his grandfather, William Dudley, who was for many years in a situation somewhat similar. But Reuben had seen too much of savage men and manners to have a wish to remain amongst them, even though he might have been elevated to the highest seat of dignity" (2:202). When *his* Indian princess, Eumea, falls in love with her English captive, he does not even notice her affection. Eumea nevertheless aids in Reuben's escape, an act of kindness that Reuben repays by establishing her as a servant in a neighboring home, where she "assiduously endeavored to conform to the European dress, customs, and manners; but she pined at being separated from Reuben, and if more than two days elapsed without her seeing him, she would give way to the most violent affliction" (2:288). Rowson here overlays the language of the sentimental abandonment plot with images of colonial exploitation and enforced conformity, reasserting the connection between the plights of Indians and of women. When Reuben finally marries an Englishwoman, Eumea drowns herself in a fit of despondency. Thus Rowson contrasts the positive results of the integration of a white woman into Indian society with the tragic results of the opposite transculturation.

The growing indifference to the state of the Indians coincides in the novel with the removal of white women from the wilderness. Beatina lives with the Peruvians; Rachel Dudley not only inhabits the New England wilderness, she hopes to marry a native warrior. But at the conclusion of *Reuben and Rachel,* white women are gone from the wilderness, returned to the domestic sphere and to their role as representatives of white "civilization." In the last wilderness tale of the novel, there are no women at all: William Dudley is taken captive with only a male companion. As long as white women are 149 permitted access to the wilderness, Rowson suggests, interracial relationships form based on love or friendship, whereas the segregation of white women results in the sexual victimization of native women. Ironically, Rowson's assertion that colonized women gain agency and sexual autonomy only in the presence of white women duplicates the colonial appropriation she seeks to challenge. That the guardianship offered by white women is "spiritual" rather than economic makes it no less appropriative, since it renders the personhood of the colonized equally contingent on white, colonial surveillance. In substituting sentiment, affection, and marriage for sex in her characterizations of interracial relationships, for instance, Rowson maps dominant representations of the desexualized white woman onto the native population. Simultaneously, however, she uses native culture as the "other" of white civilization, allowing herself a place from which to criticize those very same gender conventions as they apply to white women.

While Rowson perpetuates the metaphors of empire, she also insists that readers recognize the intertwining operations of patriarchy and imperialism. Both systems rely on representations of white men as the subjects of culture who exert power over persons figured solely as bodies, the repositories of subordinated "nature." Benedict Anderson notes that empire operates by representing the colonized not as members of cultures or self-defined nations but as bodies characterized by biological traits (skin color, eye shape). As natural(ized) bodies rather than cultural subjects, closer to the animal kingdom than to the monarchies of empire, the colonized subjects can more easily be robbed, raped, assimilated, or exterminated (1983, 143). Feminists have similarly demonstrated patriarchy's reliance on characterizations of women based not on cultural discourses that frame and define the body but on "essences" residing in the naturalized female body.[9] The objects of both colonial and patriarchal power are thus constituted as "naturally" inferior bodies (inferior due to their association with nature rather than culture).

Reuben and Rachel names and resists these constructions through the repeated image of captivity, which makes the bodies of white women and of colonized persons visible as the site of cultural inscription, surveillance, and control. In the novel, the body becomes not only a way of imprisoning white women and Indians but a prison itself, a social institution rather than a natural determinant of subordinating essences. Furthermore, white women and Indians escape captivity through communication, which requires language and collective definition, both signs of participation in culture. The colonized subject's association with a culture is arguably her greatest attraction in *Reuben and Rachel,* offering an alternative to the white heroines' representation as decultured and individuated bodies. The resistance generated through the white heroine's unruly articulation within patriarchal discourse is in turn extended to the colonized, giving rise in the novel to a resistant community. In Rowson's novel, the removal of one party weakens the power of the collective; the colonized and white women both suffer from the absence of the other.

With the "masculinization" of the American wilderness, therefore, comes the end of interracial union, bringing instead the progressive weakening of the Indians, particularly Indian women, and of white women. Just as the courage of Orrabella eventually gives way to the forlorn lovesickness and self-destruction of Eumea, so too Columbia's female descendants, removed from the wilderness, lose her original strength and determination. As the novel progresses there is less cooperation between women, particularly between daughters and mothers, who become increasingly less empowering models. While Isabelle enables Columbia's independence, Rachel's mother ultimately restricts her daughter's freedom. Following the attack on the English settlement, Mrs. Dudley returns to England with her daughter Rachel and her Indian daughter-in-law, Oberea, and sees to it that both women are properly anglicized. The result of Mrs. Dudley's removal of her daughters from the wilderness is the creation of properly Christian, yet ultimately less happy and less active women. Mrs. Dudley's benign conversion results in the early death of Oberea, who is isolated from her native culture, and the transformation of Rachel Dudley from a wilderness adventurer into a rather pathetic old maid, smiling and listening patiently as her nephew, Reuben Dudley, spews stereotypes about his savage mother, Oberea, and her heathenish race. Finally, while Mrs. Dudley proves a poor model for her daughters, Jessy Oliver has no mother at all, left solely to the will of an overbearing father who literally imprisons her.   **151**

Rowson's removal of mothers from *Reuben and Rachel* might represent her reaction to what Linda Kerber has called the ideology of "Republican Motherhood." Demonstrating her patriotism through domestic self-sacrifice, the Republican Mother insured the division between public and private spheres.

> Women could be encouraged to contain their judgments as republicans within their homes and families rather than to bridge the world outside and the world within. In this sense, restricting women's politicization was one of a series of conservative choices that Americans made in the postwar years as they avoided the full implications of their own revolutionary radicalism. (1980, 287)

By removing mothers from her novel, then, Rowson also circumvents the "conservative choice" and frees her heroines from a limited model of womanhood. As Cathy Davidson writes, "A motherless daughter [in the new Republic] is unguided, uneducated, unprotected, but also unencumbered" (1980, 120).

If the removal of mothers from the novel frees Rowson's heroines on one hand, on the other it leaves them without any models of womanhood at all except those furnished by their biological and cultural fathers. As women become more isolated, their captivities begin to seem more enduring, until, at the finish of the novel, sentimentalism and marriage supplant adventure and community. The growing importance of romance in the heroines' lives—and the threat it poses to them—is represented by the increased prominence in the novel of the abandonment plot.

As *Reuben and Rachel* progresses, the threat of abandonment encroaches both on the lives of the heroines and the text of the novel, which transforms from a frontier to a sentimental romance. Columbia's final success as an adventurous heroine is measurable by the contrast between her fate and that of her girlhood friend, Mina. While Columbia resists the temptations of romance, preferring instead to remain a prisoner with her mother, Mina surrenders to the seduction of Sir James Howard, who leaves her to die with her newborn son. In the novel's second volume, Rachel Dudley's life in the wilderness is paralleled by a second seduction plot, involving Mary Holmes, also left to die soon after giving birth to an illegitimate child. But the balance between the stories of Rachel Dudley and Mary Holmes is different from that between Columbia Arundel and Mina. Rachel's adventures end, unlike Columbia's, with the heroine returned to hearth and home, while Mina's narrative receives relatively little space in the novel compared to that of Mary Holmes, which develops into a narrative of some importance.

While the adventure plot loses ground, then, the seduction plot gains prominence, registering a loss of female agency in the novel and, by implication, in history. Yet in the narratives of both Mina and Mary Holmes, Rowson shows that the seduction and ruin of women damages not only the particular woman but America itself. The illegitimate children born of both women—Howard Fitz-Howard and Jacob Holmes—become primary villains in *Reuben and Rachel,* each threatening to disturb the generational flow (and hence the narrative continuation) of the Columbian family. Jacob Holmes, using religious rhetoric to defraud Reuben Dudley of his rightful inheritance, especially signifies the corruption of American ideals of social justice. He is also the most abusive husband depicted in the novel, again demonstrating the connection between the fate of America and that of its women.

The last pairing of a seduction and an adventure plot is the most telling as well as the most discouraging. While Jessy Oliver is held prisoner by her father and ultimately escapes in order to live her own life, the second Rachel Dudley is less fortunate. Rachel has fallen in love with Hamden Auberry, who, because his family is from a higher class than the Dudleys, at first refuses to marry Rachel. When he does marry her, he establishes Rachel in London under a false name, pregnant and alone, while he sets off to tour the continent with his wealthy aunt. Rachel soon falls victim to rumors, is forced to move to increasingly unsavory dwellings, and is left without friends and finally without money. Only at the last moment, when at her most destitute she encounters Jessy Oliver in a rural post office and together they set off to America, does Rachel discover a newly humbled Auberry and gain a traditionally respectable marriage. In the relationship of Rachel and Auberry, Rowson again equates abandonment with a betrayal of American ideals. By settling into marriage, Auberry indicates his surrender of class distinctions and his acceptance of a democratic social arrangement. Each of Rowson's seduction plots is, significantly, also set in England, suggesting that English inequality is countered by American conjugal happiness. Yet, despite the happy resolution suggested by the marriages that conclude *Reuben and Rachel,* by the end of the novel the abandonment plot, given relatively little space at the beginning of the novel, gains the forefront. Meanwhile the adventure/ captivity plot is given not to the heroine, as it is in the first two instances, but to a secondary character.

As seduction becomes a more prominent form of closure both to the heroine's life and to Rowson's text, marriage begins to seem a relatively happy resolution, and it is certainly the ending Rowson chooses. The novel ends quite traditionally, with every character married to the proper partner, indicating Rowson's indebtedness to the forms of the sentimental novel. The virtue of good women rescues men from wayward paths. Good women would rather go to prison than marry for other than love, and the virtue and happiness of good, domestic women reflect the virtue and happiness of the nation. America's destiny resides in the conjugal felicity of its inhabitants

—the one still unmarried man, Lieutenant Courtney, must return to England at the end of the novel, ruined by a false woman.

But the final marriages of Rachel Dudley and Jessy Oliver do not represent the progress of America, as Michael Davitt Bell argues happy marriages do in historical romances.[10] Rather, they signal the failure of the original spirit of adventure and equality represented by the American wilderness and by the American rhetoric of democracy and tolerance. When at the end of the novel Reuben Dudley declares America " 'a young country, where the only distinctions between man and man should be made by virtue, genius, and education' " (1798, 2:313), his representation of "democracy" is undermined by the novel's depiction of a society in which men are superior to women, the educated (that is, the wealthy) to the uneducated, whites to slaves and Indians. Rowson's final irony comes when Reuben, rejecting English titles and manners in favor of American equality and brotherhood, says he is speaking for his sister and her husband as well as for himself. Enacting the principle of coverture, which gave control of policy and property entirely to husbands, Reuben apparently considers the opinions of his wife of little consequence.

154

Cathy Davidson describes the narrative options of colonial heroines as a Scylla and Charybdis of abandonment and marriage. Due to the high childbirth mortality rate and the *feme covert* status of women, matrimony for colonial women was a risky endeavor.[11] The seduction plot, Davidson argues, therefore served as a vivid analysis of how *not* to make a marriage, while simultaneously exposing the pressures and dangers faced by all colonial women, married or not. Thus the best that can be said of the lot of married women is that it is preferable to that of abandoned heroines such as Charlotte Temple—but just barely. The unsatisfactory options offered colonial women, fictional and real, are precisely those given at the conclusion of *Reuben and Rachel.* Yet the power of Rowson's novel lies in its efforts to resist the narrative options characteristic of the sentimental novel. The choice between tragic abandonment and domestic tranquillity enters the novel only at its conclusion. Prior to the ending, however, the novel's "sentimental formula" is complicated by its status both as a historical and a captivity romance.[12] Seduction and marriage are not the only options offered by Rowson to Columbia Arundel or to the first Rachel Dudley (although they are, unfortunately, the only options Rowson offers her Indian heroines). As a historical romance, *Reuben and Rachel* suggests an alternative to the federal society in which white women are viewed only as potential wives or potential mistresses. In questioning those depictions of white women, Rowson gives the lie to the apparent inescapability or "naturalness" of those roles, showing them instead to be only two of the many potential options offered to women, and poor ones at that. Using a captivity plot, Rowson both literalizes the restrictions forced on white women by their roles in society and provides a narrative in which constriction is escaped. The sentimental heroine, Davidson implies, must eventually either settle into marriage or die abandoned. Rowson offers a third alternative. Through their captivity, Columbia Arundel and Rachel Dudley are paradoxically offered escape from the narrative paths that in other novels appeared inevitable. Bravery, adventurousness, and intelligence are characteristics not of Rowson's men only, but, in their ability to abide and even transcend their captivities, of her women as well.

155

Susanna Rowson wrote *Reuben and Rachel* at a crucial moment in American history. On March 31, 1776, Abigail Adams wrote to her husband John,

> I long to hear that you have declared an independency—and by the way in the new Code of Laws which I suppose it will be necessary for you to make I desire you would Remember the Ladies, and be more generous and favorable to them than your ancestors. Do not put such unlimited power into the hands of the Husbands. Remember all Men would be tyrants if they could. If particular care and attention is not paid to the Ladies we are determined to foment a Rebellion, and will not hold ourselves bound by any Law in which we have no voice, or Representation. (1963, 370)

Abigail Adams expresses the hope of many colonial women that the casting off of British rule might lead to the rejection of *all* subjection, that the rhetoric of democracy in America might result in the reality of a truly equitable society in which women were recognized as the equals of men. *Reuben and Rachel* initially shares Adams' optimism, positing the language of democracy and religious tolerance embodied by Columbia Arundel against political and religious tyranny. Rachel Dudley, through her firsthand experience of the American wilderness, becomes not bitter and fanatical but more openminded and sympathetic. Throughout *Reuben and Rachel* Rowson pushes against traditional hierarchies by creating strong, independent women and by showing the injustices done to natives by "superior" Christians.

Yet in response to his wife's threat of rebellion, John Adams wrote, "I cannot but laugh."

> We have been told that our Struggle has loosened the bonds of Government every where. That Children and Apprentices were disobedient—that schools and Colledges were grown turbulent—that Indians slighted their Guardians and Negroes grew insolent to their Masters. But your Letter was the first Intimation that another Tribe more numerous and powerfull than all the rest were grown discontented.—This is rather too coarse a compliment, but you are so saucy I wont blot it out. Depend upon it, We know better than to repeal our Masculine systems. (382)

Even more disastrous for his wife's hopes than his flat rebuttal is Adams' subsequent argument, in which he turns women's domestic consignment from a restriction into an exalted position.

> We Dare not exert our power in its full Latitude. We are obliged to go fair, and softly, and in Practice you know We are subjects. We have only the Name of Masters, and rather than give up this, which would completely subject Us to the Despotism of the Petticoat, I hope General Washington, and all our brave Heroes would fight. I am sure every good Politician would plot, as long as he would against Despotism, Empire, Monarchy, Aristocracy, Oligarchy, or Ochlocracy. (382)

Adams, in turning his wife's social disenfranchisement into a rhetorical "despotism" through the translation of the governmental into the domestic realm, uses the strategy of metaphoric compensation that sought to content women with their domestication and lack of economic control by granting them "home rule."

The exchange between Abigail and John Adams reflects the expectations raised in women by the American Revolution as well as their subsequent disappointment, as the rhetoric of separate spheres forced women into even more limited roles. The nonimportation and domestic production movements, designed to loosen Britain's hold on the American economy, brought a momentous, if temporary, change in American attitudes toward the home. Suddenly domestic acts—what women made, what they bought, whose products they purchased—gained enormous political importance. In order to persuade women to support these movements, men discussed politics and government with their wives and daughters for the first time on a national scale. Suddenly interested and involved in the public sphere, women dared to take a more active role in the revolution.

Yet the political importance assigned to the home, as well as the relative freedom allowed women prior to the war, was short-lived. Rather than becoming equal participants in the new democracy, women found themselves returned to their "proper sphere." In Philadelphia, for instance, women began a Ladies Association, which they hoped would become the first national women's organization. The women of the association went from door to door, collecting three hundred thousand dollars for the war effort.[13] Yet when the Ladies Association sent its funds to George Washington with suggestions of how the money should be spent, Washington acted, as John Adams hoped he would, by forcing women back into the home. Washington insisted that the money be spent on shirts for the soldiers, which the women should sew themselves. The women of the Ladies Association were thus forced from the streets back into a sewing circle (Norton 1980, 185–88). The official governmental reassertion of women's domestic nature is evident in Washington's letter of gratitude, which asserts that women's domestic nature exists prior to the dictates of nationalism: "It embellishes the American character with a new trait; by proving that the love of country is blended with those softer domestic virtues, which have always been allowed to be more peculiarly *your own*" (Norton 1980, 187).

Race as well as gender provided a locus for rhetorical and legal stabilization after the war. Michael Paul Rogin, tracing governmental policy affecting the Indians from the revolution through the presidency of Andrew Jackson, reveals a pattern of rhetorical liberation and political subjection strikingly similar to that experienced by postwar American women. Having manipulated a rhetoric of rejected slavery to justify the American revolt against England, American leaders then took great pains to control the "republican nightmares" that people of color represented (1975, 27).[14] Noting the widening gap between egalitarian rhetoric and oppressive social policy after the revolution, Rogin comments that "republican leaders were imprisoned in racial patterns to which they did not want to consent and which their revolution would not alter" (28).

It is tempting to read in the captivity stories of *Reuben and Rachel,* then, a resentment not only for the failure of the revolutionary rhetoric of equality to better the lives of white women but of people of color as well. The attraction of the captivity narrative as a fictional source perhaps lay partially in its necessary generic concern with both race and gender. Rowson's captivity romance becomes a gauge of America's failed rhetoric and of the fatal consequences of that failure for white women and for Indians. As the dust from the revolution settled it became unmistakably clear, as Davidson writes, that women "had virtually no rights within society and no visibility within the political operations of government, except as a symbol of that government—Columbia or Minerva or Liberty" (1986, 120). The power of Rowson's novel is that her Columbia is not at all a mute symbol of a repressive and misogynistic government but a lively reminder of the potential strength and ability of women. The tragedy of the novel is its realistic mirroring of the dwindling of that potential as the republic forced women into a very limiting choice—"marry or be abandoned"—a sad perversion of the revolutionary call to "Live free or die."

SIX   *A Hostage in the House: Domestic Captivity and Catharine Sedgwick's* Hope Leslie

IN HER MEMOIR, *The Life and Letters* (1872), the successful nineteenth-century novelist Catharine Maria Sedgwick describes the women in her family as captives to the discourses of sentiment and piety. In particular, Sedgwick presents her mother, Pamela Dwight Sedgwick, as the abandoned and housebound heroine featured in the sentimental literature of antebellum America. Pamela Dwight was her husband Theodore's second wife; his first, Eliza Mason, died within a year of their marriage but reportedly returned annually in spirit to restore her now remarried lover to "those days of young romantic love" (26). With his ghost-bride to keep him youthful, Sedgwick remarried not for love but for convenience: "In that time," Sedgwick writes, "marriage was essential to a man's life; there were no arrangements independent of it, no substitutions for it" (26). While obligatory for both men and women, marriage did not constrain men, either physically or professionally, as it did women. As a congressman, Sedgwick was away from his Massachusetts home for most of the year, leaving his wife "for many months in this cold northern country, with young children, a large household, complicated concerns, and the necessity of economy" (27). Although "oppressed with cares and responsibilities" and frequently "afflicted with the severest anguish, from an apprehension that her life was useless," Pamela Sedgwick uttered "no complaint" (28). Sedgwick implies that her mother, who "knew she was most tenderly beloved, and held in the very highest respect by my father"

(28), was silenced by a romantic script that called for her to give her life to a man who remained married, in fantasy if not in reality, to his first wife.

Pamela Sedgwick was further prevented from criticizing or changing her martyrdom to love, Sedgwick contends, by her religion. Sedgwick quotes her brother Harry's assertion that their mother "'seemed sweetly to repose on the pillow of Faith, and, when tortured by pain and debilitated by disease, she not only sustained herself, but was the comfort, support, and delight of her family.'" "'Such,'" he notes, "'was the strength of her submissive piety'" (37). While Harry attributes Pamela's hardships to biological illness and physical pain, Catharine, who is less willing than her brother to celebrate her mother's submission, focuses instead on the abandonment and silence sanctioned by the church and policed through cultural norms of femininity. Sedgwick directly condemns the "modesty," "self-diffidence," and "humility" of her sisters and mother, "so authorized and enforced by their religion that to them . . . [self-sacrifice] took the potent form of a duty" (33).

As described in her daughter's memoir, Pamela Dwight Sedgwick exemplifies the double bind of white, middle-class women in early America, who found themselves praised and valued by the same discourses that led them to sacrifice their vitality and their ambitions. While women such as Pamela Sedgwick were "worshiped" for their religious devotion and for their sovereignty over matters of the heart, this purported mastery of virtue and sentiment often masked the reality of women's social, legal, and economic restriction. Hearing their moral superiority extolled, women were also reminded of their subordination to the needs of their families and to the wills of their husbands. As one minister told his female congregants in 1832, "the world concedes to you the honor of exerting an influence, all but divine; but an influence you lose the power to exert, the moment you depart from the sphere and delicacy of your proper character" (Cott 1977, 158). While religion sanctified women for their centrality—and subjugation—within the limited world of their families, the rhetoric of romance, by glorifying marriage, idealized the loss of a woman's financial and social autonomy through the coverture laws. At the same time as they nominally valued women for their transcendence over the brutish standards of the marketplace, therefore, religion and sentimentalism also formed the cornerstones of the prison house of gender.

Sedgwick sought to open the door of that prison in her 1827 novel, *Hope Leslie; or, Early Times in the Massachusetts,* which exposes the coercive and debilitating power of religion and romance and seeks to loosen their hold on women. Martha Fletcher, a character whose life closely resembles that of Sedgwick's mother, plays an important role in the critique of "true womanhood" posed by *Hope Leslie.* Like Theodore Sedgwick, Will Fletcher marries Martha after losing his first, true love, Alice Leslie. Alice, like the ghost of Eliza Mason, returns to her beloved, but in the image of her daughter, Hope Leslie. Will Fletcher, like Congressman Sedgwick, marries for convenience rather than love and leaves his wife alone to manage a large household on limited means. Finally, Martha Fletcher, like Pamela Sedgwick, is reconciled to this abandonment by her sentimental devotion to her husband and by the duty assigned her by her religion. She dies an early death that Sedgwick connects to her "submissive piety."

Both Catharine Sedgwick and her fictional surrogate, Martha
Fletcher's adopted daughter, Hope, reject in their own lives the orthodox religion and heterosexual romance that conspired to kill their mothers. Like Hope Leslie, who refuses to let the Puritan brethren dictate either her romantic or her spiritual duty, Sedgwick broke free from both Calvinism and the imperative to marry and raise a family. Describing the beliefs that led her to leave the church in 1821, Sedgwick writes, "I thought myself bound not to lend sanction to what seems to me a gross violation of the religion of the Redeemer, and an insult to a large body of Christians entitled to respect and affection" (119). Shortly after her departure from the orthodox church, Sedgwick joined her "enlightened, rational, and liberal" brothers (117) in the more generous and less doctrinal Unitarian Church—"that religion which alone can give us grace in this world and life in the next" (98). Sedgwick's brothers, in addition to enabling her release from "the thraldom of orthodox despotism" (144), also provided her with a series of temporary domestic settings that allowed her to enjoy stable family life without herself having to marry and raise a family; traveling seasonally between her brothers' homes, Sedgwick, like her fictional counterpart, enjoyed

domesticity without surrendering her writing, her mobility, or her independence.

Ultimately, however, Sedgwick attributes her relative freedom not to her brothers but to the wildness of the New England landscape and to the support and comfort provided by the Sedgwicks' household servant, a freed slave named Mumbet. Just as Martha Fletcher's death in *Hope Leslie* leaves her adopted daughter to enjoy a life of adventure in the wilderness, so Sedgwick, left by her mother's death with "no regular instruction" (43), "enjoyed unrestrained the pleasures of a rural childhood" (44) that allowed her to grow up in a manner "not conventional" (75). Like Hope Leslie, who on her mother's death turns for companionship to the Indian girl Magawisca, a servant in the Fletcher home, Sedgwick "clung . . . with instinctive love and faith" (42) to Mumbet who, "though perfect in service, was never servile" (41). Encouraged in their independence at an early age by the unconventional life promised by an unsettled landscape and endorsed by strong, beloved women of color, both Sedgwick and Hope Leslie refuse the scripts that created their overburdened yet silently suffering mothers.

These parallels between Sedgwick's autobiography and her novel suggest that *Hope Leslie,* with its sustained critique of religion and romance, stands as an indictment not so much of the author's Puritan forefathers but of the cultural fathers who determined domestic femininity in her own day. The present chapter will take up this reading of the novel, exploring Sedgwick's revision of "true womanhood" through her heroine's strong identification with the "wilderness" and its inhabitants. At the same time that the apparent similarities between these texts invite such a reading, however, they also offer several cautions, urging one to take seriously the difference between "revision" and "freedom" and to rethink the relationship between an apparently transparent autobiographical text and the opaque fiction, interpretable *through* the seemingly "true" story of the author's life.[1] These cautions have important consequences for how one reads not only *Hope Leslie* but the entire genre of the captivity romance.

Both *The Life and Letters* and *Hope Leslie* reveal that final or absolute "freedom" from cultural inscription is an impossible—and dangerous—fantasy. At the same time as she attempts to escape traditional domesticity in *The Life and Letters,* for instance, Sedgwick does so only with the help of a domestic servant whose presence in the Sedgwick home relies on the very hierarchies of race and gender that Sedgwick wishes to flee. Sedgwick's flight from the home is possible, then, only within the terms of that home's power structures, with the ultimate cost displaced from the white girl to the woman of color, who is never permitted to write her own memoir or to express a desire for an extra-vagant flight from the home. The same contradictory relationship exists between Hope Leslie and her Indian "sister," Magawisca, who comes to the Fletcher home as a captive taken through the very colonial aggression that she enables Hope to condemn. In both texts, the use of the exoticized woman of color to represent the wild "other" of domesticity builds on constructions of Native and African Americans as more "natural," less "civilized" than whites, even while the white heroines criticize such constructions. In both texts, the white heroine can distance herself from dominant ideology only through the terms of white, male discourse; not surprisingly, therefore, escape from imprisonment in *Hope Leslie* leads almost inevitably to another confinement, not to a state of ultimate liberty from the dominant networks of power. To imagine that the heroine has achieved liberty would only be to rename as "freedom" the constraints of race and gender she sought to escape in the first place.

Even without *The Life and Letters,* one could read in *Hope Leslie* a critique of nineteenth-century norms of femininity and of the possibility of freedom from cultural determination. What would not be visible without both texts, however, is the degree to which captivity provides the metaphorical structure for women's life narratives. At the same time that *The Life and Letters* suggests a reading of *Hope Leslie,* one must remember that the novel predates the memoir by almost fifty years. Rather than assuming that the memoir determines the plot of *Hope Leslie,* then, one might more safely assume that the novel, in its blend of captivity narrative and domestic novel, provided the plot through which Sedgwick could represent her life as a tale of cultural capture and defiant escape. Describing to a friend her sister's flight from the "monstrous doctrines" of Calvinism (68), for instance, Sedgwick writes, "you can not even imagine what liberty to such a captive is!" (144). Reading

Hope Leslie as a precursor to *The Life and Letters,* rather than vice versa, one can see what women authors have been asserting since Ann Eliza Bleecker wrote a female audience into *The History of Maria Kittle:* captivity narratives offer women the metaphors necessary to describe their cultural imprisonment and to imagine jailbreaks into lives, if not of freedom, then of re-visionary adventure.

Hope Leslie, which stages its critique of normative race and gender through its play with literary genre, highlights both the impact of fiction on the scripts of social life and the consequent necessity of literary/social revision. Like earlier captivity romances, therefore, *Hope Leslie* combines and revises genres usually designated as "masculine" or "feminine," and hence "naturally" distinct. In order to make the wilderness a viable domain for heroines, Sedgwick first needed to redefine the frontier romance, usually associated with James Fenimore Cooper and his male contemporaries.[2] Male-authored frontier romances typically feature innately (if, in the eyes of the white hero, admirably) fierce and vengeful Indians. Motivated by natural malice, these "savages" brutalize isolated and infantilized white women who, as Nina Baym notes, "serve their civilization by sacrificing dreams of independence, repressing sexual fantasies, and acknowledging how lucky they are to be the prize possessions of white men" (1992, 26). Sedgwick's heroines, however, fight to maintain their independence, depicting "possession" by white men as a cruel captivity; although the women in *Hope Leslie,* like those in Cooper's novels, repress their sexual fantasies, their repression does not lead to the fear and loathing that are the dark counterparts of desire in Cooper's heroines, but to friendship and adventure. Providing accounts of the past that sharply contradict authorized national history, furthermore, Sedgwick's heroines specifically refuse to "serve their civilization." In *Hope Leslie,* Indian and white women articulate the historical context of their actions, reconfiguring white colonialists as the cause, not the victims, of Indian violence.[3] Comprised of naturally weak white women and innately savage Indians, Cooper's novels, as Leland Person, Jr., argues, can only "establish triangular, doubly exploitative relationships among Indian and white males and white women that reinforce male fantasies of chivalrous protection, rescue, and revenge" (1985, 671). In *Hope Leslie,* however, Indians (particularly Indian women, usually absent in Cooper's novels) and white women unite in their resistance to white, male control, forming a sympathetic and mutually supportive community.

With its idealized female community standing as a challenge to patriarchal authority and its use of female story-telling to revise masculinist and imperial history, *Hope Leslie* makes the frontier a safe haven for white heroines by rendering it in the language of popular domestic literature. Annette Kolodny has demonstrated in *The Land before Her* that pioneering women brought domesticity into the frontier territories by creating literal and metaphorical gardens from the uncultivated and "savage" terrain. Sedgwick similarly imports into the wilderness of fiction the sentimental depictions of home life, the centrality of motherhood, and the faith in Christian mercy characteristic of domestic literature.[4] Above all, *Hope Leslie* insists that the wilderness gives rise not to antisocial individualism but to the strong female communities enjoyed by the readers of and characters in domestic fiction. As Sandra Zagarell notes, *Hope Leslie* then uses its "communitarian ethic" to oppose "the rigid legalism that for Sedgwick undergirds all authoritarian male rule" (1987, 238).

At the same time that Sedgwick imports domestic conventions into Cooper's wilderness to create an environment more hospitable to female heroes, however, she also deploys the frontier romance to dismantle the limitations imposed on white womanhood by domestic literature. Sedgwick shows her heroines prospering outside the home, developing their physical and intellectual as well as their emotional powers; in the metaphorical wilderness, women draw strength from chosen, not biological, families and from friendships rather than from romance and marriage. *Hope Leslie* constitutes an extended critique of "religion, motherhood, home, and family," the four elements Jane Tompkins identifies as the mainstays of domestic fiction (1985, 145). Even as *Hope Leslie* makes clear the impact of apparently harmless fictions on the lives of women, however, it acknowledges the impossibility—even the undesirability—of ever living without such fictions. Rather than imagining a life free from cultural inscription, Sedgwick conflates and alters two genres in order to question the location of "female virtue" within a specific and potentially narrow site, thereby allowing white women to take their domesticity on the road. From *Hope Leslie* emerges a heroine who can dwell in the wilderness without becoming a "rugged" (that is, racist, misogynistic, antisocial) individualist, but who can also enjoy aspects of nineteenth-century domesticity without being, in Barbara Welter's phrase, a "hostage in the house" (1966, 151).

Sedgwick's challenge to dominant nineteenth-century assumptions about woman's "natural" character and her "proper sphere" begins with her heroines' refusal of religion and of romance, with their attendant captivities of marriage and housewifery. *Hope Leslie* resists the discursive separation of spheres, showing instead how romance and religion work together to justify and police patriarchal social order. While initially placing great stock in the promise of religion—especially Puritanism—to better the lives of women, the captivity romances eventually expose the efforts of religious leaders to control women by prescribing their (heterosexual) romantic and their (heterosocial) domestic identities. Harriet Cheney uses a pointed debate in *A Peep at the Pilgrims* to depict the disastrous consequences for women of Puritan rule. When Mrs.

Winthrop points out the hypocrisy of Roger Williams, who fought for freedom of conscience but punished his wife for disagreeing with him, one of the church elders responds that in this, anyway, Williams was correct: men owe their loyalty to God, but women owe theirs to husbands. A more serious and haunting reminder of Puritanism's subjection of women comes in Cheney's novel in the person of Anne Hutchinson, whose trial demonstrates the severe punishments church rulers inflict on women who claim the same intellectual independence and freedom of conscience for which they themselves, according to Cheney, came to America.

Opposed to this judgmental, hypocritical, and intolerant religion, the captivity romances represent the more gentle, forgiving, and open-minded theology of their heroines. In several of the novels (*Hope Leslie* is an exception), the heroine learns of a more tolerant and egalitarian faith from her mother and uses her mother's religion to rebel against her tyrannical father and to escape his constraints. While sons in these novels never explicitly rebel against patriarchal orthodoxy in the way that daughters do, they too are brought by their sisters and wives to "feminized" religion. Near the end of *A Peep at the Pilgrims,* Edward Atherton (the only character apart from the narrator to praise Hutchinson), in order to marry the novel's heroine, converts to the Puritanism he explicitly names as the faith of his mother. Although modeled on the very "domestic" traits the church elders sought to enforce, the Puritanism practiced by the novel's women ironically frees them from the home, enabling them to explore new physical and intellectual terrains. Religion and romance, rather than combining to subject daughters to the rule of the fathers, thus become the daughters' tools to displace the fathers in the name of their mothers. In Cheney's novel, matriarchal faith therefore creates independent, adventurous women and tolerant, respectful men who together constitute a more harmonious society. The father's religion serves only sons, the novels imply, but the mother's faith benefits all her children.

Less sanguine than Cheney, Sedgwick presents a more sustained indictment of the partnership of organized religion and romance. In the opening chapters of *Hope Leslie* (1827), the nefarious Englishman William Fletcher has maneuvered to have his nephew (also named Will Fletcher), a wayward Puritan-sympathizer, fall in love with his daughter, Alice. By arranging this match, William **167** hopes to force his nephew to forego his Puritan leanings and return to the established church. Will does in fact fall in love with his cousin, but when the elder Fletcher presents him with an ultimatum —disavow Puritanism or lose Alice's hand—Will resolves to flee temptation by taking passage to the New World. Alice, ignoring her father's wishes, follows her beloved to the pier, determined to emigrate with him. At the last moment, however, her father and a host of guards arrive to restrain Alice. Forced to remain within Anglican orthodoxy, Alice transforms into the conventionally abandoned heroine of sentimental fiction: "impotent," living "in absolute retirement," she "in the imbecility of utter despair, submitted to her father's commands" (13–14), ultimately marrying a respectable Anglican, Sir Leslie.

Throughout this episode, Puritanism is privileged as a means to break with the wills—and the pun is surely deliberate—of the English Fathers (even if in doing so one is subjected to another Will). Sedgwick shows Puritanism, with its promise of a community ruled by values more advantageous to women, shattering patrimonial power; in fact, the greedy and manipulative Uncle William portrays

Puritanism as a matrilineage: " 'Liberty, what is it! Daughter of disloyalty and mother of all misrule' " (8). Puritanism further carries with it an antihierarchical rhetoric of equality, democracy, and community: as Uncle William says, the Puritans in the New World " 'might enjoy with the savages that primitive equality, about which they make such a pather' " (8). Finally, by offering women the option of duty and sacrifice to God, Puritanism provides women with an escape from traditional romance plots. As Jane Tompkins observes, "By ceding themselves to the source of all power, [women] bypass worldly (male) authority, and as it were, cancel it out" (1985, 163). Subjection to God's authority clearly proves a preferable option for Sedgwick's heroines who, when distanced from the egalitarian promise of Puritanism, become fatally bound to masculine will.

Despite her early praise for Puritanism, however, Sedgwick quickly shows that any religion, in becoming institutionalized, may become an agent of patriarchal rule. The most obvious victims of the betrayal of Puritan rhetoric and of its perversion into a mode of oppression are women such as Martha, the pitiable orphan Will marries in America. Knowing that Will still loves Alice, Martha nevertheless joins him in a wilderness settlement where she raises a son, Everell, and a number of daughters. Without consulting her, Will further burdens Martha with two captive Indian children, Magawisca and Oneco, as well as with Hope and Faith Leslie, the two orphaned children of Alice Leslie who, widowed, dies during the voyage she is finally able to make to the New World. Taking custody of his new wards in Boston, Will sends Faith on to Springfield and remains with Hope in Boston for no fewer than three seasons. During his absence,

> his little community at Bethel proceeded more harmoniously than could have been hoped from the discordant materials of which it was composed. This was owing, in great part, to the wise and gentle Mrs. Fletcher, the sun of her little system. (1827, 29–30)

In Sedgwick's depiction of the first generation of settlers, only Martha Fletcher's home comes close to realizing the equality and community with which the Puritans were associated in England. It is also a world without authoritative men (there are male servants, whom, due to their low social position, Sedgwick aligns with the other disempowered members of the Fletcher household). This depiction of a peaceful, equitable domestic world devoid of the harsh and hierarchizing law of men sows the narrative seeds of a vision of a harmonious world composed of women, children, servants, and Indians that the rest of the novel struggles to realize. It also reveals Sedgwick's ties with the domestic novel, in which, as Tompkins writes, "The removal of the male from the center to the periphery of the human sphere" is "one of the most radical components" (1985, 145).

While apparently offering a domestic model, however, Martha Fletcher's community also questions the ideals of family and religion on which early nineteenth-century domesticity was based. The Fletcher home is more like an orphanage than the traditional nuclear family that became the core of domestic morality. All the central characters except Everell are either orphans or have been taken from their natural homes. The disruption of the nuclear family, furthermore, is ironically the product of religion: the death of Alice Leslie and the subsequent orphaning of her children is the result, Sedgwick implies, of her weakened state, brought about by the religious intolerance of her father. Magawisca and Oneco still have a father—the Pequod chief, Mononotto—but are separated from him by Puritan warfare against the Indians, justified by religious rhetoric. Martha's household stands, then, as a challenge to the linkage of biological kinship and social harmony, and as a critique of religions that dismember the families they claim to revere.

Central to her challenge to nineteenth-century domestic ideals is Sedgwick's skeptical depiction of "motherhood" in Martha Fletcher's "little community." As her name indicates, Martha is the woman who serves: with unwavering faith in the protection offered by men, Martha serves the myth of English, male superiority.[5] Although she has been warned by the Indians that the Fletcher home is in danger of an attack, Martha does not move her family to a nearby fort because she hears that her husband is expected from Boston shortly. Due to her trust in masculine protection, Martha and her daughters are slaughtered by Pequods, and Everell and Faith are taken hostage. Despite her ability to run a household that stands as a challenge to the core values of middle-class domesticity, Martha must be murdered—in the way Virginia Woolf writes of needing to murder the Angel in the House—if Magawisca and Hope, her surrogate daughters, are to achieve their potential as women heroes.[6] With the death of Martha Fletcher, her daughters are freed from the living proof of religion's failure to relieve women by substituting "feminine" equality for "masculine" hierarchy.

More dangerous than the restrictive religious model of womanhood, however, is the deployment of romance by the heroines' biological and cultural fathers. John Winthrop himself stoops to matchmaking in *Hope Leslie,* contriving to involve Hope with Sir Philip Gardiner, whom Winthrop sees as "the selected medium of a special kindness of Providence" (1827, 249) to the Puritans. The reader knows, however, that Sir Philip is a follower of Thomas Morton, a heretic. Winthrop is blinded to Gardiner's heresies, Sedgwick implies, because he perceives Hope Leslie, with her flouting of traditional femininity, as a greater threat to the state than the popish affectations of a male stranger. Winthrop therefore deploys romance as a mode of restriction; as he tells Will Fletcher, by arranging a match for Hope, he means to put "jesses" (155) on the "lawless girl" (154). Justifying his matchmaking to Fletcher, Winthrop comments on the wayward Hope, " 'I have thought the child rests too much on *performances;* and you must allow, that she hath not, I speak it tenderly, that passiveness, that, next to godliness, is a woman's best virtue' " (153). In showing Winthrop converting the Puritan rejection of the covenant of works into a justification for theocratically enforced female passivity, Sedgwick highlights the complicity of romance and religious orthodoxy in restricting the extra-vagant independence of women.

Despite the efforts of their fathers, however, the heroines of the captivity romances inevitably choose adventure over romance. In *Reuben and Rachel,* Jessy Oliver escapes her father's prison and joins her friend Rachel " 'in search of adventure' " (1798, 2:278), while Miriam Grey takes to the wilderness in *A Peep at the Pilgrims* rather than marry a stuffy Puritan her father has chosen to be her mate. In *Hope Leslie,* too, despite the efforts of the matchmaking brethren (Sedgwick nicely reverses gender stereotypes by making men the gossips and arrangers, while women become the agents of conscience and justice), Hope maintains her independence from all romantic entanglements. Playing the chivalric protector, Sir Philip tells Hope, " 'If I had a charmed shield, I would devote my life to sheltering you from all harm' "; she, however, deflatingly responds, " 'It's useless talking in this rattling storm, your words drop to the ground with the hail-stones' " (1827, 193). When Philip then gallantly offers Hope his cloak, she protests, " 'the cloak will but encumber me' " (193). Confronting Philip's assertion that " 'ladies must have lovers—idols must have worshippers, or they are no longer idols' " (201), Sedgwick can safely assert that *Hope Leslie* is "no romantic fiction" (12).

The ultimate marriage of Everell Fletcher and Hope Leslie might seem at odds with the consistent rejection of romance in the novel. The union does not constitute a traditional romantic ending, however, in which heterosexual coupling is rendered as the perfect and inevitable closure to a heroine's life and therefore to a woman author's text.[7] Defying narrative convention, Sedgwick minimizes the importance of the marriage: while we are told the fate of every minor character in some detail at the conclusion of the novel, we learn nothing about the wedding, except that it makes society happy. Rather than foregrounding heterosexual romance, Sedgwick concludes *Hope Leslie* by commenting of Esther Downing, Hope's friend who has escaped heartbreak by devoting her life to Christ, "She illustrated a truth, which if more generally received by her sex, might save a vast deal of misery: that marriage is not *essential* to the contentment, the dignity, or the happiness of woman" (349–50).

In the end, heterosexual romance is replaced in *Hope Leslie,* as it is in Sedgwick's autobiography, by sibling affection. Magawisca hails Everell as a brother more than as a lover. Esther, too, in the note informing Everell and Hope of her departure to England, writes that she " 'shall hereafter feel a sister's love [for Everell], who will not withhold a brother's kindness' " (347). Even Hope's feelings for Everell are described by Sedgwick in terms that stress sisterly affection over romantic passion: "It has been said that the love of a brother and sister is the only platonic affection. This truth (if it be a truth) is the conviction of an experience far beyond our heroine's" (224).

The sibling affection that develops between Everell and the

novel's heroines is less important to the plot, however, than the "sisterhood" that emerges between the women themselves. Sedgwick refuses to depict her heroines as antagonistic rivals for the novel's eligible bachelor, a convention that makes a woman's relationship to a man more important than any she might have with another woman. Rather, traditional romance is subordinated to an ideal of female friendship.[8] Magawisca, Hope, and Faith become sisters when, in the only happy interracial marriage in nineteenth-century American literature, Hope's sister, Faith, marries Magawisca's brother, Oneco.[9] But the novel's women become comrades as well, providing mutual support and sharing a spiritual motherhood: in a central scene, the reunion of Faith, Hope, and Magawisca occurs at the gravesites of their two mothers, who, Magawisca tells Hope, bless their daughters' union. Even the most remote woman in the novel, Rosa, is mourned at the end as "a fallen, unhappy sister" (348). The sisterhood that evolves in *Hope Leslie* contrasts ironically with the relationships among men—although "brethren," they rarely act as brothers. The epigraph to the final chapter, taken from La Rochefoucauld, encapsulates the novel's social vision— and Sedgwick's contribution to the frontier tradition: "Quelque rare que soit le véritable amour, il l'est encore moins que la véritable amitié" (336) (However rare true love is, it is less so than true friendship).

If orthodox religion and romance serve in *Hope Leslie* as mutually authorizing constraints on women's independence, the novel's ending literally explodes both discourses in order to free its heroines for friendship and for extra-vagant adventure. As the novel concludes, Sir Philip is escaping Boston on a pirate ship with a disguised woman the reader believes to be Hope Leslie. Also on board is Rosa, a young girl Sir Philip wooed from a convent, seduced, and then turned into a forlorn servant. Rosa, who spends the entire novel pining and sighing, is a caricature of the sentimental heroine, wasting away under the spell of romantic enthrallment and unrequited passion. Rosa's one act of disobedience, however, brings both herself and Philip to their deaths. Descending into the hull of the ship, Philip asks Rosa to hand him her lantern, which she instead flings into a powder keg, exploding the ship and killing its passengers. The kidnapped woman killed in the explosion is not, of course, Hope Leslie. Arriving at the Winthrop house late at night, the pirate sent to abduct Hope mistakenly kidnaps Jennet, the Fletchers' servant. Moralizing, judgmental, and meddlesome, Jennet represents Puritanism at its most intolerant and restrictive. She is what one might call today "male identified," seeking to out-Puritan her brethren. In simultaneously eliminating Philip and Jennet, then, Sedgwick kills off, literally and figuratively, the two New World threats to the freedom of her female hero: romantic enthrallment and religious restriction.

Once freed from the constraints of religion and romance, Sedgwick's heroines turn the Puritan errand into a female quest. The heroines' adventures center on acts of reading and revision, turning cultural stories that serve to isolate and subjugate women, and particularly women of color, into texts that draw attention to those operations of power and revise them so as to valorize women's strength and resistance. Magawisca's heroic tale begins with a demonstration of the common gender dynamics of Puritan religious discourse. Following the Pequod raid on the Fletcher home, Everell Fletcher and Faith Leslie are taken captive by the Pequod chief, Mononotto, who plans to sacrifice Everell to avenge his own son, murdered during an English attack. Magawisca, pleading for Everell's life, looks at her father with "her mother's eyes and speaketh with her voice" (84), evoking the mother as a principle of mercy in a gesture echoed by Everell, who prays as he is led to execution that "my mother and sisters are permitted to minister to me" (88). Everell's impending execution creates a tension between the male world of the Old Testament—based on violence, vengeance, and "artificial codes of law" (92)—and the feminine world of the New Testament—based on mercy and love, represented by the evoked spirits of the mothers. Mononotto uses the language of the Old Testament: " 'Nay, brothers—the work is mine—he dies by my hand—for my first-born—life for life.' " He further explains that to give up this code would be to become feminized: " 'My people have told me I bore a woman's heart towards the enemy. Ye shall see, I will pour out this English boy's blood to the last drop, and give his flesh and bones to the dogs and wolves' " (92).

As a result of Mononotto's stern adherence to his patriarchal imperative, the reader is presented with the first in a series of prison breaks. Afraid that Magawisca will help Everell escape, Mononotto has her placed under guard in the dwelling of his elderly and ailing sister. Magawisca, who feels that "if she were to remain pent in that prison-house, her heart would burst" (91), attempts to spring past her guard, but he "caught her arm in his iron grasp," forcing her back into the hut. It is then that Magawisca devises a plan that enacts one of the prominent themes of the novel: the "art" of the mother-figure allows the younger woman to escape her imprisonment by men. The ailing woman has been brewing a sleeping remedy to ease her pain, some of which Magawisca now slips into the guard's drink, enabling her to escape. While Everell prepares for execution, Magawisca runs through the forest, scaling rocks and leaping over precipices until, at the very moment that Mononotto brings his tomahawk down toward Everell's exposed neck, Magawisca leaps from a clearing and interposes her arm. As the "lopped, quivering member dropped over the precipice," Everell hugs her "as he would a sister that had redeemed his life with her own" (93) and makes his escape.

174   Magawisca's rescue of Everell uses gender difference to revise one of Anglo-American imperialism's central myths. In the legend of Pocahontas, the Indian princess lays her head on John Smith's to protect his life from the wrath of her father. Mary Dearborn discusses the metaphoric implications of Pocahontas' sacrifice, noting that if the act represents, as critics have claimed it does, a "ritual marriage" between the Indian princess and the white man, it does not speak well of the benefits of interracial matrimony for Indian women, who, literally or symbolically, risk their necks for white husbands who are free to desert them (1986, 97–98). In revising that legend, Sedgwick implies that the law of the Old Testament— the law of the Fathers—ultimately punishes not the sons but the daughters. Under the law of an eye for an eye, when a woman engages in the masculine plot of heroism, thereby transgressing the boundaries of gender, her transgression must be repaid with a mutilation of the body on which those boundaries are inscribed. When Magawisca attempts to escape her father's prison, a guard catches her by the arm; her symbolic act of liberation from that patriarchal hold is brutally literalized, then, in her painful loss of the site of control.

Magawisca's actions so successfully revise cultural scripts that none can accommodate her actions. Witnesses attempt to recontain her agency in a traditional narrative of heavenly intervention: "To all it seemed that this deliverance had been achieved by miraculous aid. All—the dullest and coldest—paid involuntary homage to the heroic girl, as if she were a superior being, guided and upheld by supernatural power" (1827, 93). Here Sedgwick again shows religious rhetoric returning Magawisca to divine passivity and rendering her implicitly inferior to her male witnesses, who hail her *as if* she were a superior being. Sedgwick further suggests that history, authored for a white male audience, will erase the heroism of women, and of women of color in particular. A painting commemorating Everell's rescue depicts a man saving the sleeping boy from the attack of wild beasts. *This* version—in which female heroism is masculinized and the Indians, so often metaphorized as animals, literally become them—will endure, we are told, and become the official story, " 'a kind of history for Mr. Everell's children' " (96). The purported objectivity of male-centered "history" is undermined, however, by the inclusion of a description of the painting *and* of Magawisca's actions within a letter Hope writes to Everell, in which Hope's sarcasm undercuts the legitimacy of the painting. Acts of female writing and revision thus subvert the narratives of masculinized history, rendering visible the women and Indians that tales of male heroism erase or subjugate, even while history remains in both cases the privileged domain of whites.[10]

Sedgwick extends the critical reading and revision of male myth/history—for the two are shown to be indistinguishable—through Hope's heroism on a trip to the newly forming settlement at Northampton. Hope's actions in this episode mirror Magawisca's, redeeming her suffering and rendering it fruitful. First, while Magawisca loses a limb to the unequal system of male power and female confinement, Hope gains "a right godly and suitable appendage to a pilgrim damsel" (98). That "appendage" is Craddock, the most ineffectual male in the novel. But whereas Magawisca loses an "appendage" due to her agency, Hope can travel because of Craddock's presence. When subsequently this appendage is "sacrificed"—Hope moves too quickly for Craddock and soon leaves him behind—it will be not as punishment inflicted on Hope for her heroism but as a self-willed act to allow freer movement. Furthermore, whereas Magawisca is a victim of the Old Testament, Hope subverts one of its most misogynistic myths, the fall of Adam and Eve. In the descent from Mount Holyoke, Craddock is bitten by a rattlesnake. Hope offers to suck the venom from the wound, "for I well knew it could not harm me, and I believed it to be life or death to my poor tutor" (102). The serpent no longer has power to harm Eve in this New World paradise; rather, it wounds the American Adam, no longer a powerful namer, but a comic scholar of dead languages and a "poor tutor."

Finally, whereas Magawisca is able to escape her imprisonment because of the art/magic of the disempowered mother, Hope is now able in turn to free the imprisoned mother. The old Indian woman, Nelema, cures the poisoned tutor with a snake dance, assuming "the living form of the reptile whose image she bore" as a "sign of honour" (104). As a consequence, however, Nelema is arrested, condemned as a witch, and imprisoned in Governor Winthrop's basement. It is from this prison that Hope Leslie sets her free. The release of the mother/artist is essential to the formation of female community; if Nelema is killed, Hope Leslie writes Everell, "you will never again hear of Magawisca, I shall never hear more of my sweet sister" (110). In Hope's letter relating her rescue of Nelema, Sedgwick thematizes the generational coming to legibility of women in the novel. From the mothers, who work in perishables (potions, food, weavings) or write, like Nelema, "hieroglyphics on the invisible air" (104), springs the daughter, Hope, who begins to create an encoded text, her letter. Finally the nineteenth-century narrator writes publicly in a published novel.

The visibility achieved generationally in *Hope Leslie* involves the rescripting of classic (male-authored) literature into an adventure story that differs from conventional American mythology in several significant ways. First, no adventure is resolved in *Hope Leslie* by a single heroic agent; rather, the two heroines' stories collectively depict the dangers women face and the means they use to prevail. Second, the result of the heroines' adventures is not a final and complete "freedom" that overturns the restrictive rule of patriarchal colonialism; instead, the heroines escape one prison only to encounter another. These generic differences constitute one of the most important insights of the captivity romance as a genre: since confinement (within bodies constructed by white, patriarchal discourse, and hence by language itself) cannot be finally escaped, least of all in a novel, women must read critically in order to revise the terms of those discourses, an activity most usefully undertaken as a community action. Collective reading becomes a way, then, of naming the ideological investments in conventional stories, and of offering alternatives that make women the subjects as well as the objects of language.[11]

Sedgwick is not naive, however, about the dangers of revisionary adventure in a social world where power, despite the most clever of readings, remains unequally distributed and maintained by dominant narratives. While Hope's adventures redeem the sacrifices made by Magawisca, for instance, the benefits nevertheless accrue to the white and not to the Indian heroine who, at the novel's conclusion, must return to the "wilderness" that is still presented as her natural habitat.[12] Hope, too, continues to face the dangers of gender inequality, as one of her most dramatic adventures demonstrates. At the midnight rendezvous of Hope, Faith, and Magawisca, the women are surprised by the governor's guards, who seize Faith and Magawisca. Hope is carried away in a canoe by Oneco and Mononotto, however, until the latter is struck by lightning. While Oneco frantically attempts to revive his father, Hope makes her escape, running through the forest until she stumbles on a troop of drunken pirates who try to rape her. Hope again escapes and, seeing a dinghy moored nearby, leaps aboard and sets to sea. No sooner does she push off from shore, however, than she is surprised by another pirate, who has been sleeping in the boat. Convinced that Hope is a sacred apparition, the pirate agrees to row the "saint" back to Boston where Hope, wet and exhausted, faints into Rosa's arms and is carried to the Winthrop home. All the forces Hope encounters threaten to immobilize and put her at the mercy of men, who command the means of movement (the canoe, the ship, the dinghy). Rather than denying the restraints placed on women's movement in the social world—entrapment, sexual violation, and an idealization that puts the fetishized woman at the mercy of the purported adorer—Sedgwick acknowledges these dangers as part of her adventure plot, showing that moving in a world framed by masculinist discourse is, for Sedgwick, every woman's "adventure."

Despite the potential dangers, however, the heroines of *Hope Leslie* continue, through their revisionary adventures, to challenge nineteenth-century definitions of "womanhood" by revising masculine narratives and their increasingly rigid division of masculine and feminine spheres. Above all, *Hope Leslie* deconstructs the "natural" division between "home and the world" (Cott 1977, 64), giving women a plot outside the house without denying the empowerment of domestic constructs such as the "sisterhood" gained through collective identities. Jane Tompkins has argued that the genre of the western arose in the early twentieth century as a reaction to the "feminine culture" of the nineteenth century. Tompkins contends that the western "*answers* the domestic novel," becoming "the antithesis of the cult of domesticity that dominated American Victorian culture" (1987, 371). The captivity romance, I am arguing, is another response to the "cult of domesticity." Like the western, the captivity romance challenges orthodox religion and privileges frontier adventure over the romance plot and its seemingly inevitable domestic closure. But while the western denies adventure to women as the apparently natural representatives of religion and the home, *Hope Leslie* rejects religion and the home as discursive tools men use to deprive women of their independence. While the western sees home and frontier as inherently antagonistic, the captivity romance creates a female hero who embodies the best of both discursive worlds, thereby refuting the notion that the public and private spheres were ever, as they are popularly labeled, separate.

Dissatisfaction with conventionally defined "womanhood" is perhaps best represented in the captivity romance through the trope of captivity, which, as my analysis of *Hope Leslie* demonstrates, was stressed—even overstressed—as women's experience in America. Sandra Gilbert writes that "women writers have frequently responded to sociocultural constraints by creating symbolic narratives that express their common feelings of constriction, exclusion, dispossession" (1985, 35). Through the trope of captivity, these romances suggest an American version of the madwoman in the attic. But novels such as *Hope Leslie* create neither madwomen nor dutiful, devout housewives, but adventurous and daring heroines who, far from being constricted, excluded, and dispossessed, read and revise cultural stories so as to become *self*-possessed agents *included* in communities that enable their adventures. Above all, the captivity romances suggest not only that sociocultural constraint gives rise to narratives of imprisonment, as Gilbert suggests, but that revisionary adventure *within* those narratives can provide women with strategies to resist restriction in their everyday lives. The continuing influence of the captivity story on women's life narratives becomes even more evident in the texts discussed in the following chapter, feminist and popular narratives that also offer the story of confinement and escape as significant for women's revisionary self-imaginings. In so doing, they follow Catharine Sedgwick in producing, through the captivity romance, America's most striking expression of female extra-vagance, of women granting each other permission to enter the world.

CONCLUSION *Contemporary Captives*

IN THE FIRST PARAGRAPHS of one of her earliest stories, "The Maid of Saint Phillippe" (1891), Kate Chopin perpetuates a nineteenth-century dichotomy between the wilderness and a civilization tended by a totalizing category of inhabitants called "housewives." Between the two traditional realms, however, Chopin creates a middle ground, walked by the story's heroine, Marianne Laronce.

> Marianne was tall, supple, and strong. Dressed in her worn buckskin trappings she looked like a handsome boy rather than like the French girl of seventeen that she was. As she stepped from the woods the glimmer of the setting sun dazzled her. An instant she raised her hand—palm outward—to shield her eyes from the glare, then she continued to descend the gentle slope and make her way toward the little village of Saint Phillippe that lay before her, close by the waters of the Mississippi.
>
> Marianne carried a gun across her shoulder as easily as a soldier might. Her stride was as untrammelled as that of the stag who treads his native hill-side unmolested. There was something stag-like, too, in the poise of her small head as she

turned it from side to side, to sniff the subtle perfume of the Indian summer. But against the red western sky curling columns of thin blue smoke began to ascend from chimneys in the village. This meant the housewives were already busy preparing the evening meal; and the girl quickened her step, singing softly as she strode along over the tufted meadow where sleek cattle were grazing in numbers. (1969, 1:116)

Although the boyish Marianne, with buckskin trappings and a rifle slung over her shoulder, is clearly not a conventional heroine, the beginning of "The Maid of Saint Phillippe," in which the call of hearth and home brings Marianne from the "wild," seems to promise a domestic *Bildungsroman,* the story of a girl who gives up her tomboyish youth to become a "housewife."

Yet the remainder of Chopin's story resists the domestication of the gun-toting Marianne. Chopin first eliminates the town altogether, and with it the model of femininity represented by its housewives. Under the threat of an English raid (the story is set in 1763), the French inhabitants of Saint Phillippe quit the village, moving to a more secure trading post in western Louisiana. Only Marianne's father stays behind. While this plot frees Marianne from the potential influence of the domestic mothers, it also leaves a heroine who is the sole servant of her father, with no choice "but to follow his will; whatever that may be" (119). Chopin liberates Marianne by reversing dependencies between father and daughter: "Marianne worked and hunted and grew strong and stronger. The old man was more and more like a child to her. When she was not with him, he would sit for hours upon a rude seat under the apple-tree, with a placid look of content in his old dim eyes" (120). When her father finally dies, Marianne finds herself "with no will to obey in the world but her own. Then her heart was as strong as oak and her nerves were like iron" (120). Chopin's story suggests that only life in a wilderness that demands the development of physical and emotional self-reliance and strength can enable a woman to recognize her own will.

Orphaned and independent, Marianne, like Hope Leslie, faces one final threat to her autonomy: romance. When the former inhabitants of Saint Phillippe hear of her father's death, they urge

181

Marianne to join them in the new village. Most persistent in his en-treaties is Captain Vaudry, who uses the threat of an untamed wil-derness to coerce Marianne into her "proper" domestic role.

> "Ah, Marianne, you do not know what life is, here in this wild
> America. Let the curé of Kashashia say the words that will
> make you my wife, and I will take you to a land, child, where
> men barter with gold, and not with hides and peltries. Where
> you shall wear jewels and silk and walk upon soft and velvet
> carpets. Where life can be a round of pleasure. I do not say these
> things to tempt you; but to let you know that existence holds
> joys you do not dream of—that may be yours if you will."
> (121–22)

In reducing the strong and iron-nerved heroine to a "child," Vaudry
reveals the infantilizing nature of his wish to remove Marianne from
the wilderness in which she has physical and economic autonomy,
and to place her instead in a socioeconomic sphere in which "men
barter with gold," while women are superfluous domestic orna-ments. Chopin's desire to escape the romance plot, with its seem-ingly inevitable ending in marriage and motherhood, is represented
by Marianne's response to Vaudry's proposal.

> "Do you not know, Captain Vaudry," she said with savage resis-
> tance, "I have breathed the free air of forest and stream, till it is
> in my blood now. I was not born to be the mother of slaves."
> "Oh, how can you think of slaves and motherhood! Look
> into my eyes, Marianne, and think of love."
> "I will not look into your eyes, Captain Vaudry," she mur-
> mured, letting the quivering lids fall upon her own, "with your
> talk and your looks of love—of love! You have looked it before,
> and you have spoken it before till the strength would go from
> my limbs and leave me feeble as a little child, till my heart
> would beat like that of one who has been stricken. Go away,
> with your velvet and your jewels and your love. Go away to
> your France and to your treacherous kings; they are not for
> me." (122)

Through Marianne, Chopin exposes the debilitating consequences
of women's "proper" roles as wives and mothers. She notes, too,

that the sacrifices women must make in marriage—associated by Marianne with slavery—are veiled by the rhetoric of love and romance.

In place of the romance plot offered by Vaudry, Marianne chooses the wilderness tale, which Chopin presents as a more enabling narrative for female heroes. Marianne's final rhetorical flourish literalizes Chopin's phrase, "savage resistance": " 'Freedom is left for me!' exclaimed the girl, seizing her gun that she lifted upon her shoulder. 'Marianne goes to the Cherokees! You cannot stay me; you need not try to. Hardships may await me, but let it be death rather than bondage' " (122). The conclusion of the story reverses the direction of Marianne's quest. Turning her back on the village, Marianne undergoes a frontier and not a domestic initiation. Through her wilderness plot, Chopin liberates her heroine from domesticating models of femininity, from restriction by patriarchal will, and from the seduction of romance. By choosing the forest over the home, independence over romance, and Indians over whites, Marianne breaks free from her "bondage" to the constraining gender conventions of her day.

183

When Kate Chopin wrote "The Maid of Saint Phillippe" in 1891, extra-vagance in nature was still a powerful metaphor for women's potential to break from the conventions that formed their social prisons. The ease with which Chopin sends her heroine to the Indians with the expectation not of captivity and torture but of peace and independence, shows the continuing influence on later American women writers of authors such as Rowson and Sedgwick, who used the captivity narrative and its wilderness setting to demonstrate the constraints placed on women in white culture and to question white women's "proper" character and domain. By the time Chopin published *The Awakening* in 1899, however, extra-vagance no longer seemed as feasible for a woman hero. The novel's protagonist, Edna Pontellier, signals the inoperability for women of extra-vagance in nature when she falls asleep reading its greatest proponent: Ralph Waldo Emerson. This scene, depicting Edna ironically "deadened" by the poet of enthusiasm, prefigures the end of the novel, in which the heroine, attempting to break from social convention by venturing forth like Marianne into nature, drowns in the ocean. Escape into nature is no longer possible for a Chopin heroine: to offer resistance, even one no longer "savage," is ulti-mately self-destructive.

While escape into nature—and particularly to life among the Indians—may have lost its appeal for late-nineteenth-century women writers as a metaphorical release from the bondage of white womanhood, it did not disappear forever. Almost fifty years later, the "vanishing American" (as Leslie Fiedler termed Indians) re-turned in pages authored by white women, again helping white he-roines criticize and revise mainstream American gender roles. The reappearance of captivity in white women's writing is not surpris-ing, for the late twentieth century shares several important charac-teristics with the period when captivity romances flourished. First, many white women of the early nineteenth century and feminists of the late twentieth century share a belief in the existence and power of women as a community. Nancy Cott argues that modern Ameri-can feminism in fact arises from the "separate sphere" ideologies that first classed women together as a distinct, interpretable social unit.[1] In addition, both periods witnessed the emergence of orga-nized movements on behalf of African Americans: the abolition movement in the early nineteenth century and the civil rights move-ment of the mid-twentieth century. These antiracist efforts provided white women with practical and representational tools to express and rectify their own marginalization and victimization, even while, in speaking for and about people of color, they often rein-scribed racist stereotypes and reaffirmed a race hierarchy in which whites are the subjects and African Americans the objects of dis-course.[2] Finally, women in both eras produced a large body of liter-ature criticizing the condition of women and imagining a more equitable social order. Whether it is the wilderness extra-vagance of *Hope Leslie* or the otherworldly religious authority of domestic novels such as Susan Warner's *The Wide, Wide World* (1850) and Harriet Beecher Stowe's *Uncle Tom's Cabin* (1852), the visionary resolution typical of novels such as Alice Walker's *The Color Purple* (1982) or Gloria Naylor's *The Women of Brewster Place* (1983), the adoption of romantic American myths for women heroes in Mar-ilynne Robinson's *Housekeeping* (1980), or the sexual exuberance of Erica Jong's *Fear of Flying* (1973), women's literature in both pe-riods questioned patriarchal prescription and explored new narra-

184

tives, new communities, and new expressions of subjectivity for women. In the preceding chapters I have discussed the centrality of these three factors—faith in female community, belief in the power of a liberating literary vision, and the representational importance of people of color—to the captivity romances of the late eighteenth and early nineteenth centuries. In concluding, I will suggest how the captivity narratives' dialectics of imprisonment and extra-vagance, restriction and community, inscription and revision continue to animate white women's writing in America into the close of the twentieth century.

In the previous chapter, I argued that *Hope Leslie* shows captivity in the wilderness to be less threatening to white women than imprisonment by white men; Chopin's "The Maid of Saint Phillippe" stylized Sedgwick's story, removing the possibility of Indian capture altogether and thereby focusing on the white heroine's flight from the prison of dominant gender roles. Barbara Deming's *Prisons That Could Not Hold* brings captivity full circle, featuring *only* imprisonment by white men and explicitly attributing her captivities to the operation of patriarchy. Deming's text collects her auto-biographical accounts of two marches—one for civil rights in 1964, the other for women's rights in 1984—both resulting in her arrest and imprisonment. While Deming never enters the "wilderness" or experiences kidnapping by captors of color, her narrative charts her awakening to feminism through her recognition of and challenge to her culture's racist stereotypes, occasioned by her increased awareness of her imprisonment in dominant discourse. In deploying the intersection of race and gender ultimately to reimagine the status of nation, Deming's text takes its place in a long tradition of captivity writing by white women in America. It articulates more explicitly than any previous work captivity's social implications and its subversive potential.

When Deming is first arrested in Albany, Georgia, for participating in a 1964 civil rights march, she sees imprisonment as a sign of the dominant culture's belief in strategic repression. "The act of putting a man in jail," she writes, "remains essentially the act of trying to wish that man out of existence" (1985, 2). By jailing blacks, women, and other protesters, white male authority attempts to repress difference based on race, gender, or ideology.

> The cop locks the door on us and walks off. Now we're out of mischief. The barred steel door has banged shut; the big key has made a lot of noise. They have "put us away." People still believe there is some magic in the turning of a key. (1)

Yet the fantasy of successful repression held by agents of cultural power is doomed to fail, as Deming shows with gentle irony.

> I am reminded of a fairy tale I once heard about a miser and his old slippers. One day they cause him embarrassment and he tries to throw them away. He isn't able to. He throws them out the window, he buries them in the garden, he tries to burn them, he travels to a distant country and drops them in a pond; but each time fate returns them to him, and each time in a way that causes him mischief. They are too much a part of him. If the miser could not get rid of his old slippers . . . But people persist in believing that they can put other people from them. (1–2)

Deming's fable suggests again what has been repeatedly demonstrated in the captivity story: far from becoming silenced, effaced, or buried by the act of imprisonment, society's "cast offs" instead gain a subjectivity that allows them to make even more "mischief." In short, imprisonment is constitutive and not repressive. Deming further suggests, by making her point through a fable, that the control claimed by the police is fictional, open to interpretation and revision; these acts are most successfully undertaken in *Prisons,* as in the captivity romances, by the collectives formed, not repressed, by imprisonment.

Membership in that revisionary community is offered to Deming, as it had been to earlier captives, by the circulation of life narratives among the nonconforming (that is, nonwhite, nonmale, nonmilitaristic) citizens whom the police sought to divide and regulate. After her release from the Georgia jail, Deming still feels

> bound . . . to the people of the Negro community of Albany, whose situation we had in some small measure shared during the two months we spent there, in and out of jail—those of us who were white better able now to imagine ourselves in their place, and they better able to feel close to us. (177)

Imprisonment removes people from the mainstream as *individuals*, but returns them as members of a *class;* while that collective identity permits the surveillance of its members, it also renders them capable of articulating connections between life experiences and subsequently of revising the assumptions fostered by the dominant culture (in Deming's case, for instance, the assumption that whites and blacks have no point of connection, no common experiences). Due to her new group consciousness, Deming is able to revise and elude, at least momentarily, the confines of identity written on and therefore limited to the individual body.

> Down the corridor I hear the small sounds of prisoners turning in bed or stirring, sighing. I sit there a long time, a peculiar joy rising in me, my sense of distance from all the others here more and more dissolving, a sense of kinship with them waking in me more and more. I reach out and grasp one of the bars of the cage with my hand. I have only to remember that gesture . . . I have a queer stirring in me, and it is as though my heart first bursts the bars that are my ribs, then bursts the bars of this cell, and then travels with great lightness and freedom down the corridor and into each stinking cell, acknowledging: yes, we are all of us one flesh. (22)

As in *Hope Leslie*, patriarchal, racist acts of imprisonment paradoxically result in acts of liberation and extra-vagance enacted, not by rugged individualists, but by members of a new community.

In earlier narratives, the captive's awareness of racial injustice gives her the distance from her home culture's ideology to begin questioning her position as a woman within dominant gender ideology. Deming's narrative repeats this pattern, using her participation in the civil rights movement to articulate and challenge her own status within patriarchy. Deming invokes the tactics of civil rights activism to argue that female separatism is a "new way, but a way that owes very much to that earlier movement" (194). The structure of her text, which pairs the narrative of her arrest in Georgia with an epistolary defense of "women-only" communities, also suggests that out of her experiences as a civil rights activist in the 1960s came Deming's faith in the power of female community, evident in her feminist writings of the 1970s and 1980s. Deming particularly links

187

the two narratives with the central image of bondage and release. In a passage worth quoting at length, Deming responds to the charge that women-only actions ignore fundamental and biological heterosocial bonds:

> When we come together in our women-only circles it is not to try to deny our bond with men; it is to *affirm* our bond with one another. The bond between male and female—yes, of course, it is fundamental. But let me add, Norma: it is not under any threat. It never has been. The bond that *has* been under threat—for centuries and centuries, for all the centuries of the patriarchy—is the bond between women and women. That bond, too, is fundamental. And biological. (Isn't it?) But we have been *forbidden* to affirm it. Our gathering together as we do now amounts in effect to civil disobedience—whether or not we decide, while together, to climb some military fence, block some entrance, commit some act for which we can be sent to jail. For the First Commandment patriarchy expects women to obey is: THOU SHALT BOND WITH MEN—AND MEN *ONLY*. THOU SHALT BOND WITH NO OTHER. . . . It's not irrelevant, I think, that you should have used the word "inescapable" to describe our relation to men. For they have tried to make a natural bond into something more than that—or rather, less than that: tried to make it bondage. The word "bond" itself is a tricky one, I find. I have just looked it up in the dictionary. "That which binds or restrains: fetter, shackle . . . confinement." Though a little later: "that which binds, joins . . . connecting link . . ." There really should be two distinct words, shouldn't there?— one for the link which does not confine, one for the link which does? The fact that there are *not* two words says much about the patriarchy. (192)

Like earlier captives and the women novelists who adapted their narratives, Deming sees female "bonding"—the formation of female community—as the surest means to dissolve patriarchal "bondage." "If we can hope to win something in the struggle in which we are engaged," Deming concludes, "it is perhaps above all with this love-for-more-than-one that we are armed" (121).

By resisting racism and misogyny, Deming's "struggle" ultimately involves revising the meaning of America itself. On their walk in celebration of women's history, the marchers are stopped by a hostile group of Vietnam veterans, who jab flags at them "like brandished weapons" (214). "So there on the bridge at Waterloo," Deming writes, "the question was asked us again and again: 'Why didn't we love our country?' The question within that question, I'd say: 'Why don't we love the patriarchy?'" (215). Deming argues that "we could best act out of love of our country by challenging it to make some necessary changes" (215).

Deming, like Rowson, Cheney, and Sedgwick before her, contends that America's betterment, its growth, can best be achieved through the well-being of its women. For women to be happy, Deming joins her predecessors in claiming, they must have revisionary extra-vagance. It is significant that both events described by Deming, organized to rouse America's conscience, are marches. "It felt good to be on the road like this again," Deming says after commencing the Seneca march.

> Yes, it recalled the miles I had walked in the sixties. Our signs speaking in one way. Our feet speaking without words. Speaking our refusal to sit still and let things stay as they are. Speaking our dismay and speaking our hopes. Blue and Quinn had learned a song from the women at Northwoods which we slow-chanted: WALK, WALK, WALK FOR PEACE. WALK OVER THE LAND—a stride taken for each accented word. (197)

189

Like Sedgwick, Deming is well aware of the dangers that attend female extra-vagance: rape, physical and verbal abuse, imprisonment. Deming also makes clear, however, the revisionary significance of her actions: to walk is to "take strides," to refuse passivity. Deming's ultimate faith that women's activity will revise the narratives that imprison them is represented by the image she uses to end her narrative. On leaving prison, Deming writes, "At the first steps I had taken, outside the cell, I had felt that I had to learn all over again how to put one foot in front of the other. Again the world seemed all new. To walk! I feel as changed as though I had found that I could fly" (125). "To walk" is to be acquitted, freed from the charges for which one has been imprisoned. For Deming, as for other captives, extra-vagance (the ability "to walk") is to be released from one's bondage, and to escape the patriarchal charge that a woman is "guilty" by virtue of her gender.

The captivity narrative has most clearly survived as a literary form in a genre apparently quite different from Deming's text, yet very similarly structured: romance novels mass-marketed for female consumers. Romance plots in which innocent white heroines learn to love noble Indian braves are so popular that one journal catering to the genre, *Romantic Times,* offers a Lifetime Achievement Award for Best Indian Series. In a survey of romance novels containing white-Indian love relationships, Peter Beidler reports finding eight published in 1990 alone that feature Indian captivities. These novels differ from the captivity romances of the late eighteenth and early nineteenth centuries in their focus on sex between white women and Indian men, an emphasis that suggests that Indians and white women are primarily "sexual" beings whose relationship to culture comes only through (hetero)sexuality. In contrast, Rowson and Sedgwick favored other relationships, particularly those between white and Indian women, using "romance" only as a second-string strategy for culture-crossing. In the modern romances, however, heterosexual romance, rather than homosocial bonds between women, remains the prime, although not the exclusive, means for women to discover their extra-vagance.

Despite this difference, however, captivity appears to function for the heroines of modern romances much as it did for Deming and for earlier captive heroines, creating metaphorical distance from white "civilization." Above all, the modern romance continues to offer, through its representation of captivity, a description and revision of the atrocities imposed on women of all races not by Indians, but by white men. Beidler notes that in almost all the Indian romances he surveyed, the principal villains are white men (100). In a novel typical of the genre, Cassie Edwards' *Savage Sunrise* (1993), Ashley Bradley, following the accidental death of her mother and stepfather, is taken in by her stepbrother, Calvin Wyatt, a wealthy New Orleans businessman. Calvin gazes with "a look of possession, of ownership" (32) at his young ward, forcing her to accept expensive presents in return for which he expects sex. When Ashley refuses, Calvin tries to rape her. This scene ties Ashley's fate to that of Star Woman, the Indian who, in the novel's opening, is abducted and sold in New Orleans' Indian slave trade, also operated by Calvin Wyatt. Indian and white women are represented and linked as commodities, bodies bought and sold for the pleasure and profit of white men. This association between the degradation of white and Indian women continues throughout the novel. When Ashley escapes from her stepbrother during the attempted rape, for instance, she is abducted by slave traders, thereby showing that women of all races are the victims of white male greed and lust. Demonstrating (as *Hope Leslie* had begun to do) that Indian "captivity" is a relative freedom compared to the slavery imposed on women by white men, the romance novels make explicit the more subtle critique of white patriarchy offered by earlier authors.

Romance novelists such as Cassie Edwards give their heroines the distance to criticize the operations of white patriarchy by allowing them to cross cultures; from their imagined place "outside" white America, contemporary heroines, like their captive predecessors, unlearn their racist stereotypes and reassess their identifications with white men on the basis of shared racial identity. Ashley is rescued from the slave trade by an Osage warrior, Yellow Thunder, whom she initially distrusts, for "she was guilty of the prejudices of all white people who felt that Indians were *savages*." She quickly overcomes her distrust, however, for "she was finding out who was the true savage among those whom she knew, and his skin was not of a copper color!" (61). Asking that Ashley give him not her body but "every essence of her moods, of her hopes and desires, of her *dreams*" (64), Yellow Thunder, who operates from the principles taught him by his mother, wins Ashley's heart. Together they return to the Osage village where, unlike earlier fictional captors and captives, they marry, raise a family, and live happily ever after.

The heroine's revision of "the prejudices of all white people," here as in the captivity romances, is a prerequisite and ultimately a pretext for the white woman's more sustained mission: the reimagining of white womanhood and the formation of bonds with other women. Like Hope Leslie and Rachel Dudley, Ashley falls "instantly in love with this wilderness" (196) where she discovers new strengths, primarily through her attachments to other women, both white and Osage. Ashley and Yellow Thunder escape Calvin's imprisonment with the help of Juliana, a white woman Ashley befriends after witnessing Juliana's abduction and rape by her step-brother. Juliana later joins them at the Osage village, where she too falls in love with an Indian warrior. Along their escape route, Yellow Thunder and Ashley are aided by a series of independent women, from the innkeeper Anna to the voodoo witch Petulia. Once among the Osage, Ashley worries that her white gender socialization will make her a burden to the "active, hard-working people," until an Indian woman teaches her the Indian customs and "made her feel as though she belonged" (247). The novel resolves as its many captive women—Star Woman, Juliana, Bright Eyes—are released from bondage and their captors punished, both acts accomplished through the strong friendships among women.

At the same time as it employs the earlier captivity romances' vision of the heroine's escape from the constraints of white woman-hood through the interracial and mostly female communities she develops while crossing cultures, *Savage Sunrise* also shows more clearly than its fictional predecessors that neither white authors nor their heroines can ever be "free" of dominant discourses of race and gender. In her effort to create a contrast with greedy, possessive white men, for instance, Edwards characterizes Indian men by using either white advertising's image of the "modern man" (emotional and giving, the Indian brave always ensures that his partner achieves orgasm) or nineteenth-century imperialism's image of the "noble savage" (217). More disturbing is Edwards' appropriation of slavery and the brutal experiences of Indian women to metaphorize white women's less easily named constraints. Not only does she equate the ordeals of white and Indian women, Edwards implies that the former are in greater need and are more deserving of rescue: given the choice of rescuing Ashley or his sister who is held in bondage, Yellow Thunder chooses to save the white heroine.

Not surprisingly, since it is published, advertised, and sold by companies owned and operated almost entirely by white men, *Savage Sunrise* is no more capable of eluding dominant gender discourses than it is of escaping racial stereotypes. Ashley moves from the "ownership" of her stepbrother to the possessive custody of Yellow Thunder, who repeatedly refers to Ashley as "my woman." In the end, Ashley, who "felt as though she were in heaven, having a husband, a true home, and now a child" (444), is reinscribed in the language of domestic femininity that granted Calvin ownership of her and from which, therefore, she has fled in the first place. Unlike Deming's narrative, furthermore, these contemporary romances, in retaining the trope of captivity, imply that white women still need an excuse for investigating their whiteness and their womanhood, particularly in relationship to one another: women cannot simply choose to have adventures outside their cultural "homes."

At the same time as these novels demonstrate the impossibility of ever completely crossing (out) the borders of one's cultural discourses, however, their tremendous popularity with women readers shows the continuing appeal of stories of racial crossing that allow white heroines to resist being controlled—sexually or textually—by white men. As texts as different as *Prisons That Could Not Hold* and *Savage Sunrise* demonstrate, the dynamics of the captivity story —challenges to racial identity leading to a strong gender critique, imprisonment and captivity giving rise to empowering community, enforced confinement bringing about revisionary extra-vagance— remain central to white women's writing in twentieth-century America. "WE WILL CONNECT OUR WOMEN'S PAST TO OUR FEMINIST FUTURE," promises a flier quoted by Deming (287). In studying the captivity stories written by white women in America, *Bound and Determined* has attempted just such a project. To explore white women's persistent concern with containment and community— with the shifting boundaries of culture and identity—is to understand the threads that connect contemporary women writers with their predecessors and to provide the basis for a different tradition in American literature: the tradition of the captivity narrative.

1. Mary Rowlandson's narrative has remained popular since its initial publication in 1682. Editions of Rowlandson's narrative were printed in 1720, 1773, 1792, 1828, and 1913, and the narrative was included in anthologies edited by Charles Lincoln (1930), Richard VanDerBeets (1973), and Alden Vaughan and Edward Clark (1981) (Vaughan 1983, 55–56). Patty Hearst's story equally "captured" the national imagination. Hearst was the subject of 103 articles between March 1974 and February 1977, in journals ranging from the *National Review* to *The Ladies Home Journal* and *TV Guide,* and authored by "authorities" ranging from Hearst's attorney, F. Lee Bailey, to the Hearst family cook. Between February 1974 and November 1976, *Time* carried twenty-nine stories about Hearst, while *Newsweek* in the same period featured forty stories. While the drama of Patty-Turned-Tania appeared to hold the public's interest, the more foregrounded story was of Tania Punished. *Newsweek* featured Hearst on its cover three times during the court case, under the banners "Patty on Trial" (February 2, 1976), "Patty's Defense" (March 1, 1976), and "Guilty!" (March 29, 1976).

2. Roy Harvey Pearce first expressed the opinion that captivity literature authored after the eighteenth century is unworthy of critical study (1947, 16), thereby severing earlier texts from nineteenth-century women authors. Pearce also expressed the critical assumption that the captivity narratives resurfaced in the work of male authors. Claiming that the captivity narrative "enters literary history proper in *Edgar Huntly*" (1), Pearce denies women their place in the founding of literary history "proper." This assumption is repeated in the most extensive study of the captivity tradition in American literature, Richard Slotkin's *Regeneration through Violence.* Slotkin accords only one page to Lydia Maria Child's *Hobomok* and four to Catharine Sedgwick's *Hope Leslie.* In comparison, Slotkin accords Cooper's Leatherstocking tales over one hundred pages of text. After the Puritans, then, the captivity narrative apparently disappeared, to emerge again most importantly in the pages of male authors. Slotkin's chapter titles, including "The Search for a Hero and the Problem of the 'Natural

Man,'" "Evolution of a National Hero: Farmer to Hunter to Indian," and "Man without a Cross: The Leatherstocking Myth," explain why Slotkin may not have recognized wilderness mythologies authored by women, and show what a difference such a recognition might have made to the categories that Slotkin claims have shaped our national mythology.

Even feminist analyses of the captivity narratives can work with assumptions detrimental to post-seventeenth-century women authors. In her insightful analysis of Puritan captivity narratives, for instance, Tara Fitzpatrick assumes that, while the narratives she studies—particularly those of Rowlandson, Duston, and Swarton—are subversive of cultural hegemony, narratives authored after 1800 are not worth attention, not, as Pearce and VanDerBeets assert, because they are overly sensational, but because they are overly hegemonic. After the narrative of John Williams (1707), Fitzpatrick writes, "the promise of personal salvation in the wilderness, outside the hedge, would be no longer subversive but instead triumphal" (1991, 19). There have been excellent considerations of the individual captivity romances, especially *Hope Leslie,* by critics such as Barbara Ann Bardes and Suzanne Gossett, Nina Baym, Mary Kelley, Lucy Maddox, Dana Nelson, Carroll Smith-Rosenberg, and Sandra Zagarell, and two critics, Dawn Lander Gherman and Leland Person, Jr., have examined the captivity novels as a genre. There has also been groundbreaking feminist work on the captivity narratives, especially by Mitchell Breitwieser, Tara Fitzpatrick, Annette Kolodny, June Namias, Teresa Toulouse, and Laurel Thatcher Ulrich, to all of whom I am indebted.

3. See, for example, Pearce (1947) and VanDerBeets (1973).

4. On the imperialist association of Indians and nature, see Richard Drinnon, who argues that for white Anglo-Americans "'going native' has always been tantamount to 'going nature.'" To prevent "going native/nature," Drinnon argues, Puritans converted bodies "from instruments of rhythmic pleasure into instruments of domination and aggression" (1980, xv). Americans can undo the "correlation between repression and violence," Drinnon asserts, by imagining "the relatively free body in a less repressive society" (xv). Drinnon still locates freedom in the body, whereas for the women under discussion here the persistent em-bodiment of freedom becomes part of their constraint, leading them to assert that identity and cultural belonging are determined in the realm of discourse and inscribed on bodies; freedom can therefore only ever be, as Drinnon acknowledges, relative.

5. See my discussion of the Hearst narrative in chapter 3, below.

6. Captivity literature was never generically static, nor did it do consistent "cultural work." Early narratives, for example, centered on the biblical metaphor of the captive Israel waiting patiently to be delivered from bondage by divine intervention. Given that metaphorical structure, the most "proper" attribute of the Puritan female captive was passivity, all agency belonging to God and His masculine deputies. In contrast, popular anthologies of the nineteenth century celebrated women who took up axes and even rifles to resist or escape their Indian attackers. Generic differences such as these suggest regional and historical changes in the relative agency accorded frontier women, especially with their husbands away at war. The increased insistence on women's active resistance to capture may also indicate a desire to reinscribe the antagonism between white women and people of color at a time when abolition attempted to diminish the distance between those groups.

Even within each period there are significant differences between narratives. Seventeenth-century captive Hannah Duston, for instance, who took up a tomahawk and murdered her captors while they slept, seems more like the "heroic mothers" of the nineteenth-century frontier than a passive captive awaiting divine rescue. These changes register and shape changing conceptions of female authorship and appropriately "feminine" style, different proximities to the colonial/Native American encounter, various uses made of the narratives (religious sermons, anti-French propaganda, financial gain for the captive/author), and shifting attitudes toward "race" and "gender" in American culture. Other critics such as Pearce, VanDerBeets, and Derounian-Stodola and Levernier have noted the changes in captivity narratives over time. But the changes critics note tend to serve the interests of white men (by reinforcing ministerial authority in the seventeenth century, for instance, and by justifying white violence against Indians in the nineteenth). I wish to explore the changes brought about by women on their own behalf.

7. For a compelling discussion of how narrative genres, particularly autobiography, shape gender identity, see L. Gilmore (1994).

8. I take the concept of "interpellation" from Louis Althusser, who argues in "Ideology and Ideological State Apparatuses" that "*all ideology has the function (which defines it) of 'constituting' concrete individuals as subjects*" (1971, 171). Althusser argues that power rests on the invisibility of ideological interpellation (those most invested in ideology believe themselves most outside its effects); therefore, social struggle relies on the consciousness of one's "naming" as subjects within an ideological discourse (175).

9. The inscription of a cross-cultural female community framed to strengthen white female subjectivity is what Laura Donaldson in *Decolonizing Feminism* (1992) calls the "Miranda Complex": the reduction of the native female "other" to a domesticated figure who consolidates and unifies the imperialist white female. Gayatri Chakravorty Spivak has criticized this textual gesture, which she calls the mainstay of "the project of imperialism" (1991, 907), arguing that as "the female individualist, not-quite/not-male, articulates herself in shifting relationship to what is at stake, the 'native female' as such (*within* discourse, *as* a signifier) is excluded from any share in this emerging norm" (799). Spivak further suggests that imperialism perpetuates itself in part by insisting on a single, "individualist" subjectivity divorced from collective profit (if whites are "individuals," then they are innocent of the acts committed by, for instance, the United States Army or the Bureau of Indian Affairs). In constructing communal identities and demonstrating that their social status depends on how and with whom they identify, the captives make clear the ideological and social (one could say "political") stakes of identity formation without proposing a utopian life based on no "identity" at all.

10. See Axtell, "The White Indians," in Axtell (1985), and Kolodny (1993). Linda Kerber has argued that "one of the major factors in the colonists' perception of Indians as uncivilized was the Indians' tendency to define gender relations differently than did Europeans. Europeans were particularly dismayed when Indian women played roles that were not subservient or when Indian societies did not display a separation of spheres as Europeans understood them" (1988, 19).

11. For a fascinating study of the association of "whiteness" and "Americanness," and of the ways both are rendered invisible in order to maintain their normative status, see Ruth Frankenberg (1993), especially 191–235. Eric Cheyfitz makes clear that whiteness and its imperialist roots can only become visible and be made comprehensible when whites are "in transition between cultures and between groups within our own culture" (1991, xvi). My thinking about the critique enabled by captives' culture-crossing is indebted to his insightful analysis.

12. I take the facts of the BLO action from David Firestone, "While Barbie Talks Tough, G.I. Joe Goes Shopping," *New York Times*, sec. A (December 31, 1993), 12, and from a National Public Radio Weekend Edition segment done by Scott Simon on January 1, 1994.

13. I take the phrase "compulsory heterosexuality" from Adrienne Rich's 1980 essay, "Compulsory Heterosexuality and Lesbian Existence." In that essay, Rich addresses the modes in which patriarchal society has

NOTES TO PAGE 14

"imposed, managed, organized, propagandized, and maintained by force" (1986, 50) women's dependence on men through heterosexual structures that women can never freely "choose." As a counterstructure, Rich proposes "lesbian existence," which she names as any erotic, emotional, or intellectual relationship between women. My own thoughts on the empowerment women in captivity literature derive from other women are clearly indebted to Rich's influential essay.

14. I have decided not to consider men's captivity narratives here. One reason for focusing on the narratives by women is that they far outnumber those of men: June Namias documents that between 1673 and 1763, 771 women were taken captive in New England, but only 270 men (1988, 131). Laurel Thatcher Ulrich provides a useful analysis of this fact, suggesting that women were more adaptive than men, who tried to escape more frequently and certainly resisted adoption and acculturation more thoroughly than women. Ulrich argues that women, who were brought up to expect that they would marry and thereby become a member of a "clan" perhaps socially alien to them and for whom they would be expected to perform several menial tasks, did not find captivity as disorienting as did men (1980, 202–14).

More to the point, Namias points out that male and female captives told different kinds of stories: "In the end, he *wins* and there are few real losses, no reconsideration of the project's worth, and no thoughts of what might be the personal consequences for the 'other'" (1988, 131). In contrast, women's narratives "leave the reader with the sense that even in the worst of situations, women can muster religious, physical, social, and psychological resources on their own. These messages of strength and independence for the 'weaker' sex were surely the gendered messages readers could find in these unusual stories of the American frontier" (90). While both sets of narratives thus contain "gendered messages," the male-coded tale—about solitary heroics in which nothing is compromised but the integrity of the "othered" enemy—has been celebrated and analyzed frequently enough, while the story of interracial knowledge and agency gained without the fiction of "freedom" has only begun to be explored.

My focus on white womanhood has also led me to exclude slave women's narratives—an even more potent testimony to gender and racial confinement—from consideration in this book. Many of my topics—the community that can arise from confinement, the collective revision of identity, the play with literary genres in order to revalue subjugated subjectivities—have already been explored in relation to women's slave narratives by critics such as Valerie Smith and Frances Smith Foster. I would like to think that the present study continues their work, insisting that white subjects too have a stake in revising discourses of race and gender in order to analyze and remedy the physical and discursive confinement and constraint of all peoples.

CHAPTER ONE

1. For a fuller discussion of the role of biology and science in nineteenth-century imperialism, see Cheyfitz's discussion in the first chapter of *The Poetics of Imperialism* (1991).

2. One of the earliest and most eloquent assessments of the deployment of the figure of the captive white woman to uphold patriarchal and imperialist ideology was made by Susan Howe, who addresses Mary Rowlandson directly: "You are a passive victim, captured and threatened by a racial enemy until God's providence (later a human hero) can effect your deliverance. You must shelter the masculine covenant as lost lady and lofty idol. You will water the American venture with your tears" (1991, 97). A number of critics have recently joined Howe in challenging the position that Puritan captives represent social and religious hegemony. See Breitwieser (1990), Fitzpatrick (1991), Kolodny (1984), Toulouse (1992), and Ulrich (1980).

3. Susan Howe points out that while critics have been quick to condemn Rowlandson's narrative for its racist stereotypes of Native Americans, no one has noted what she labels as an "equally insulting stereotype, that of a white woman as passive cipher in a controlled and circulated idea of Progress at whose zenith rides the hero-hunter (Indian or white) who will always rescue her" (1991, 96). My intention in this study is to continue Howe's work of noting the "insulting stereotypes" of white women circulated in accounts of captivity narratives, while also demonstrating the ways in which women "rescued" themselves from patriarchal inscription.

4. The "typical" captivity narrative, furthermore, expresses several paradoxical assumptions about the position and character of women, as Laurel Thatcher Ulrich has most persuasively argued. While ministers presented the captives' stories as tales of passive suffering, the narratives are also extraordinary documents of survival. Female captives such as Mary Rowlandson, Ulrich argues, survived captivity largely through their housewifery skills (Rowlandson takes her place in the community through her ability to sew), but also because of their familiarity with servility. Although Rowlandson hated and feared her captors, Ulrich writes, she "knew how to please them. Growing up in a hierarchal society, she had learned what it

meant to be an inferior" (1980, 228). While Ulrich's work is important in its recasting of the captive's "passivity" in light of the social training of women, one can go further to examine how, even in the most traditional narratives, women not only passively endure but discover active talents their home environment would never have brought to light, much less nurtured.

5. The narrative of Experience Bozarth, for instance, appears in the Drake (1851), the Frost (1854), and the Withers (1895) anthologies. Mrs. Merrill's narrative appears in Withers and in both the 1854 and 1859 Frost anthologies, as does that of Elizabeth Zane. Rarely does the narrative of a female captive appear in three anthologies (Jemima Howe, Mrs. Clendennin, and Mercy Harbison, the last two being women who escaped, share that honor). In contrast, neither Drake, Frost, nor Withers anthologizes the narratives of women who stayed among the Indians, such as Frances Slocum or Eunice Williams. On the uses of captivity literature as propaganda, see Axtell (1985), Pearce (1947), Sieminski (1980), and Slotkin (1973).

6. For a fuller discussion of the differences between Mather's depiction of Duston and "the flesh-and-blood woman," see Ulrich (1980), 168–70, and Fitzpatrick (1991), 12–17.

7. Howard Peckham, who includes the Jemison narrative in his 1954 collection, *Captured by Indians,* notes that Seaver, a local physician, took down Jemison's narrative in the first person, although "clearly succumbing to frequent rhetorical flourishes beyond the expression of Mary Jemison" (78).

8. For a fuller discussion of the captivities of Jemison, Slocum, and Williams, see Dawn Lander Gherman, who argues that Williams chooses neither to return nor to remain. Williams, Gherman asserts, had no choice (no voice) at all (1975, 77–78). I agree that one must be cautious about assuming that, at least as a youth, Williams or any other female captive was allowed much imput in the tug-of-war over her identifications; Williams, however, expresses a preference for Indian manners, thereby evincing more agency than Gherman is willing to concede.

9. Annette Kolodny addresses "notions that a woman simply could not master the skills necessary for survival at the edge of the frontier without becoming either masculinized or Indianized" (1982, 167). Kolodny attributes this to the fact that men simply didn't believe women *could* thrive in the wilderness. As I will argue at the conclusion of this chapter, men knew, through the captivity narratives, a variety of stories in which women

prospered in the wilderness without becoming brutal or immoral; they went to considerable lengths to ignore and discredit such stories. The issue is not, as Kolodny argues, one of disbelief, but of anxiety and willed blindness. On the "Indianization" of white women, see also James Axtell's groundbreaking work (1985), especially 302–27, and Namias (1988).

10. When the editor of *The American Preceptor* included Howe's story in both its 1801 and 1818 editions, he excised the story of her trials at the hands of her "rescuers," apparently not considering it fit reading matter for future Americans.

11. Cheyfitz similarly argues throughout his excellent study, *The Poetics of Imperialism,* that "translation was, and still is, the central act of European colonization and imperialism in the Americas" (1991, 104).

CHAPTER TWO

1. In *Regeneration through Violence,* Richard Slotkin makes the compelling argument that Mather took up Mercy Short's cause with such relish because it afforded him a way to deal with the forces previously attributed to the Indians without the necessity of conquering the wilderness. "Now the devil was coming forth," Slotkin writes, "and the battle could be fought in the limited wilderness of a girl's mind and a small room, instead of the dark and limitless wilderness outside" (1973, 131). Timberg also suggests a connection between witchcraft and kidnapping.

2. On the captives' disruption of boundaries that the ministers used their narratives to uphold, see Fitzpatrick (1991), 21.

3. On the "Indianization" of the white captive, see Axtell (1985), 302–27.

4. Several critics have noted the "double" nature of Rowlandson's perspective. Gherman refers to the "Allegorical and the Realistic" (1975, 56) levels of Rowlandson's text; Kolodny traces separate "spiritual" and "physical" journeys that "get progressively sorted out" (1984, 18); and Breitwieser finds in Rowlandson's tale "a collision between cultural ideology and the real" (1990, 4). Susan Howe notes, "Mary Rowlandson's thoroughly reactionary figuralism requires that she obsessively confirm her orthodoxy to readers at the same time she excavates and subverts her own rhetoric" (1991, 100). Arguing that "God's text in Rowlandson's text is counterpoint, shelter, threat" (124), Howe concludes that the "trick of her text is its mix" (127). In what is to my mind the most persuasive discussion of the divided narrative, Teresa Toulouse claims that Rowlandson's text re-

veals "an angry woman's self-abnegating means of expressing compliance and at the same time voicing accusation and condemnation" (1992, 667), concluding that Rowlandson thereby represents "the anger and desire for defining specialness of the socially (and sexually) disenfranchised expressed in ways that both use and strain the boundaries of orthodoxy" (672). Tara Fitzpatrick has argued, as I do at the conclusion of this chapter, that the dual, "sometimes dueling," voices of Rowlandson's narrative may more logically be attributed to two distinct speakers: Rowlandson and Increase Mather (1991, 2). I am also indebted to a paper on Rowlandson's "two narratives" given by Laura Henigman in the advanced American literature seminar, Columbia University, spring 1986.

5. Susan Howe has similarly argued that Rowlandson's narrative demonstrates that "all individual identity may be transformed—assimilated" (1991, 96), thereby challenging Puritan faith in the fixity of character.

6. Here I am also taking issue with the argument advanced by Nancy Armstrong and Leonard Tennenhouse in *The Imaginary Puritan* (1992). Armstrong and Tennenhouse contend that Rowlandson's consistent desire to return to her home culture caused her to recreate "Englishness" in writing, thereby giving rise to modern authorship as the individual representative of a collectivity. While I agree that Rowlandson ultimately comes to speak for a collectivity—white women (see my discussion in chap. 4)—I disagree that she expresses consistent desire for her home culture or that she successfully reintegrates into that culture. The tentative language Armstrong and Tennenhouse use to describe Rowlandson's return—"Rowlandson ends up *pretty much* where she begins, in the bosom of her family and friends. Indeed, she *seems* to return to the same community that was in place before the Indian uprising, and her return *appears* to restore that community's original state of wholeness" (211, emphasis mine)—suggests their inability to resolve Rowlandson's closing assertion of her separateness from English culture with their claim of her represented wholeness.

7. For details of the Great Sioux Uprising of 1862, I am indebted to Duane Schultz's excellent history.

8. On the pressures placed on captives to confess to being raped, see Brownmiller (1975); see also Namias (1988), 81–82.

9. See chapter 4 for a fuller discussion of the dangers of exciting "sympathy" in soldiers.

10. On the ideology of "true womanhood," see Welter (1966), Kelley (1984), Tompkins (1985). For a full discussion of how that ideology en-

abled "bonds of womanhood," see especially Cott (1977) and Smith-Rosenberg (1985).

11. I borrow from Rachel Blau DuPlessis (1985) the concept of "writing beyond the ending"—particularly the acceptable narrative endings of marriage and death—in order to inscribe new and more empowering subjectivities for women.

12. See Pearce (1947), 9–13, and VanDerBeets (1973), xx–xxiv. Both critics argue that the "sensationalized" narratives put an end to the captivity tradition in America. After the eighteenth century, VanDerBeets writes, "for all practical purposes and with few exceptions, the development of the narratives of Indian captivity culminated—in the travesty of the penny dreadful" (xxiv).

13. On popular accounts of the "noble savage," see Fiedler (1968), Nash (1967), 65, and Slotkin (1973).

14. In *Woman in the Nineteenth Century,* Margaret Fuller documents the close alliance between those working for abolition and those working for women's rights: "Of all its banners, none has been more steadily upheld, and under none have more valor and willingness for real sacrifices been shown, than that of the champions of the enslaved African. And this band it is, which, partly from a natural following out of principles, partly because many women have been prominent in that cause, makes, just now, the warmest appeal on behalf of Woman" (1971, 28). Fuller argues that "there exists in the minds of men a tone of feeling toward women as toward slaves" (33), and that men treat women accordingly: "It may well be an Anti-Slavery party that pleads for Woman, if we consider merely that she does not hold property on equal terms with men; so that, if a husband dies without making a will, the wife, instead of taking at once his place as head of the family, inherits only a part of his fortune, often brought him by herself, as if she were a child, or ward only, not an equal partner" (31). For a full discussion of white women's appropriation of women of color through analogies such as Fuller's, see Sanchez-Eppler (1991).

15. On the connection of discourses of race and gender on the American frontiers, see Barnett (1975), Herzog (1983), and especially Riley (1984), who similarly argues that when frontier life caused women to reconsider stereotypes that cast them as frail and helpless, they felt freer to reconsider stereotypes about Indians as well (122).

16. Tara Fitzpatrick notes a similar subversive power of authorship in Puritan women's narratives. As "the primary tellers of their tales," Fitzpatrick argues, "the women captives became the active authors of their

own histories, defying if never escaping the traditionally masculine authority and authorship central to the Puritan sexual order" (1991, 5).

17. For accounts of "initiation" patterns in the captivity narrative, see Pearce (1947), VanDerBeets (1984), and Vaughan (1983). James Axtell has documented that captives were frequently adopted as members of Indian families (1985, 302–4). The captives, Axtell writes, "were taught not only to speak and to endure as Indians but to act as Indians in the daily social and economic life of the community" (324). Since captives were also taught Indian gender socialization, Axtell concludes that "the boys enjoyed the better fate" (324).

18. Other captives report that captivity narratives they had read previous to their own capture influenced their expectations and perceptions of the Indians. Ann Coleson had read that the Sioux cut off women's breasts, roast them, and make their captives eat them, and seems surprised when this does not happen to her. Eliza Swan has read of numerous tortured captives. Consequently, when, bound to a tree early in her captivity, she sees an Indian hastening toward her with a lifted tomahawk, she sticks out her neck so he will not miss. Instead the Indian kisses her forehead in a token of friendship and frees her. Glenda Riley chronicles the horror stories of Indian atrocities circulated among white women on the frontier (1984, 83–119). Riley suggests that many of the so-called Indian massacres may have been caused when white settlers, rendered tense and fearful by these stories, overreacted to their new Indian neighbors.

19. Many captives note the unusually difficult labor performed by Indian women. Theresa Gowanlock, taken captive by Cree in 1885, notes that Indian women do all the tribe's work "while the big, lazy, good-for-nothing Indian looks about in idleness" (1885, 12). Sarah Larimer writes that Indian men consider work to be "unmanly" (1871, 178).

It seems to be a stretch of imagination to represent an Indian woman as an artist, when we contemplate her surroundings, recalling all her unsightliness—a creature who chops wood, carries water, brings home game, skins animals, dresses hides, attends horses, secures the pony for her husband to ride, assists him to mount, and then trudges after him on foot, carrying his youngest child on her back—finally, beaten, cuffed, and kicked to complete her degradation. It might be almost concluded that something by way of reform might be done for those unfortunate sisters of our own continent. It is believed that the Indian can never be enslaved, yet the Indian woman is already a slave of the worst kind, held by ignorance and love. Still, these unfortunate

squaws, unlovely though they appear, have gleams of womanly kindness, dull and perverted, doubtless; but, however small, the
Promethean spark glitters through the ashes of their lives. (183–84)

"The female, in many respects, is her husband's superior" (185), Larimer
concludes. Dawn Lander Gherman has noted that tales of the hardships
endured by Indian women have been a mainstay of early American political
propaganda. "The insidious side-effect of this propaganda in white culture," Gherman argues, "was that white women were implicitly told to be
content with their lot, for, among aboriginal people, they would be treated
even worse" (1975, 160). For a similar argument, see Axtell (1985), 324.

20. The phrase is taken from Eve Kosofsky Sedgwick's *Between Men*.
In that study, Sedgwick argues that patriarchal power is created and perpetuated through male homosocial desire, in which the principal bond exists
between the male rivals and not between either of the men and the desired
woman. Through their traffic in the shared female object, the men ensure
their own position as subjects in control of a symbolic economy in which
the woman figures only as a prized commodity.

21. In 1967, David Richards first proposed that Mather served as editor of Rowlandson's narrative. See also Vaughan and Clark (1981), 32;
Minter (1974), 336–37; Breitwieser (1990), 198; and Toulouse (1992),
656.

22. Several critics have commented on ministerial "improvements" on
colonial captives' narratives, particularly Rowlandson's and Duston's. See,
for instance, Slotkin (1973), 112–15; Ulrich (1980), 167–72; Toulouse
(1992), 656; and Fitzpatrick (1991), 1–27.

23. The popularity of the captivity anthologies is attested to by their
frequent reprintings. Drake's anthology alone appeared in seven editions
between 1841 and 1870 (Vaughan 1983, 23).

24. Although Frost did not admire the Indians, he seems less threatened by a challenge to racial than to gender identity.

Numerous instances are on record of Indians abandoning their wig-
wams, throwing off their habits and religion, and becoming creditable
members of civilized society. Examples of the opposite change are rare;
yet some few have occurred. But it has oftener happened, that white
children, when captured and brought up by the Indians, have forgotten
early associations, or if too young to forget, have often disregarded the
differences of color, and become real Indians. (1854, 227)

Frost admits that "racial" identity is constructed and therefore mutable (if a white child can become a "real" Indian, can there be an essential racial difference between whites and Indians?), but remains firm in his sense that gender identity is fixed and stable.

CHAPTER THREE

1. Occasionally the press itself drew the implicit connection between the oil crisis and its "villains" (Arabs) and manifest destiny and its "villains" (Indians). On March 14, 1974, for instance, *Newsweek* reported, "The annual summer re-enactment of Custer's Last Stand, a tourist spectacle presented by local boosters in Big Horn County, Montana, will be scratched this year. Cash shortages, together with fears that the gasoline crisis will scare tourists away from the scene, are combining to ring down the curtain of the year's restaging of the famous 1876 massacre" (15). Now Arabs, taking the place of their nineteenth-century counterparts, are scaring white "tourists" from the frontier and are "scratching" the "spectacle" of white male heroism—even failed heroism—in the west.

2. See Slotkin (1973), 116–20.

3. For a fuller discussion of Short and Hearst, see Timberg (1983).

4. *The Exorcist* was written by William Peter Blatty and directed by William Friedkin. Hearst's autobiography had a male coauthor, Alvin Moscow.

5. One of the "black" captors was actually a white man, Bill Harris, in disguise. Perhaps due to Steven Weed's mistaken report that two black men had abducted Hearst, the press repeatedly characterized the SLA as a black militant group, even though its leader, Cinque Maume (Donald DeFreeze), was the only black member.

6. In *The Making of Tania Hearst,* David Boulton similarly argues that Hearst, a "gun-toting Barbie-doll stalking the fascist insect which preys on the life of the people" (1975, 149), was by the end of her captivity "no longer a little girl but a grown woman, no longer a helpless victim of uncomprehended social forces but a shaper and moulder of those forces. Her parents had taught her to be a 'nice' girl; the SLA had taught her to be a 'bad' girl, and she liked that better" (218).

7. For a description of the FBI campaign and its terminology, see Weed (1976). Weed's book makes clear both how attractive the rescue plot remains for men and how impossible that plot is rendered in the twentieth century. While Weed's title, *My Search for Patty Hearst,* suggests an active quest to retrieve his kidnapped fiancée, the text itself is a story of frustrating inactivity with more pacing than searching.

8. Hearst was indicted for armed robbery on March 11, 1976; the Harrises were indicted for kidnapping on September 29, 1976. See Hearst (1982), 424.

CHAPTER FOUR

1. For a fuller discussion of how women's autobiographies, particularly those employing cultural "crossing," blur distinctions between fact and fiction in order to achieve agency for women, see Leigh Gilmore (1994).

2. Nancy Cott notes that literacy among women approximately doubled in the period between 1780 and 1840 (1977, 15); this growing literacy, Cott argues, "swelled the audience for female journalists and fiction writers" (7). See also Davidson (1986) and Kelley (1984).

3. See Pearce (1947), 13, and Haberly (1976), 432.

4. The elaborate nature of White's opening metaphor, as well as its depiction of White appearing before the "bar of criticism," would seem to suggest that the narrative bears touches of artistic embellishment. If White did indeed experience the adventures she narrates—duels, lesbian engagements, court hijinx and all—she lived an extraordinarily unusual life for an early-nineteenth-century woman. That White dwells so briefly on the captivity experience indicates, however, that she was never herself taken captive.

5. Roy Harvey Pearce voices the opinion of many critics when he claims the captivity narrative "enters literary history proper in *Edgar Huntly*" (1947, 1). Even Annette Kolodny, who has provided one of the most helpful feminist analyses of the captivity tradition, names *Edgar Huntly* as the text that ushered the captivity story into American fiction (1979, 228). In her recent study, *Feminism and American Literary History,* Nina Baym acknowledges women authors' formative place in wilderness literature by claiming that Lydia Child's *Hobomok* influenced Cooper's *Last of the Mohicans,* and that Catharine Sedgwick's *Hope Leslie* altered the thematics of Cooper's later fiction, showing him "that martial white women, Indian-white marriage, and Indian women could exist within the scope of this worldview" (1992, 35). See also Fitzpatrick (1991), 16.

6. Despite his narrow definition of masculinity as shaped solely by "rivalry and fears of humiliation" (1989, 41), David Leverenz convincingly presents the works of Emerson, Thoreau, Whitman, Hawthorne, Melville, and Douglass as representations of "the prison house of manhood," in which "conventional manliness becomes a cage of iron, barred from

within, where egotism twists into frightening perversions of desire" (246). See as well the work of Michael Gilmore (1985) and David Pugh (1983).

7. On the perceived "feminization" of authorship, see Buell (1986), 429–30. In "The American Scholar" (1837), for instance, Emerson expresses the male author's feelings of dispossession and feminization, noting, "I have heard it said that the clergy,—who are always more universally than any other class, the scholars of their day,—are addressed as women: that the rough, spontaneous conversation of men they do not hear, but only a mincing and diluted speech. They are often virtually disenfranchised; and, indeed, there are advocates of their celibacy. As far as this is true of the studious classes, it is not just and wise. Action is with the scholar subordinate, but it is essential. Without it, he is not yet man" (1940, 52). "The so-called 'practical men' sneer at speculative men," Emerson complains, "as if, because they speculate or see, they could do nothing" (52). Seen as effeminate and unproductive within a society that increasingly privileged only financial success—which was not to be the lot of most male writers in America—Emerson used art to recoup his losses. After naming several landowners in "Nature" (1836), for instance, Emerson asserts that "none of them owns the landscape" (5), for according to Emerson it can only be truly possessed by the eye. Emerson's vision thus turns the speculative man into a land speculator, reinscribed in the language of public, competitive manhood. Above all, Emerson, like Whitman after him, advocates roughness and spontaneity as the attributes of masculinity, defining a kind of transcendental machismo.

8. Critics and historians have documented the deployment of the wilderness as an alternative to the male writer's culture, a mythological and generic "world elsewhere." The "essential quality of America," Nina Baym notes, "comes to reside in its unsettled wilderness and the opportunities that such a wilderness offers to the individual as the medium on which he may inscribe, unhindered, his own destiny and his own nature" (1992, 71). The paradigmatic hero of this wilderness is the American Adam who is, in R. W. B. Lewis's formulation, "an individual emancipated from history, happily bereft of ancestry, untouched and undefiled by the usual inheritances of family and race; an individual standing alone, self-reliant and self-propelling, ready to confront whatever awaited him with the aid of his own unique and inherent resources" (1955, 5).

9. For fuller discussions of "separate sphere ideologies," see especially Cott (1977), Kelley (1984), Tompkins (1985), and Welter (1966).

10. Mary Kelley has argued that women in fact often pursued literary

careers in order to escape domesticity and to enter the "public" and commercial sphere.

11. Several scholars, especially Chambers-Schiller, Erkkila, Kerber, Norton, and Smith-Rosenberg, have noted the vigorous reassertion of women's "proper role" after the revolution and have argued that control over women's "sphere" became a strategy for limiting the revolutionary zeal threatening the newly formed government.

12. In *Love and Death in the American Novel,* Leslie Fiedler notes that the association of women with the "domestic virtues" of purity and piety "led to an unfortunate series of misunderstandings."

> With no counter-tradition, cynical or idealizing, to challenge it, the sentimental view came to be accepted as quite *literally* true, was imposed upon actual women as a required role and responded to by men as if it were a fact of life rather than of fancy. (1969, 63)

Caught in this literalization of their fictional, domestic identities, women could not escape home so easily, because they *were* home, ideologically and metaphorically.

13. R. W. B. Lewis notes, "The proposition implicit in much American writing from Poe and Cooper to Anderson and Hemingway [is] that the valid rite of initiation for the individual in the new world is not an initiation *into* society, but given the character of society, an initiation *away from it*" (1955, 115).

14. See Cott (1977), 201.

15. In Richardson's novel, Pamela does not return to her preindividuated family; rather, she marries the man who separated her from that communal security and threatened her with rape. If one continues the parallels with the Rowlandson narrative, then, the captive may be said to "marry" her captors, thus signaling a desire not to return, but to remain. Where Rowlandson's text expresses longing for her home culture, Armstrong and Tennenhouse grant her generative authorial intention; when the narrative divides the author from that community and imagines alternative social configurations, however, the schism arises not through textual design but from "one of the great ironies of Western history" (1992, 207).

16. Kelly again refers to herself in the third person throughout the concluding chapter of her narrative, in which she recounts General Sully's campaign against the Indians. Whenever she enters the discourse of struggle "between men," as Eve Kosofsky Sedgwick notes, a woman can be no more

than an object of exchange; Kelly's choice of pronouns registers that objectification in her text.

17. "In a world ordered by sexual inbalance," Laura Mulvey writes, "pleasure in looking has been split between active/male and passive/female. The determining male gaze projects its fantasy onto the female figure, which is styled accordingly. In their traditional exhibitionist role women are simultaneously looked at and displayed, with their appearance coded for strong visual and erotic impact so that they can be said to connote to-be-looked-at-ness" (1989, 19).

18. The claim that Indians did not rape white women captives is made by Ulrich (1980) and by Vaughan and Clark (1981). James Axtell attributes the Indians' lack of sexual interest in white female captives to a different aesthetic standard ("the New England Indians, at least, esteemed black the color of beauty"), a strong incest taboo (most captives were adopted into families as female relatives), and to "a religious ethic of strict warrior continence" (1985, 310). Susan Brownmiller argues that materials published subsequent to the Kelly narrative suggest that she and other captives *were* raped (1975, 140–53). Among the narratives I have read, one captive—Ann Coleson—reports being raped by her Sioux captors, while several claim they never experienced or heard reports of Indian rape. Gertrude Morgan writes that "the crime of ravishing captive women, so common and hellish a vice among civilized nations, *is entirely unknown*. That statement may dissipate the romance many writers have imparted to their stories of the Indians and beautiful white captive maidens, but it is nevertheless a fact" (1866, 29).

As Morgan indicates, at work in reports of Indians raping white women is less a concern for white women's safety than a prurient white fantasy. The sexualization of the captive's vulnerability can be analyzed through Catharine MacKinnon's connection of stereotypical female gender roles and the subordinated position women occupy in heterosexuality. As MacKinnon writes, "Vulnerability means the appearance/reality of easy sexual access; passivity means receptivity and disabled resistance, enforced by trained physical weakness; softness means pregnability by something hard. Incompetence seeks help as vulnerability seeks shelter, inviting the embrace that becomes the invasion, trading exclusive access for protection . . . from the same access" (1982, 530). That the terms MacKinnon chooses to describe women's sexual position—"seeks help," "invasion," "trading exclusive access for protection"—so closely parallel the language of "rescue" is itself telling. The narratives of Rowlandson, Kelly,

211

and Hearst bear out MacKinnon's thesis, as each shows the narrative of masculine rescue leading to the discourse of sexual desire and ultimately of rape.

19. I borrow the concept of the "imagined community" from Benedict Anderson's 1983 study of the rise of nationalism. For a fuller discussion of Anderson's argument and its relationship to the imagined gender communities inscribed in the captivity romances, see chapter 5.

20. Subsequent captivity romances explore the bonds between white women and Indians left unexamined in Bleecker's text. See chapters 5 and 6.

21. In "The Spirit of Place," D. H. Lawrence writes, "Men are free when they belong to a living, organic, *believing* community, active in fulfilling some unfulfilled, perhaps unrealized purpose. Not when they are escaping to some wild west. The most unfree souls go west, and shout of freedom. The shout is a rattling of chains, always was" (1923, 6).

22. Pearce first made the case for Bleecker's text as "simply a captivity narrative turned novel of sensibility" (1947, 13).

23. While some critics, most notably Jane Tompkins and Nancy Armstrong, have persuasively argued that sentimentalism potentially empowers women, Bleecker, working within a wider repertoire of genres, appears to have associated the language of sentimentalism with female frailty and domestic confinement.

24. Annette Kolodny is one of the few critics to consider carefully women's writings on the American frontier; yet even Kolodny argues that frontier women never left their homes behind, striving to create domesticated gardens in the wilderness.

25. For a fuller critique of Tompkins' argument, see Myers (1988).

26. Gillian Brown's *Domestic Individualism* (1990) argues that nineteenth-century gender ideologies were far more complex than "separate sphere" history would lead contemporary readers to believe.

CHAPTER FIVE

1. See Kerber (1980) and Norton (1980).

2. See, for instance, Kerber (1980), 47, or Erkkila (1987), 190.

3. Carroll Smith-Rosenberg has similarly noted Rowson's creation for

America of "a matriarchal origin myth" that leads to a national present dedicated to "ennobling and entitling" female values (1993, 496–97). Smith-Rosenberg also argues that Rowson deploys the captivity story in order to imagine cooperation between white women and Indians, and hence to create an American subject "constituted through fusion, not confusion" (497). I do not agree, however, with Smith-Rosenberg's claim that Rowson "misreads" (503) the inherently racist narratives of women such as Mary Rowlandson in order to constitute her vision of national fusion; rather, as I have argued in earlier chapters, the "illusion of a coherent subjectivity" (504) is challenged in Rowlandson's captivity narrative precisely through the image of intercultural fusion. Rowson, therefore, appears to have been an extremely careful reader of Rowlandson's text.

4. My argument differs here from Smith-Rosenberg's conclusion that Rowson undertakes the "final effacement of American Indians" (1993, 497) in order to legitimize white claims to Indian land (501) and to authorize herself "as a representative of the new Euro-American middle classes" and as a "professional writer" (503). As I have argued, Rowson depicts white women losing agency and authorization in direct relation to the rise of the middle-class and its appropriation of Indian land. Rowson also shows that the stability of middle-class values ends her ability to rewrite genres, confining her instead within the conventions of sentimentalism.

5. My discussion of the pleasures of community owes much to Dennis Foster, who argues that community "emerges from what resists the communal, the gathering of all people in an essential spirit" (1994, 375). Recognizing the difference at the core of community, Foster argues, "will open us to communication, to an awareness of our 'exposure' before the world, and crucially (lest you think this is all bleak stuff) ecstasy" (176).

6. In arguing for an organic and significant structure in *Reuben and Rachel,* I am taking issue with Henri Petter (1971), the only critic to consider the composition of the novel, who dismisses Rowson as a mere sensationalist:

> Her Indian chapters are insufficiently coordinated with the more usual parts of the novel; they read like an element deliberately introduced to give the story a dash of the uncommon and are not so much a part of the narrative as a picturesque feature, rather like the Columbus material in the opening chapters. *Reuben and Rachel* is clearly not a historical novel but a poorly organized book, setting fashionable plots against a sketchy background of historical fact. (35–36)

213

7. On the sexualization of Indian women, see Barnett and Herzog. See especially the excellent discussion by Dawn Lander, who writes, "In the wilderness, the 'otherness' of sexual opposites, of male-female polarity, is reinforced or even replaced by polarities of class or race. In fact, the foreignness of class or race is an indispensible component of eroticism in the wilderness" (1977, 201).

8. On the formation and importance of female community in nineteenth-century America, see Cott (1977) and Smith-Rosenberg (1985).

9. Feminist critics have been particularly concerned to reverse the assumption that sex determines gender, arguing instead that cultural discourses of gender inscribe sex on the body. See, for example, Butler (1990) and de Lauretis (1987).

10. Bell writes that Catharine Sedgwick's *Hope Leslie* expresses its author's optimism "by means of a conventional romantic narrative plot, found again and again in historical romance, in which historical progress becomes identified with the romantic attachment of hero and heroine" (1970, 214).

11. For a detailed account of the origins of and changes in the *feme covert* status of married women in eighteenth-century America, see Salmon (1986) and also Kerber (1980), who notes the connection between political and domestic hierarchies in the *feme covert* laws (119). "Set within a specific context of limiting marriage laws and restrictive social mores," Cathy Davidson has argued, eighteenth-century women's novels therefore present "less a story of the wages of sin than a study of the wages of marriage" (1986, 143).

12. The phrase is used by Herbert Ross Brown (1940) to encapsulate the entire Richardsonian narrative of seduction and abandonment.

13. Both Kerber (1980) and Norton (1980) discuss the "domestication" of revolutionary politics, including accounts of the Philadelphia Ladies Association.

14. Betsy Erkkila has noted the similar effects the metaphors of the revolution had on women and blacks in America. The rhetoric of justifiable revolt, Erkkila writes, led to "a certain openness and indeterminacy in black/white relations during the revolutionary era" (1987, 210), an openness Erkkila reads in Phillis Wheatley's poems. Yet, just as the freedoms granted women during the war were undermined by renewed emphasis on "proper" domesticity, so racial "indeterminacy . . . would begin to close and rigidify once the war was over and slaves were written into the constitution as three-fifths human" (210). And while the situation of slaves and of

Indians in postwar America was of course significantly different, Michael Rogin notes that in the imagination of those seeking to restore social hierarchy, all people of color in America posed a similar metaphorical and political threat (1975, 27).

CHAPTER SIX

1. For a fuller discussion of how fiction shapes autobiographical narratives and hence identity, see L. Gilmore (1994).

2. In Cooper's novels, Nina Baym argues, "the white man does not need a woman fighting by his side to inspire him, still less a woman mediating between him and the Indian enemy; he needs a woman to fight *for* and *about*" (1992, 26). In contrast, the novels of Lydia Maria Child and Catharine Sedgwick create strong, independent women, suggesting that "if women's values were implemented a more tolerant, more imaginative, more gracious civil state . . . would come into being" (25). Sandra Zagarell has similarly argued that by playing with generic boundaries, *Hope Leslie* challenges "the collusion between established narrative structures and racist, patriarchal definitions of the nation" (1987, 233).

3. Ann Douglas has argued that as "she defies the stern edicts of Governor Winthrop and his peers, frees witches, and defends Indians, Hope Leslie suggests counter-history; she is an *ex post facto* protest against the masculine solidities of the past" (1977, 221-22). On Sedgwick's historical revisions, also see Nelson (1993), 73-75, and Maddox (1991), 96-110.

4. On the conventions of domestic fiction, see Baym (1978).

5. On Martha Fletcher's ethnocentrism, see Mary Kelley's introduction to *Hope Leslie* (Sedgwick [1827] 1984), xxx. See also Bardes and Gossett for a discussion of Martha's "obedient passivity" (1985, 21) and the subsequent punishment inflicted on her by Sedgwick. Baym (1992) offers an insightful critique of the function of "protection" in Indian romances, noting that the "gendered interrelation of dependency and protection called 'love'" (29) is generated by white men in the face of supposed Indian "threats" to ensure that women remain "artless, thoughtless, childlike, cheerful, and incompetent" (29) and to undermine white women's "attempts to intervene in the world" (32).

6. Woolf writes that the Angel "was intensely sympathetic. She was immensely charming. She was utterly unselfish. She excelled in the difficult arts of family life." In order to avoid becoming such a martyred woman herself, Woolf concludes, "I turned upon her and caught her by the throat. I did my best to kill her . . . I acted in self-defense. Had I not killed her she

would have killed me" (1979, 59). In killing off Martha Fletcher as a way of circumventing traditional domesticity, Sedgwick follows the lead of previous captivity romances, most of which feature heroines who either have no mothers at all—Jessy Oliver in *Reuben and Rachel* and Miriam Grey in Harriet Cheney's *A Peep at the Pilgrims* are cases in point—or have at best ambivalent feelings toward a mother who soon dies, as in Lydia Maria Child's *Hobomok* and Eliza Cushing's *Saratoga*.

7. See Bell (1970), 214.

8. For an extended analysis of how friendships between women circumvent the heterosexual romance that typically closes women's texts, see DuPlessis (1985).

9. William Dudley and Oberea in Rowson's *Reuben and Rachel* have a loving marriage, but William is killed because he cannot surrender his English background. In Lydia Child's *Hobomok,* Mary respects her Indian husband but never truly loves him. Child ends the novel by returning Hobomok to the forest when Mary's true love, an Englishman who has been reported killed at sea, returns to claim Mary's hand. For an excellent discussion of interracial romance in *Hope Leslie,* see Leland Person, Jr. (1985). To Person's analysis I would add only that, for Sedgwick, interracial "sisterhood" seems more important than interracial marriage; the relationship between Hope and Magawisca is much more developed than that between Faith and Oneco, although, as Person notes, the latter relationship is characterized as more loving and respectful than any marriage between whites.

10. Lucy Maddox contends that at the conclusion of *Hope Leslie,* "Indians, the companions of white women in the struggle against white patriarchal oppression, seem doomed to disappear into 'deep voiceless obscurity,' . . . unless they can be persuaded to accept full assimilation into white culture" (1991, 110). Dana Nelson similarly argues that *Hope Leslie* "never successfully challenges the euphemistic Anglo construction of the ultimate 'fate' of the Indians" (1993, 77).

11. On the feminist possibilities of collective reading, see de Lauretis' discussion in *Alice Doesn't* (1984) of consciousness raising, 159–84.

12. Like Lucy Maddox, Nina Baym argues based on Magawisca's return to the wilderness that Sedgwick's innovations in *Hope Leslie* "serve no culturally radical purpose. In mocking Cooper's martial hysteria, *Hope Leslie* proposes that Indian removal need not have been, nor need be in the future, so bloody: The Indians will be willing or at least acquiescing agents of their own removal" (1992, 34–35). I would certainly agree that Sedgwick seems unable to imagine a plot for her Indian heroine that doesn't

NOTES TO PAGE 184

require her return to the wilderness, but I disagree with Baym's implication that Sedgwick therefore endorses policies of Indian removal. Sedgwick would arguably have done more to support such policies by having Magawisca happily assimilate into white society, a conclusion equally condemned by Maddox (1991, 110). Whether Magawisca stayed in Boston or returned to her own culture, her actions bode ill for the future of Indian culture because of the reader's knowledge of historical outcome.

CONCLUSION

1. See Cott (1977), 197–206.

2. For an insightful analysis of white abolitionists' appropriations of African American women and their narratives, see Sanchez-Eppler (1991).

REFERENCES

Adams Family Correspondence. Volume 1: *December 1761–May 1776.*
    1963. Ed. L. H. Butterfield, Wendell D. Garrett, and Marjorie E.
    Sprague. Cambridge, Mass.: Harvard University Press.
Althusser, Louis. 1971. *Lenin and Philosophy.* New York: Monthly Re-
    view Press.
Anderson, Benedict. 1983. *Imagined Communities: Reflections on the
    Origin and Spread of Nationalism.* London: Verso.
Anzaldua, Gloria. 1987. *Borderlands/La Frontera: The New Mestiza.* San
    Francisco: Spinsters Ink.
Armstrong, Nancy. 1987. *Desire and Domestic Fiction: A Political History
    of the Novel.* New York: Oxford University Press.
Armstrong, Nancy, and Leonard Tennenhouse. 1992. *The Imaginary Puri-
    tan: Literature, Intellectual Labor, and the Origins of Personal Life.*
    Berkeley and Los Angeles: University of California Press.
Axtell, James. 1985. *The Invasion Within: The Contest of Cultures in Colo-
    nial North America.* New York: Oxford University Press.
Bakhtin, M. M. 1981. *The Dialogic Imagination: Four Essays.* Ed. Michael
    Holquist. Trans. Caryl Emerson and Michael Holquist. Austin: Uni-
    versity of Texas Press.
Barber, Eunice. 1818. *Narrative of the Tragical Death of Mr. Darius Barber
    and His Seven Children.* Boston: Printed for David Hazen.
Barber, Mary. 1873. *The True Narrative of the Five Years' Suffering and
    Perilous Adventures.* Philadelphia: Barclay.
Bardes, Barbara Ann and Suzanne Gossett. 1985. "Women and Political
    Power in the Republic: Two Early American Novels." *Legacy* 2: 13–
    30.
Barnett, Louise. 1975. *The Ignoble Savage: American Literary Racism,
    1790–1890.* Westport, Conn.: Greenwood Press.
Baym, Nina. 1992. *Feminism and American Literary History.* New
    Brunswick, N.J.: Rutgers University Press.
———. 1985. "Melodramas of Beset Manhood: How Theories of Ameri-
    can Fiction Exclude Women Authors." Pp. 63–80 in *The New Femi-*

nist Criticism: Essays on Women, Literature and Theory, ed. Elaine Showalter. New York: Pantheon.

———. 1978. *Women's Fiction: A Guide to Novels by and about Women in America, 1820–1870.* Ithaca: Cornell University Press.

Beidler, Peter G. 1991. "The Contemporary Indian Romance: A Review Essay." *American Indian Culture and Research Journal* 15: 97–125.

Bell, Michael Davitt. 1970. "History and Romance Convention in Catharine Sedgwick's *Hope Leslie.*" *American Quarterly* 22: 213–21.

Berlant, Lauren. 1991. *The Anatomy of National Fantasy: Hawthorne, Utopia, and Everyday Life.* Chicago: University of Chicago Press.

Bleecker, Ann Eliza. 1793. *The Posthumous Works of Ann Eliza Bleecker, in Prose and Verse.* Ed. Margaretta V. Fangeres. New York: T. and J. Swords.

Boulton, David. 1975. *The Making of Tania Hearst.* London: New English Library.

Bozarth, Experience. 1775. Untitled narrative. Pp. 334–35 in Drake (1851); also reprinted in Frost (1854) and Withers (1895).

Bradley, Isaac. 1695. Untitled narrative. Pp. 281–84 in Frost (1854).

Breitwieser, Mitchell Robert. 1990. *American Puritanism and the Defense of Mourning: Religion, Grief, and Ethnology in Mary White Rowlandson's Captivity Narrative.* Madison: University of Wisconsin Press.

Brown, Gillian. 1990. *Domestic Individualism: Imagining Self in Nineteenth-Century America.* Berkeley and Los Angeles: University of California Press.

Brown, Herbert Ross. 1940. *The Sentimental Novel in America, 1789–1860.* Durham, N.C.: Duke University Press.

Brown, Jane. 1851. "Historical Traditions of Tennessee." *American Whig Review* 15:235–49.

Brownmiller, Susan. 1975. *Against Our Wills: Men, Women and Rape.* New York: Simon and Schuster.

Buell, Lawrence. 1986. *New England Literary Culture: From Revolution Through Renaissance.* Cambridge and New York: Cambridge University Press.

Butler, Judith. 1990. *Gender Trouble: Feminism and the Subversion of Identity.* New York: Routledge.

Carleton, Phillips. 1943. "The Indian Captivity." *American Literature* 15:169–80.

Carrigan, Minnie Bruce. 1912. *Captured by the Indians: Reminiscences of Pioneer Life in Minnesota.* Buffalo Lake, Minn.: The News Print.

Carter, Angela. 1986. *Saints and Strangers.* New York: Penguin.

Cattermole, E. G. 1926. *Famous Frontiersmen, Pioneers and Scouts: The Romance of American History.* Tarrytown, N.Y.: William Abbatt.

Chambers-Schiller, Lee Virginia. 1984. *Liberty, A Better Husband: Single Women in America: The Generations of 1780–1840.* New Haven, Conn.: Yale University Press.

Cheney, Harriet. 1824. *A Peep at the Pilgrims.* Boston: Phillips, Samson.

Cheyfitz, Eric. 1991. *The Poetics of Imperialism: Translation and Colonization from "The Tempest" to "Tarzan".* New York: Oxford University Press.

Chopin, Kate. [1899] 1976. *The Awakening.* New York: Norton.

———. 1969. *The Complete Works of Kate Chopin.* Vol. I. Ed. Per Seyersted. Baton Rouge: Louisiana State University Press.

Clendennin, Mrs. 1763. Untitled narrative. Pp. 22–25 in Frost (1859); also reprinted in Drake (1851) and Withers (1895).

Coleson, Ann. 1864. *Miss Coleson's Narrative of Her Captivity among the Sioux Indians.* Philadelphia: Barclay.

Cooper, James Fenimore. [1826] 1962. *The Last of the Mohicans: A Narrative of 1757.* New York: Signet.

Cott, Nancy F. 1977. *The Bonds of Womanhood: "Women's Sphere" in New England, 1780–1835.* New Haven, Conn.: Yale University Press.

Cunningham, Mrs. 1785. Untitled narrative. Pp. 368–71 in Withers (1895).

Davidson, Cathy. 1986. *Revolution and the Word: The Rise of the Novel in America.* New York: Oxford University Press.

———. 1980. "Mothers and Daughters in the Fiction of the New Republic." Pp. 115–27 in *The Lost Tradition: Mothers and Daughters in Literature,* ed. Cathy Davidson and E. M. Broner. New York: Frederick Ungar.

Dearborn, Mary. 1986. *Pocahontas's Daughters: Gender and Ethnicity in American Culture.* New York: Oxford University Press.

de Lauretis, Teresa. 1987. *Technologies of Gender: Essays on Theory, Film, and Fiction.* Bloomington: Indiana University Press.

———. 1984. *Alice Doesn't: Feminism, Semiotics, Cinema.* Bloomington: Indiana University Press.

Deming, Barbara. 1985. *Prisons That Could Not Hold.* San Francisco: Spinsters Ink.

Dennis, Hannah. 1761. Untitled narrative. Pp. 45–49 in Frost (1854); also reprinted in Withers (1895).

Derounian-Stodola, Kathryn Zabelle and James Arthur Levernier. 1993. *The Indian Captivity Narrative, 1550–1900.* New York: Twayne.

Dickinson, Emily. 1960. *The Complete Poems.* Ed. Thomas H. Johnson. Boston: Little Brown.

Donaldson, Laura. 1992. *Decolonizing Feminism.* Chapel Hill: University of North Carolina Press.

Douglas, Ann. 1977. *The Feminization of American Culture.* New York: Oxford University Press.

Drake, Samuel Gardiner. 1851. *Indian Captivities; or, Life in the Wigwam.* Auburn: Derby and Miller.

———. 1842. *Tragedies of the Wilderness.* Boston: Antiquarian Bookstore and Institute.

Drimmer, Frederick. 1961. *Scalps and Tomahawks: Narratives of Indian Captivity.* New York: Coward-McCann.

Drinnon, Richard. 1980. *Facing West: The Metaphysics of Indian-Hating and Empire-Building.* Minneapolis: University of Minnesota Press.

DuPlessis, Rachel Blau. 1985. *Writing beyond the Ending: Narrative Strategies of Twentieth Century Women.* Bloomington: Indiana University Press.

Durham, Mrs. 1779. Untitled narrative. Pp. 28–32 in Frost (1854).

Duston, Hannah. 1697. Untitled narrative. Pp. 162–64 in Vaughan and Clark (1981).

Eastlick, Lavina. 1901. Untitled narrative. Pp. 314–29 in Drimmer (1961).

Edwards, Cassie. 1993. *Savage Sunrise.* New York: Dorchester Publishing.

Elliott, Emory. 1986. *Revolutionary Writers: Literature and Authority in the New Republic, 1723–1810.* New York: Oxford University Press.

Emerson, Ralph Waldo. 1940. *Selected Writings of Emerson.* Ed. Brooks Atkinson. New York: The Modern Library.

Erkkila, Betsy. 1987. "Revolutionary Women." *Tulsa Studies in Women's Literature* 6:189–223.

Fiedler, Leslie A. 1969. *Love and Death in the American Novel.* New York: Laurel.

———. 1968. *Return of the Vanishing American.* New York: Stein and Day.

Finney, Molly. N.d. Untitled narrative. Pp. 103–26 in Cattermole (1926).

Fitzpatrick, Tara. 1991. "The Figure of Captivity: The Cultural Work of the Puritan Captivity Narrative." *American Literary History* 3:1–26.

Foster, Dennis A. 1994. "Pleasure and Community in Cultural Criticism." *American Literary History* 6, no. 2 (summer): 371–82.

Foster, Edward Halsey. 1974. *Catharine Maria Sedgwick.* New York: Twayne.

Foster, Frances Smith. 1993. *Written by Herself: Literary Production by African American Women, 1746–1892.* Bloomington: Indiana University Press.

Foucault, Michel. 1979. *Discipline and Punish: The Birth of the Prison.* Trans. Alan Sheridan. New York: Vintage.

Frankenberg, Ruth. 1993. *White Women, Race Matters: The Social Construction of Whiteness.* Minneapolis: University of Minnesota Press.

Frost, John. 1859. *Pioneer Mothers of the West; or, Daring and Heroic Deeds of American Women.* Boston: Lee and Sheppard.

———. 1854. *Thrilling Adventures among the Indians.* Philadelphia: J. W. Bradley.

Fuller, Emeline. 1892. *Left by the Indians: Story of My Life.* Mount Vernon, Iowa: Hawk-eye Steam Print.

Fuller, Margaret. 1971. *Woman in the Nineteenth Century.* New York: Norton.

Gardner, Abigail. 1885. *History of the Spirit Lake Massacre and Captivity of Miss Abbie Gardner.* Des Moines: Mills.

Gerish, Sarah. 1689. Untitled narrative. Pp. 68–70 in Drake (1851).

Gherman, Dawn Lander. 1975. *From Parlour to Tepee: The White Squaw on the American Frontier.* Ph.D. diss., University of Massachusetts/Amherst.

Gilbert, Sandra M. 1985. "What Do Feminist Critics Want? A Postcard from the Volcano." Pp. 29–45 in *The New Feminist Criticism: Essays on Women, Literature and Theory,* ed. Elaine Showalter. New York: Pantheon.

Gilmore, Leigh. 1994. *Autobiographics: A Feminist Theory of Women's Self-Representation.* Ithaca, N.Y.: Cornell University Press.

Gilmore, Michael T. 1985. *American Romanticism in the Marketplace.* Chicago: University of Chicago Press.

Godfrey, Mary. 1836. *An Authentic Narrative of the Seminole War; and of the Miraculous Escape of Mrs. Mary Godfrey, and Her Four Female Children.* New York: D. F. Lanchard.

Gowanlock, Theresa. 1885. *Two Months in the Camp of Big Bear: The Life and Adventures of Theresa Gowanlock and Theresa Delaney.* Parkdale, Canada: Times Office.

Haberly, David. 1976. "Women and Indians: *The Last of the Mohicans* and the Captivity Tradition." *American Quarterly* 28 (fall): 431–41.

Hanson, Elizabeth. 1728. "God's Mercy Surmounting Man's Cruelty." Pp. 230–44 in Vaughan and Clark (1981); also reprinted in Drake (1851) and VanDerBeets (1973).

Harbison, Mercy. 1792. Untitled narrative. Pp. 210–40 in Kephart (1915); also reprinted in Drake (1851), Frost (1859), and VanDerBeets (1973).

Hawthorne, Nathaniel. 1900. "The Duston Family." *The Complete Writ-*

ings of Nathaniel Hawthorne. Vol. 17, pp. 229–38. New York: Houghton, Mifflin.

Hearst, Patricia Campbell. 1988. *Patty Hearst.* With Alvin Moscow. New York: Avon.

————. 1982. *Every Secret Thing.* With Alvin Moscow. Garden City, N.Y.: Doubleday.

Herzog, Kristin. 1983. *Women, Ethnics, and Exotics: Images of Power in Mid-Nineteenth-Century American Fiction.* Knoxville: University of Tennessee Press.

Hicks, Elizabeth. 1902. *A True Romance of the American War of Independence, 1775–1783.* London: W. Harwick.

Horn, Sarah Ann. [1839] 1955. *Narrative.* Ed. Carl Coke Rister. Glendale, Calif.: Arthur H. Clark.

How, Nehemiah. 1745. Untitled narrative. Pp. 127–38 in Drake (1851).

Howe, Jemima. 1755. Untitled narrative. Pp. 10–16 in Frost (1859); also reprinted in Drake (1851) and Peckham (1954).

Howe, Susan. 1991. *The Birth-mark: Unsettling the Wilderness in American Literary History.* Hanover, N.H.: University Press of New England for Wesleyan University Press.

Jemison, Mary. 1758. Untitled narrative. Pp. 62–79 in Peckham (1954).

Johnson, Susannah. 1907. *A Narrative of the Captivity of Mrs. Johnson.* Springfield, Mass.: H. R. Huntting.

Kelley, Mary. 1984. *Private Woman, Public Stage: Literary Domesticity in Nineteenth-Century America.* New York: Oxford University Press.

Kelly, Fanny. 1871. *Narrative of My Captivity among the Sioux Indians.* Hartford: Mutual Publishing. Also reprinted in Drimmer (1961) and Peckham (1954).

Kephart, Horace. 1915. *Captives among the Indians.* New York: Outing Publishing.

Kerber, Linda K. 1988. "Separate Spheres, Female Worlds, Woman's Place: The Rhetoric of Women's History." *Journal of American History* 75, no. 1 (June): 9–39.

————. 1980. *Women of the Republic: Intellect and Ideology in Revolutionary America.* New York: Norton.

Kinnan, Mary. [1795] 1973. "A True Narrative of the Sufferings of Mary Kinnan." Pp. 317–32 in *Held Captive by Indians: Selected Narratives, 1642–1836.* Ed. Richard VanDerBeets. Knoxville: University of Tennessee Press.

Kolodny, Annette. 1993. "Among the Indians: The Uses of Captivity." *The New York Times Book Review,* January 31, 1, 26–29.

————. 1984. *The Land before Her: Fantasy and Experience of the Ameri-*

can Frontiers, 1630–1860. Chapel Hill: University of North Carolina Press.

———. 1982. "Turning the Lens on 'The Panther Captivity': A Feminist Exercise in Practical Criticism." Pp. 159–75 in *Writing and Sexual Difference,* ed. Elizabeth Abel. Chicago: University of Chicago Press.

———. 1979. "Review Essay" [of *Narratives of North American Captivities,* ed. Wilcomb E. Washburn]. *Early American Literature* 14:228–35.

Lander, Dawn. 1977. "Eve among the Indians." Pp. 194–211 in *The Authority of Experience: Essays in Feminist Criticism,* ed. Arlyn Diamond and Lee Edwards. Amherst: University of Massachusetts Press.

Larimer, Sarah. 1871. *The Capture and Escape; or, Life among the Sioux.* Philadelphia: Claxton, Remsen and Haffelfinger.

Lawrence, D. H. [1923] 1969. *Studies in Classic American Literature.* New York: Viking.

Leverenz, David. 1989. *Manhood and the American Renaissance.* Ithaca, N.Y.: Cornell University Press.

Lewis, R. W. B. 1955. *The American Adam: Innocence, Tragedy, and Tradition in the Nineteenth Century.* Chicago: University of Chicago Press.

Lincoln, Charles. 1913. *Narratives of the Indian Wars, 1675–1699.* New York: Charles Scribner's Sons.

MacKinnon, Catharine A. 1982. "Feminism, Marxism, Methodology, and the State: An Agenda For Theory." *Signs* 7 (spring): 515–44.

Maddox, Lucy. 1991. *Removals: Nineteenth-Century American Literature and the Politics of Indian Affairs.* New York: Oxford University Press.

Manheim, Frederick. 1851. "Narrative of the Manheim Family." Pp. 333–34 in Drake (1851).

Mather, Cotton. 1914. "A Brand Pluck'd Out of the Burning." Pp. 259–87 in *Narratives of the Witchcraft Cases, 1648–1706,* ed. Charles Lincoln Burr. New York: Charles Scribner's Sons.

M'Coy, Isabella. 1747. Untitled narrative. Pp. 143–47 in Drake (1851).

Merrill, Mrs. 1791. Untitled narrative. Pp. 43–45 in Frost (1854); also reprinted in Frost (1859) and Withers (1895).

Miller, Nancy K. 1988. *Subject to Change: Reading Feminist Writing.* New York: Columbia University Press.

Millet, Kate. 1970. *Sexual Politics.* Garden City, N.Y.: Doubleday.

Minter, David. 1974. "By Dens of Lions: Notes on Stylization in Early Puritan Captivity Narratives." *American Literature* 45:335–47.

Mitchell, Elvis. 1988. "Patty Hearst: The Movie." *Rolling Stone* (September 8): 31, 160.

Morgan, Gertrude. 1866. *Gertrude Morgan; or, Life and Adventures among the Indians of the Far West.* Philadelphia: Barclay.

225

Mulvey, Laura. 1989. *Visual and Other Pleasures*. Bloomington: Indiana University Press.

Myers, D. G. 1988. "The Canonization of Susan Warner." *The New Criterion* (December): 73–78.

Namias, June. 1988. *White Captives: Gender and Ethnicity on Successive American Frontiers, 1607–1862*. Ph.D. diss., Brandeis University.

Nash, Roderick. 1967. *Wilderness and the American Mind*. New Haven, Conn.: Yale University Press.

Nelson, Dana. 1993. *The Word in Black and White: Reading "Race" in American Literature, 1638–1867*. New York: Oxford University Press.

Norton, Mary Beth. 1980. *Liberty's Daughters: The Revolutionary Experience of American Women, 1750–1800*. Boston: Little, Brown.

Oatman, Olive. 1851. Untitled narrative. Pp. 195–214 in Peckham (1954).

Pearce, Roy Harvey. 1947. "The Significances of the Captivity Narrative." *American Literature* 19:1–20.

Peckham, Howard H. 1954. *Captured by Indians: True Tales of Pioneer Survivors*. New Brunswick, N.J.: Rutgers University Press.

Person, Leland, Jr. 1985. "The American Eve: Miscegenation and a Feminist Frontier Fiction." *American Quarterly* 37: 668–85.

Petter, Henri. 1971. *The Early American Novel*. Athens: Ohio State University Press.

Plummer, Clarissa. 1838. *Narrative of the Captivity of Mrs. Clarissa Plummer*. New York: Perry and Cooke.

Plummer, Rachel. 1839. Untitled narrative. Pp. 334–66 in VanDerBeets (1973).

Poirier, Richard. 1966. *A World Elsewhere: The Place of Style in American Literature*. New York: Oxford University Press.

Poovey, Mary. 1984. *The Proper Lady and the Woman Writer: Ideology as Style in the Works of Mary Wollstonecraft, Mary Shelley, and Jane Austen*. Chicago: University of Chicago Press.

Porter, Mrs. N.d. Untitled narrative. Pp. 20–21 in Frost (1859).

Pugh, David. 1983. *Sons of Liberty: The Masculine Mind in Nineteenth-Century America*. Westport, Conn.: Greenwood Press.

Rich, Adrienne. 1986. "Compulsory Heterosexuality and Lesbian Existence." *Blood, Bread, and Poetry: Selected Prose 1979–1985*. New York: Norton.

Richards, David. 1967. "The Memorable Preservations: Narratives of Indian Captivity in the Literature and Politics of Colonial New England, 1675–1725." Honors thesis, Yale College.

Riley, Glenda. 1984. *Women and Indians on the Frontier, 1825–1915*. Albuquerque: University of New Mexico Press.

Rogin, Michael Paul. 1975. *Fathers and Children: Andrew Jackson and the Subjugation of the American Indian.* New York: Knopf.

Rowan, Mrs. 1784. Untitled narrative. Pp. 65–67 in Frost (1859).

Rowlandson, Mary. 1682. "The Sovereignty and Goodness of God." Pp. 31–75 in Vaughan and Clark (1981); also reprinted in Drake (1851), Peckham (1954), and VanDerBeets (1973).

Rowson, Susanna Haswell. 1798. *Reuben and Rachel; or, Tales of Olden Times.* 2 vols. London: Minerva.

Salmon, Marylynn. 1986. *Women and the Law of Property in Early America.* Chapel Hill: University of North Carolina Press.

Sanchez-Eppler, Karen. 1992. "American Houses: Constructions of History and Domesticity." *American Literary History* 4 (Summer): 345–53.

———. 1991. *Touching Liberty: Abolition, Feminism and the Politics of the Body.* Berkeley and Los Angeles: University of California Press.

Schrader, Paul, dir. 1988. *Patty Hearst.* Atlantic/Zenith.

Scott, Frances. 1786. Untitled narrative. Pp. 338–42 in Drake (1851); also reprinted in Frost (1854).

Sedgwick, Catharine Maria. [1827] 1984. *Hope Leslie; or, Early Times in the Massachusetts.* Introduction by Mary Kelley. New Brunswick, N.J.: Rutgers University Press.

———. 1872. *The Life and Letters of Catharine M. Sedgwick.* Ed. Mary E. Dewey. New York: Harper and Brothers.

Sedgwick, Eve Kosofsky. 1985. *Between Men: English Literature and Male Homosocial Desire.* New York: Columbia University Press.

Sewell, David R. 1993. "'So Unstable and Like Mad Men They Were': Language and Interpretation in Early American Captivity Narratives." Pp. 39–55 in *A Mixed Race: Ethnicity in Early America,* ed. Frank Shuffelton. New York: Oxford University Press.

Shultz, Duane. 1992. *Over the Earth I Come: The Great Sioux Uprising of 1862.* New York: St. Martin's.

Sieminski, Greg. 1980. "The Puritan Captivity Narratives of the American Revolution." *Journal of American Culture* 2:575–82.

Slocum, Frances. 1778. Untitled narrative. Pp. 116–32 in Peckham (1954); also reprinted in Frost (1854).

Slotkin, Richard. 1973. *Regeneration through Violence: The Mythology of the American Frontier, 1600–1860.* Middletown, Conn.: Wesleyan University Press.

Smith, Mary. 1815. *The Affecting Narrative of the Captivity and Sufferings of Mrs. Mary Smith.* Providence, R.I.: L. Scott.

Smith, Valerie. 1987. *Self-Discovery and Authority in Afro-American Narrative*. Cambridge, Mass.: Harvard University Press.

Smith-Rosenberg, Carroll. 1993. "Subject Female: Authorizing American Identity." *American Literary History* 5, no. 3 (fall): 481–511.

———. 1988. "Domesticating Virtue: Coquettes and Revolutionaries in Young America." Pp. 160–84 in *Literature and the Body: Essays on Populations and Persons. Selected Papers from the English Institute, 1986*, ed. Elaine Scarry. Baltimore: The Johns Hopkins University Press.

———. 1985. *Disorderly Conduct: Visions of Gender in Victorian America*. New York: Knopf.

Spivak, Gayatri Chakravorty. 1991. "Three Women's Texts and a Critique of Imperialism." Pp. 798–814 in *Feminisms: An Anthology of Literary Theory and Criticism*, ed. Robin Warhol and Diane Price Herndl. New Brunswick, N.J.: Rutgers University Press.

Stowe, Harriet Beecher. [1852] 1960. *Uncle Tom's Cabin; or, Life among the Lowly*. New York: Signet.

Swan, Eliza. 1815. *An Affecting Account of the Tragical Death of Major Swan, and of the Captivity of Mrs. Swan, and Infant Child, by the Savages*. Boston: H. Stationary [*sic*] Store.

Tarble, Helen. 1904. *The Story of My Capture and Escape During the Minnesota Indian Massacre of 1862*. St. Paul: Abbot.

Ter Amicam. 1913. "Preface to the Reader." Pp. 112–17 in *Narratives of the Indian Wars, 1675–1699*, ed. Charles Lincoln. New York: Scribners.

Thoreau, Henry David. [1854] 1958. *Walden; or, Life in the Woods*. New York: Harper and Row.

Timberg, Bernard M. 1983. "Patty Hearst and Mercy Short: An Analogue Critique." *Journal of American Culture* 6:60–64.

Tompkins, Jane. 1987. "West of Everything." *South Atlantic Quarterly* 86:357–77.

———. 1985. *Sensational Designs: The Cultural Work of American Fiction, 1790–1860*. New York: Oxford University Press.

Toulouse, Teresa A. 1992. "'My Own Credit': Strategies of (E)valuation in Mary Rowlandson's Captivity Narrative." *American Literature* 64:655–76.

Turner, Frederick Jackson. 1920. *The Frontier in American History*. New York: Henry Holt.

Turner, Victor. 1974. *Dramas, Fields, and Metaphors: Symbolic Action in Human Society*. Ithaca, N.Y.: Cornell University Press.

Ulrich, Laurel Thatcher. 1980. *Good Wives: Image and Reality in the Lives of Women in Northern New England, 1650–1750.* New York: Oxford University Press.

VanDerBeets, Richard. 1984. *The Indian Captivity Narrative: An American Genre.* Latham, Md.: University Press of America.

————. 1973. *Held Captive by Indians: Selected Narratives, 1642–1836.* Knoxville: University of Tennessee Press.

Vaughan, Alden. 1983. *Narratives of North American Captivity: A Selective Bibliography.* New York: Garland.

Vaughan, Alden T. and Edward W. Clark. 1981. *Puritans among the Indians: Accounts of Captivity and Redemption, 1676–1724.* Cambridge, Mass.: Harvard University Press.

Wakefield, Sarah. 1864. *Six Weeks in the Sioux Tepees: A Narrative of Indian Captivity.* 2d ed. Shakopee, Minn.: Argus Book and Job Printing Office.

Waters, John, dir. 1994. *Serial Mom.* Savoy.

————, dir. 1990. *Cry Baby.* Universal.

Weed, Steven. 1976. *My Search for Patty Hearst.* With Scott Swanton. New York: Crown.

Weil, Dorothy. 1976. *In Defense of Women: Susanna Rowson (1762–1824).* University Park: Pennsylvania State University Press.

Welter, Barbara. 1966. "The Cult of True Womanhood: 1820–1860." *American Quarterly* 18:151–74.

White, K. 1809. *A Narrative of the Life, Occurrences, Vicissitudes and Present Situation.* Schenectady, N.Y.: Printed for the Authoress.

Williams, Eunice. 1704. Untitled narrative. Pp. 32–49 in Peckham (1954).

Winnett, Susan. 1990. "Coming Unstrung: Women, Men, Narrative, and Pleasure." *PMLA* 105 (May): 505–18.

Withers, Alexander Scott. 1895. *Chronicles of Border Warfare.* Cincinnati: Robert Clarke.

Woodward, Kenneth. 1974. "The Exorcism Frenzy." *Newsweek,* February 11, 60–66.

Woolf, Virginia. 1979. "Professions for Women." Pp. 57–63 in *Women and Writing,* ed. with an introduction by Michele Barrett. New York: Harcourt Brace Jovanovich.

Zagarell, Sandra. 1987. "Expanding 'America': Lydia Sigourney's *Sketch of Connecticut,* Catharine Sedgwick's *Hope Leslie.*" *Tulsa Studies in Women's Literature* 6:225–45.

Zane, Elizabeth. N.d. Untitled narrative. Pp. 37–46 in Frost (1859); also reprinted in Frost (1854) and Withers (1895).

Zanger, Jules, ed. [1873] 1962. *Narrative of My Captivity among the Sioux Indians.* By Fanny Kelly. New York: Corinth.

229

Bakhtin, M. M., 15, 132, 133
Barber, Eunice, 30, 62, 107
Barber, Mary, 62
Barbie dolls, 11
Bardes, Barbara Ann, 196n. 2, 215n. 5
Barlow, Joel, 140
Barnett, Louise, 204n. 15, 214n. 7
Baym, Nina, 134, 164, 196n. 2, 208n. 5, 209n. 8, 215nn. 2, 5, 216n. 12
Beidler, Peter, 190
Belknap, Dr., 79
Bell, Michael Davitt, 154
Berlant, Lauren, 9
Between Men (Sedgwick), 206n. 20
Bird, Captain, 65
black nationalism, 3
Blair, Linda, 88
Blatty, William Peter, 207n. 4
Bleecker, Ann Eliza, 14, 125–27; authorship of first captivity fiction, 125; conflicts between sensibility and wilderness genres, 131–32; critique of male rescuers, 125–26; depiction of first literary consciousness-raising group, 127–28; female readership, 127, 128, 164; use of wilderness genre, 112, 114
BLO (Barbie Liberation Organization), 11
Blynn, Mrs., 123
Boone, Daniel, 134, 137
Boulton, David, 98, 207n. 6
Bozarth, Experience, 30, 32, 201n. 5
Bradley, Isaac, 33
brainwashing, 98, 99

Breitwieser, Mitchell, 50–51, 196n. 2, 202n. 4
Brown, Charles Brockden, 2, 112, 195n. 2, 208n. 5
Brown, Gillian, 212n. 26
Brown, Herbert Ross, 214n. 12
Brownmiller, Susan, 211n. 18
Burstyn, Ellen, 88

Calvinism. *See* Puritanism
camp aesthetic, 102, 104, 105
Cannes Film Festival, 102
captivity: alternative cultural models of, 68–69; American colonies as victims of collective, 137; Arab oil crisis as, 3, 88; domesticity as, 114–15, 159–79; of gay-identified man, 13; liminars versus marginals, 44–45; as metaphor for women's cultural confinement, 4, 12, 164, 183; as metaphor in Hearst kidnapping, 88; as metaphor in twentieth-century women's writing, 184–85; as metaphor of restrictive national policy, 114, 144; modern prison system experiences, 94, 185, 186–87; sexual vulnerability associated with, 122–23, 211n. 18; of woman narrator's voice, 79–86. *See also* rescuers; slavery; white culture, women's captivity within
captivity narratives: anthologies of (*see* anthologies); appeal of, 2; atypical, 25, 30–31; as battle between grammars, 39, 100; borrowing from other narratives, 107; "classic" ac-

234

about women's agency, 32–33, 84–86; of captives who remained with Indians, 34, 36; and discrepancies with women captives' accounts, 20–21, 24–26, 34–36, 80–82, 86, 100–102; emergence of captive's voice despite, 80; of Hearst story, 8, 89, 100–102, 105, 207n. 4; of Howe narrative, 79–80; of nineteenth-century anthologies, 82–86; objectives of changes by, 20–21, 80, 105; overtaking voice of narrator, 79–86, 105, 203n. 4; of Rowlandson narrative, 46, 80–82

Edwards, Cassie, 190–93

effeminacy, 112, 113

eighteenth-century captivity narratives: acculturated captives in, 35–36; first fictional, 125–28; popularity during and after American Revolution, 140; resistance and escape in, 30–31; and shared "femaleness" notion, 63. *See also* captivity romance; *names of specific authors*

Elliott, Emory, 139–40

Emerson, Ralph Waldo, 112, 135, 183, 208n. 6, 209n. 7

epistolatory form, 127, 130, 187

Erkkila, Betsy, 139, 210n. 11, 214n. 14

eroticism. *See* sexuality

escape accounts, 30–31, 34, 37, 197n. 6

Every Secret Thing (Hearst), 89–91, 93–94, 97–99, 100, 105

Ewbanks, Mrs., 60

Ewing, George, 34, 36

Exorcist, The (film), 87, 88, 89

extra-vagance: as captivity plot device, 113–17, 134, 136, 172, 179; Chopin's use of, 183; defined, 113; Deming's use of, 189; heroine's problems returning from, 119; masculine versus feminine, 116, 117, 129, 164–66, 215n. 2; Sedgwick's use of, 172, 179, 184, 185; women's dangers from, 189–90

"family values," 88

FBI (Federal Bureau of Investigation), 90, 91, 96–97, 99, 207n. 7

Fear of Flying (Jong), 184

federal period: captivity narrative's influence on women's fiction, 14–15; domestication of women, 113, 138–39, 151; egalitarian rhetoric versus oppressive social policy, 158, 214n. 14; emergence of women-authored wilderness novel, 14–15, 112–14; historical novels as mainstays of, 139–40; Indian policy, 157–58; women's denial of legal and social rights, 138, 140, 155–57; women's group consciousness, 116–17

female separatism, 187–88

female strength. *See* strength, female

feme covert status, 138, 154, 214n. 11

Feminism and American Literary History (Baym), 205n. 5

parallels with Sedgwick's autobiography, 161–62; portrayal of interracial matrimony, 172, 216n. 9; revisionary adventures in, 177–78; and thematics of Cooper's later fiction, 208n. 5; on ultimate fate of Indians, 216–17nn. 10, 12

Horn, Sarah, 38, 57, 66

Housekeeping (Robinson), 184

Howe, Jemima, 38, 79–80, 83, 201n. 5, 202n. 10

Howe, Susan, 200n. 3, 202n. 4, 203n. 5

Hutchinson, Anne, 42, 166, 167

identity: captivity romance issues of, 136, 141; collective gender versus national, 142–43; fixed versus acquired, 49; formation through opposition, 137; invisibility of whiteness, 7, 11; literacy linked with civilized, 39; national, 9, 142; naturalized, 50. *See also* culture-crossing; gender identity

identity-based community, 13, 128

Imaginary Puritan, The (Armstrong and Tennenhouse), 203n. 6

imagined community, 124–25, 142, 212n. 19

imperialism: and assumptions about colonized peoples, 2, 150; and assumptions about gender and race, 5–7, 39, 54, 58, 59, 150; captivity narrative justifying, 2, 20, 123; hierarchies of, 5–6; linguistic images and, 39; nationalistic,

2, 5–7, 55, 58, 150, 198n. 9; patriarchal, 21, 66; and threatened sexualization of white women, 123. *See also* westward expansionism

imprisonment (modern), 94, 185–87

incest taboo, 211n. 18

Indian Captivities; or, Life in the Wigwam (anthology), 82, 109

Indians. *See* Native Americans

initiation rite, 210n. 13

institutional protection, captivity narrative condemnation of, 66–67

interpellation, 197n. 8

interracial marriage: of acculturated captive, 35; in captivity romances, 112, 172, 216n. 9; in contemporary mass-marketed romance novels, 190; *Reuben and Rachel* portrayals of, 148–50, 190, 216n. 9; vulnerability of Indian women within, 174

Israelites' captivity, as captivity narrative parallel, 80

Jemison, Mary, 8, 34–38, 84, 201nn. 7, 8

Johnson, Captivity, 68

Johnson, Susannah, 60, 66–68

Jong, Erica, 184

Kelley, Mary, 196n. 2, 209n. 10, 215n. 5

Kelly, Fanny Wiggins, 14, 69–79; biographical background, 69–70; conciliatory policy toward captors, 76–77; on drudgery of Indian women, 77, 84; fic-

voice (*continued*)
  overriding of captivity narrator's, 79–86, 105, 203n. 4

Wakefield, John, 52
Wakefield, Sarah, 14, 52–57, 61, 123; narrative compared with Rowlandson's, 55, 56, 57; on "rescue" initiating greater trials, 67; self-definition as stronger than traditional women, 62; on sympathy for Sioux, 53, 60
Walden (Thoreau), 113
Walker, Alice, 184
Warner, Susan, 184
"War-Woman," 84–85
Washington, George, 157
Watergate affair, 87

Waters, John, 102, 104, 105
Weed, Steven, 89, 95, 96, 99, 207nn. 5, 7
Welter, Barbara, 166
western genre, captivity romance contrasted with, 178
westward expansionism: assumptions about Indians, 58–59; captivity narratives justifying, 2, 20, 37, 54, 82; captivity narrative's revisionist mythology of, 5, 58; effects on white women, 6, 55, 57–59, 61, 69–70, 77, 78; glamorized rhetoric of, 70; and reconsideration of gender and racial stereotypes, 56, 57–59, 66–67, 74–75, 204n. 15; white cultural justification of, 54, 59; and white women's sisterhood, 73; and wilderness fiction genre, 134;

and women's domesticity, 212n. 24
Wheatley, Phillis, 214n. 14
White, K., 110, 111, 119
white culture: captives' distrust of, 36, 59, 64–65, 67, 94; and challenges to racial stereotypes, 91–92; fears of sexual tainting, 123; Indian captivity as preferable to constraints of, 115; as invisible identity, 7, 11; male abuse of women within, 64–67, 73, 190, 191; males as sole possessors of divinely sanctioned agency, 24; male villains in "redeemed" captives' returns, 37–38, 41–42; modern romance novels' portrayal of, 190–91; narratives revealing conflicts within, 25; nineteenth-century frontier women's disillusionment with, 61; post–American Revolution rigidifying gender roles, 112, 138–39; repression of racial and gender differences, 185, 186; as "rescuers" of captives, 119; threatening women's economic independence, 36–38; triumphing over nature, 5–6; women's captivity within, 4, 8, 19, 20, 25, 37–38, 41–42, 57, 65–67, 89, 94–96, 99, 107, 114, 115, 129, 131, 141, 144, 160–61, 178, 183, 185–90, 191, 193. *See also* culture-crossing; imperialism; patriarchal culture
Whitman, Walt, 208n. 6, 209n. 7